Chinese Constitutionalism in a Global Context

Over the course of the last four decades, as China's ideological realm has been transformed, it has become significantly more complicated. This is well illustrated in the current discourse concerning China's constitutional future. Among Chinese intellectuals, the liberal constitutional paradigm is widely accepted. However, more recently, this perspective has been challenged by mainland New Confucians and Sinicized Marxists alike. The former advocate a constitutionalism that is based upon and loyal to the Confucian tradition, while the latter has sought to theorize the current Chinese constitutional order and reclaim its legitimacy. This book presents a discussion of these three approaches, analyzing their respective strengths and weaknesses and looking to the likely outcome. The study provides a clear picture of the current ideological debates in China, while developing a platform for the three schools and their respective constituencies to engage in dialogue, pluralize the conceptions of constitutionalism in academia, and shed light on the political path of China in the 21st century. The consequences of this Chinese contribution to the global constitutionalism debate are significant – notions of the meaning of democratic organization, of the nature of the division of authority between administrative and political organs, of the nature and role of political citizenship, of the construction of rights are all implicated. It is argued that China's constitutional system, when fully theorized and embedded within the global discourse might serve, as the German Basic Law did in its time, can be a model for states seeking an alternative approach to the legitimate construction of state, political structures, and institutions.

Peng Chengyi is currently a full-time research fellow of the Institute of World Economics and Politics at the Chinese Academy of Social Sciences in Beijing. Previously, he attained his PhD degree from the Department of Public and Social Administration at the City University of Hong Kong and his BA and MA degrees in political science at St. Thomas University and the University of British Columbia in Canada. His research interests include constitutionalism, comparative political philosophy, world political thoughts, and corruption prevention in contemporary China.

Globalization: Law and Policy

Globalization: Law and Policy builds an integrated body of scholarship that critically addresses key issues and theoretical debates in comparative and transnational law and the principles governance and policy on which they are developed. Volumes in the series focus on the consequential effects of globalization, including emerging frameworks and processes for the internationalization, legal harmonization, juridification, and democratization of law among increasingly connected political, economic, religious, cultural, ethnic, and other functionally differentiated governance communities. Legal systems, their harmonization and incorporation in other governance orders, and their relationship to globalization are taking on new importance within a coordinated network of domestic legal orders, the legal orders of groups of states, and the governance frameworks of non-state actors. These legal orders engage a number of important actors, sources, principles, and tribunals – including multinational corporations as governance entities, contract, and surveillance as forms of governance that substitute for traditional law, sovereign wealth funds, and other new forms of state activity; hybrid supra national entities like the World Bank and the International Monetary Fund; and international tribunals with autonomous jurisdiction, including the International Criminal Court, the World Trade Organization, and regional human rights courts. The effects have been profound, especially with respect to the role of states, and especially of developed states as their long time position in global affairs undergoes significant transformation. Comparative and transnational law serve as natural nexus points for vigorous and sometimes interdisciplinary approaches to the study of state and non-state law systems, along with their linkages and interactions. The series is intended as a resource for scholars, students, policy-makers, and civil society actors, and includes a balance of theoretical and policy studies in single-authored volumes and collections of original essays.

Larry Catá Backer is the W. Richard and Mary Eshelman Faculty Scholar, Professor of Law and International Affairs at the Pennsylvania State University. Previously he served as Executive Director of the Comparative and International Law Center at the University of Tulsa. He has published widely on comparative and transnational law.

Also in the series

Power, Procedure, Participation and Legitimacy in Global Sustainability Norms
A Theory of Collaborative Regulation
Karin Buhmann

Chinese Constitutionalism in a Global Context
Peng Chengyi

For more information about this series, please visit: www.routledge.com/Globalization-Law-and-Policy/book-series/GLOBLP

Chinese Constitutionalism in a Global Context

Peng Chengyi

Routledge
Taylor & Francis Group
LONDON AND NEW YORK

First published 2019
by Routledge
2 Park Square, Milton Park, Abingdon, Oxon OX14 4RN

and by Routledge
52 Vanderbilt Avenue, New York, NY 10017

First issued in paperback 2020

Routledge is an imprint of the Taylor & Francis Group, an informa business

British Library Cataloguing-in-Publication Data
A catalogue record for this book is available from the British Library

Library of Congress Cataloging-in-Publication Data
Names: Chengyi, Peng author.
Title: Chinese constitutionalism in a global context / Peng Chengyi.
Description: New York : Routledge, 2018. | Series: Globalization : law and policy | Includes bibliographical references and index.
Identifiers: LCCN 2018016875 | ISBN 9781409454106 (hardback)
Subjects: LCSH: Constitutional law—China.
Classification: LCC KNQ2070 .C4355 2018 | DDC 342.51—dc23
LC record available at https://lccn.loc.gov/2018016875

ISBN 13: 978-0-367-58754-3 (pbk)
ISBN 13: 978-1-4094-5410-6 (hbk)

Typeset in Galliard
by Apex CoVantage, LLC

To all those who are concerned about the development of China and the future of the world!

Contents

Figures and tables

Figures

Tables

Preface

My interest in the research took shape in part from my participation in two conferences. The first was "The 100th Anniversary of Constitution Setting-up in China and the Future of Chinese Constitutionalism" (*zhongguo lixian yibai zhounian ji zhongguo xianzheng de weilai* 中国立宪100周年及中国宪政的未來), held at the City University of Hong Kong on October 17–18, 2008. At this conference, I discovered Larry C. Backer's interesting and path-breaking theorization of Chinese constitutional development since Deng Xiaoping's reform and opening-up. In contrast to the mainstream contempt of the Chinese constitution as a sham, Backer develops a legitimate framework for understanding the construction of Chinese constitutionalism. While his theory is not the mainstream, nor supported by the authority of China, it provides a new perspective for China's constitutional development in the future and poses a challenge both to the dominant Western Liberal Constitutionalism and to the emerging Traditional Confucian Constitutionalism. The other conference I attended was a conference of devout Confucian practitioners entitled "The Unfolding of reform and opening-up and China's Future – Principles, Values, Motivations of Confucianism, and Contemporary Explorations" (*gaigekaifang yu zhongguodeqiantu – rujia de yili, jiazhi, dongli, ji dangdai tansuo* 改革开放与中国前途 – 儒家的义理，价值，动力及当代探索) held at Confucius' hometown – Qufu, Shandong, on April 25–26, 2009. Jiang Qing, the leading figure of the so-called "mainland Neo-Confucians," gave the keynote address at this conference, "Reflections on 'Confucian Religious Constitutionalism'" (*guanyu rujiao xianzheng de sikao* 关于儒教宪政的思考), in which he shared his latest thoughts on the issue of constitutionalism for China. Even though some "mainland new Confucians" such as Chen Ming immediately expressed doubts about Jiang Qing's specific constitutional framework, Jiang Qing's call for and justification of developing a form of constitutionalism based on China's own cultural tradition did find resonance among members of the audience. reform and opening-up As a result of attending these two conferences and consequently discovering these new developments in the discourse concerning China's constitutional development, I think it would be enlightening and important to sort these three constitutional discourses out, explore their respective strengths and weaknesses, and shed light on the likely outcomes. The result is a 2-year research project on this topic as my PhD dissertation focus. The current book at hand is mainly a result of that research, with some updated reflections on the issue in light of the new development since then.

The significance of the research is quite obvious. A century ago, Chinese intellectuals were facing the same choices of Western liberal path, traditional Confucian path and Sinicized Marxism path. The ideological chaos was regarded as unprecedented in the long Chinese history. The ideological battle ended with the victory of Sinicized Marxism in mainland China. After nearly four decades of reform and opening-up, the ideological realm in China, however, has been jumbled again. History seems to repeat itself in the sense that proposals of Western liberal path and traditional Confucian path have been advocated again by some intellectuals. How the ideological game will evolve and end up certainly have significant implications for both China and the world, especially with China's rapid rise in the West-dominated liberal world order, despite that the Western liberal order itself is under significant transformations due to the challenge of rising populism. This book will be a mapping of the ideological realm in China as well as a search to the answer to the billion-dollar question about China's future path and its implications. Thus, anyone concerned about China's future and its impact on the world should have a careful reading of this book.

In celebration of the completion of this book, I want to make a number of acknowledgements here. First of all, I want to thank my parents who have not only given me the physical body but also injected in me a clairvoyant soul. Their humbleness, simplicity, hard-working as well as unconditional love, typical to all those living at the bottom layer of Chinese society, have always touched me to tears and inspired me with inexhaustible powers to pursue my dreams. Second, I want to thank the Project of Hope in China, which had provided financial supports to over 5.7 million students and built up nearly 20,000 "Primary Schools of Hope" in impoverished areas by 2017. Without the support of the Project of the Hope for its sponsorship of attending the Peipei Foreign Language School (培培外国语学校) in Zhejiang Province in China, as well as the financial support of Gao Qi (高崎) from Shanghai, I would not have had the opportunities to study in China's first "Stars of Hope" class in the beautiful harbor-city Wenzhou and receive my tertiary education in the beautiful Canada and the modern Hong Kong. Without all these supports, I would certainly not have arrived at my current stage today. Third, I want to thank Prof. Philip Ivanhoe, for his guidance in writing my dissertation each step along the way and his meticulous editing of a previous version as well as careful comments on various arguments of the book. I would also like to thank Prof. Larry Backer for his consistent support as well as encouragement for turning the dissertation into a book, without which the book would have not been possible at the current stage. I am also thankful to Dr. Sungmoon Kim, Prof. Julia Tao, and Prof. Hon-mun Chan for their support as well as feedback on various sections of the work. Despite the lessons and inputs from them, I need to acknowledge that any errors in the book are my own and I alone am responsible for the contents of the work.

1 Introduction

Background

With nearly four decades of rapid economic growth, China has emerged as a great power on the world stage with rising impact throughout the world. Meanwhile, China also faces enormous challenges domestically due to its sheer size and rapid development amid drastic societal and economic transitions. Can the current political structure cope with those challenges? What would be a socialist China's impact on the West-dominated liberal world order? These million-dollar questions have attracted the attention of many outsiders and insiders alike. For some, the answers to these questions hinge on the political path the Chinese leadership would steer China towards. Perhaps few would disagree that the Chinese leadership has no realistic choice other than constitutionalism. But which constitutionalism, since in China there is more than one constitutionalism discourse, such as liberal constitutionalism, Confucian constitutionalism, and socialist constitutionalism? This book thus will seek to examine China's constitutionalism choice and its implications for the world.

Indeed, a prominent event in China's ideological realm has been a heated debate on constitutionalism after the new leadership taking office in 2012. Not long after the new political leadership of China was elected in the 18th National Congress of the Chinese Communist Party in November 2012, the 2013 *Southern Weekly* incident occurred. The incident led to the threat of strikes by the newsroom staff of the *Southern Weekly*,[1] as well as actual demonstrations outside the newspaper's headquarter in Guangzhou, China. On the surface, it was about press freedom, a conflict between the Propaganda Department of Guangdong Province and the *Southern Weekly*, in which the original New Year's special editorial was changed under the pressure from the propaganda officers. On a deeper level, however, it is an ideological competition related to constitutionalism, since the special New Year's editorial tried to graft the hot notion of "Chinese Dream" made popular by the new General Secretary Xi Jinping with the heavily value-laden Western political terminology of constitutionalism. As a result, the title of the editorial changed from "Chinese Dream, Constitutionalism Dream" to "We are Closer to the Dream than Any Other Times."

The reason for the incident to emerge is the liberals' partly wishful and partly strategic optimism about the prospects of Xi's political reform as inspired from his open-minded remarks in a speech delivered on the 30th anniversary of the 1982 Constitution in December

1 Also referred to as *Southern Weekend*, which is one of the most influential media outlets in China based in Guangzhou China. Although it is a part of the Nanfang Media Group, a provincial government-owned media corporation, it is well-known for its outspokenness as well as pro-liberal views and stances.

2012. Xi's remarks that "No organisation or individual has the privilege to overstep the Constitution and the law, and any violation of the Constitution and the law must be investigated" and that "the life of the Constitution lies in its implementation" excited the liberal reformists who read the speech as a sign of his determination to undertake a liberal overhaul of the political system. This triggered an open letter of constitutional reform demands signed by 72 liberal intellectuals,[2] as well as the *Southern Weekly* incident mentioned earlier. They urged the Chinese Communist Party (CCP) to uphold constitutional government, ensure the rights enshrined in the Chinese Constitution, and set up checks and balances on the power of the party-state. In response, a loose coalition of conservatives, including party ideologues and leftist intellectuals, responded by unleashing a spate of ferocious counterattacks in a number of key party publications. Adopting an ideological stance, they argued that constitutional government was a by-product of Western capitalism, incompatible with China's own practice of socialism, and that China's political system must reflect the country's social and cultural conditions. They argued that the campaign for constitutional government was part of a malicious Western plot to subvert the CCP, just as Gorbachev's constitutional reform brought about the dissolution of the Soviet Union.

Even as China has entered the New Era with the successful completion of the 19th congress of the CCP in the autumn of 2017, the debate is still going on with neither side convincing the other side, which is a well reflection of the ideological nature of the debate. There is almost no systematic or theoretic engagement among the arguments of the different constituencies. This is particularly the contribution the current work seeks to make. In terms of the background of the debate, if we locate it within the larger ideological context of China since the reform and opening-up, as well as its recent history, we can see that the debate is by no chance accidental and in fact has deep historical reasons.

As we all know, after nearly four decades of economic reform and opening-up to the outside world, it is clear that China's ideological realm has been significantly transformed and complicated. This is well manifested in the wide acceptance of the liberal constitutional paradigm among Chinese intellectuals, which is so deep and profound that it is fair to say the notion of "constitutionalism" has become a pronoun for Western Liberal Constitutionalism in mainland China. This has induced some established[3] political scholars in China to call for a banning of "constitutionalism" as a basic political terminology in China and for state leaders to shy away from the notion as early as the turn of the new millennium. This is also why contents related to "constitutionalism" face stricter scrutiny in the mainland press.

As a matter of fact, the aspiration of constitutionalism as an ideology dates back to about a hundred years ago, when Chinese intellectuals were aspiring and trying to help China recover from the chaos inflicted by colonialism, imperialism, and civil war and transform it into a stable and strong state. Nevertheless, while China has doubtlessly succeeded in finding a way for rejuvenating its national strength, the aspirations for constitutionalism has persisted among the liberals, who seek to build a constitutional government based on Western models. Some of them have issued *Charter 08* (*lingba xianzhang* 零八宪章) in 2008 in China and generated some significant impact both domestically and overseas. For example, Liu Xiaobo, one of the main drafters, received the Nobel Peace Prize in 2010 for largely the

2 Chen Hongguo et al., "A Proposal for a Reform Consensus" (《改革共识倡议书》), last retrieved at http://club.china.com/data/thread/1011/2755/18/60/3_1.html on Oct. 21, 2016.

3 "Established" is a translation of the term "tizhinei" (体制内) in Chinese, which refers to those embedded into the regime and, hence, mostly in accordance with the official lines and ideologies.

same acts that led him to an 11-year prison sentence in China. To some, the latest proposals of the liberal camp in the recent heated debate of constitutionalism has not gone beyond the tenets of the Charter (Tong, 2015).

The dominance of Western Liberal Constitutionalism in China, however, has been challenged from two unexpected quarters. One is from the cultural conservatives. Historically it is widely thought that Confucianism and constitutionalism are incompatible, even antithetical, since Confucianism is usually associated with authoritarianism, rule of man instead of rule of law, collectivism, hierarchical role-based order, over-emphasis on obligation, and so on, while constitutionalism is founded on the rule of law, individual rights, equality, and so on. This view is indeed a prominent feature of Chinese thought from the New Cultural Movement of the early 20th century to the "Asian Values" debates of recent decades. Even today it still holds some currency among many intellectuals both in and outside China. For example, those subscribing to the view of the overseas New Confucians do not question whether liberal democracy, as practiced in the West, should be the form and direction of China's political future, but rather focus on the compatibility between the two traditions and the liberal democratic roots found within the Chinese tradition, centered on Confucianism.[4] This view was first well expressed in the ***Manifesto to the World on Behalf of Chinese Culture*** issued in 1958 by the four great New Confucian philosophers, and since then, many works have been devoted to this endeavor, for example, Joseph Chen, Li Minghui, Lee Seung-hwan, Cheng Chung-ying, Yu Kam-por, Heiner Roetz, and Huang Chun-chieh all have written on some aspects of this theme. However, in recent years, some intellectuals are breaking the yoke of this dominant view by exploring the constitutional resources within Confucianism and challenging previous conceptual frameworks. And we can identify three main approaches on the issue of Confucian Constitutionalism in contemporary academia, namely the institutional approach, the ritualistic approach, and the religious approach. These various approaches all make valid discoveries and have unearthed excellent constitutional resources within the Confucian tradition; however, each approach seems to have its respective limitations, and only a combination of them could render a full picture of Traditional Confucian Constitutionalism, which would have some significant implications.

The second challenge to the dominance of Western Liberal Constitutionalism in China comes from the established orthodox school of Sinicized Marxism. Because both the liberal and tradition-based schools display a certain level of hostility toward Marxism, they implicitly deny the legitimacy of the current constitutional framework of China and consequently ignore its achievements particularly in the past four decades, such as the progress in regard to the rule of law. However, in recent years, in light of the significant progress of the constitutional framework of China, including its values and practices regarding the rule of law, this dominant liberal perspective has been challenged. Stephanie Balme and Michael Dowdle (2009), for example, have devoted their book ***Building Constitutionalism in China*** to exploring the empirical impacts of the emerging constitutionalism on many aspects of Chinese society, including its juridical, political, and social realms. A US constitutional scholar, Larry C. Backer, has also sought to establish a party-state model to grant legitimacy to China's current constitutional development in the international community. This effort has been echoed by the separate articulations of Jiang Shigong, Lin Feng, Chu Jianguo, Randall Peerenboom, and so on as well. Mainstream

4 For a full list of the works, see notes 3 and 20 of Chen (2007).

legal scholars in China have made similar efforts and convened a conference on "Socialist Constitutionalism with Chinese Characteristics" in May 2010 in Changsha City of Hunan Province, although many scholars attending the conference are still thinking within the liberal constitutional paradigm. As a result, we can see that a new Sinicized Marxist constitutional paradigm is emerging.

While not utilizing the notion of "constitutionalism" to the same degree, the notions of Western Liberal Constitutionalism, Traditional Confucian Constitutionalism, and Sinicized Marxist Constitutionalism indeed represent well three "flags" in the ideological realm of contemporary China that have each attracted its own large constituencies. It is in this sense that I compare the three constitutional discourses to three "kingdoms," the competition of which to some extent resembles the *Romance of the Three Kingdoms* (*Sanguo yanyi* 三国演义) actually occurred in the Chinese history.[5] In this research project, my task has thus been seeking to sort the three "constitutional kingdoms" out and help the audience to have a clearer picture of them as well as attain a more informed forecast of the result of the grand game.

The importance of this research project is quite obvious. It has the potential to make contributions in regard to five primary issues. First, since China's current regime is perceived to lack legitimacy by some critics both in the West and within China, especially those hard-core advocates of Western Liberal Constitutionalism and Traditional Confucian Constitutionalism, a clarification of the criteria used for making such a judgment could shed light on the issue of legitimacy. Second, facing perhaps a new wave of democratization ushered in by recent Middle East and North Africa uprisings, Chinese politics seems to have come to a crossroads once again, and a report of the state of play among the three constitutional discourses certainly would shed light on the political path that China will undertake in the future. Third, through a careful sorting out of the contents of each school's constitutional discourse, as well as a cautious evaluation of their respective strengths and weaknesses, this research seeks to construct a platform for engendering genuine dialogues among the schools that currently remain in a polemic and largely unproductive atmosphere. Fourth, given that the three constitutional blueprints introduced earlier, namely liberal, religious, and Marxist, can also be found at the global level (Backer, 2009a), this research can serve as an in-depth case study for the latter. Finally, given China's sheer size and development speed, the choice of China's political path in the 21st century certainly would have profound implications for the world, especially the Western world that holds a different ideology amid a possible turning point in history with the rise of populism. This would also impact the relationships between China and the rest of the world.

Methodology

The methods for conducting this research mainly include literature review, post-modern critical analysis, and comparative perspective. For the first method, the literature mainly consists of those that are directly related to the notion of constitutionalism. In the few

5 I need to acknowledge that the metaphor may not be very precise, partly because each of the "three kingdoms" in actual Chinese history had the same kind of political organization; nevertheless, their vying for power and increasing independence as well as exclusivity towards each other in the ideological realm do match the points of the metaphor here to some extent.

cases where the notion is not directly used, the criteria for inclusion depend on its relevance to the idea of constitutionalism as well as the themes of the respective chapters. The second method is used because it is crucial to have a critical stance, especially in examining each perspective's unconscious pre-conceptions, for examining their arguments objectively and engaging in a genuine dialogue. In fact, according to Tian (2005) and Jung (2002), post-modern thought is the most critical of modernity's dominance and, hence, has some potential to bridge the gap between Western and Chinese views, which is why they have painstakingly called for the construction of such a bridge. Third, a comparative perspective is justified not only because it is crucial to move beyond the monologue of the dominant Western paradigm (Dallmayr, 2010; Jung, 2002), but also because by "mirroring" each other we can understand better each side's hidden prejudices and consequently the barriers for a genuine dialogue.

The insights of hermeneutics and the wisdom of ancient Chinese epistemology are also utilized to guide the application of the three methods. According to the advocates of hermeneutics, "all understanding inevitably involves some prejudice," where "prejudice" does not have the negative connotation familiar to us since the Enlightenment, but refers to our fore-having, fore-sight, fore-conception, or "a judgment that is rendered before all the elements that determine a situation have been finally examined" (Gadamer, 2004, pp. 272–273). It is thus very important to develop "a hermeneutically trained consciousness," which requires us "to be aware of one's own bias, so that the text can present itself in all its otherness and thus assert its own truth against one's own fore-meanings" (Gadamer, 2004, pp. 271–272). Accordingly I have tried to keep at bay all my previous conceptions on the subject as well as the three schools unless each of the conceptions had been independently examined and secured.

Another closely related insight from hermeneutics is the notion of the "hermeneutic circle." Following Schleiermacher's original usage of the term, it refers to the relation of the whole and the parts in interpretation, more specifically the necessary mutual reference between the whole and the parts in the process of understanding ("Hermeneutic circle," 2004). The notion is further developed by Heidegger and Gadamer. Heidegger uses it to denote his fundamental ontology, which relies on the "back-and-forth movement between a pre-understanding of *Being* and the uncovering of the structural features of *Dasein*," while Gadamer emphasized the interplay between the movements of tradition and interpreter in the process of understanding ("Hermeneutic circle," 2004). For my current research, it means that I have sought to understand the ideas and arguments of each work within the broader traditions behind them and to access their meanings with mutual reference between the whole and its parts. In fact, as we will see, these insights are echoed in the wisdom of ancient Chinese epistemology as well.

Ancient Chinese epistemology is certainly very broad and profound, but what is most relevant to the research here is its insights about partial views or half-truths (*bi* 蔽). Ancient Chinese sages not only described the prevalence of the problem, its root causes, harms, and dangers, but also prescribed solutions to the problem. As Zhuangzi points out, the problem with the myriad schools is not so much that they are invalid but that they are partial, just as the faculties of ears, eyes, noses, and mouths, all of which provide certain valid insights and have their individual merits, but cannot communicate with each other (天下多得一察焉以自好。譬如耳目鼻口，皆有所明，不能相通) ("All Under Heaven" of *Zhuangzi* 《庄子-天下篇》). Xunzi also devotes a whole chapter "Resolving Partiality" (*Jiebi* 《解蔽》) analyzing the causes and the dangers of the problem of "partiality" and offering the solutions.[6] There is no need to review his arguments in detail here, but I just mention his prescription of attaining the Way as the panacea, namely to empty, unify, and tranquilize our never-empty, always plural, and restless heart,[7] with the rich self-cultivation tactics personally certified (*tizheng* 体证) by the ancient sages. However, given that our current project is an academic endeavor, which requires demonstration rather than just a kind of mystic, tacit understanding, in the following, I will seek to describe both the full pictures as well as the details of each school, and reach the state captured by the ancient Chinese: "when talking about something big, nothing in the world would be able to embrace [it], and when talking about something minute, nothing in the world would be able to penetrate [it]" (语大，天下莫能载焉; 语小，天下莫能破焉) (*The Doctrine of the Mean* 《中庸》).

Plan

Given that the dominant Western liberal understanding of constitutionalism is deeply entrenched in the readers' minds both in and outside China, which may well act as a non-justified hidden barrier for the comprehension of alternative visions, Chapter 2 will clarify the key concepts of "constitution" and "constitutionalism," as well as the various possible conceptual frameworks towards constitutionalism in China. This is crucial as it could help the reader to have a panoramic view of the outlooks at the issue and, hence, be better prepared to understand the seemingly oxymorons of "Confucian constitutionalism" and "Marxist constitutionalism."

After this, Chapter 3 of the book will review the expansionist history of Western Liberal Constitutionalism in China, the core claims of its contemporary advocates as well as the main challenges it faces in China today. It will set up the foundation for the development of Chinese schools of constitutionalism as both an indigenous development and as part of the global discourse of the parameters of the ideology of constitutionalism and its expression in China.

6 It is worth pointing out that this is actually where Xunzi transcends Gadamer, since Xunzi contends that the Way offers the ultimate objective "criteria," while Gadamer is suspicious of any such absolute truth. Zhuangzi also holds a similar absolutist view as he contends that "non-action could serve as the ultimate criteria of rights and wrongs" (*wuweikeyidingshifei* 无为可以定是非) ("The Ultimate Joy" chapter of *Zhuangzi* 《庄子-至乐篇》).

7 The elaboration is well expressed by Xunzi:

> By what can human beings know the Way? By heart. Through what methods does the heart know? By being empty, holistic, and tranquil. The heart has never stopped storing, yet there is the calling of emptiness; the heart has never ceased to be plural, yet there is the calling of oneness; the heart has always been in motion, yet there is the calling of tranquility. People are born with the ability to perceive and memorize, with memory implying storage, yet there is the calling of emptiness, which thus means the stored not to persecute the incoming; people are born with the ability to perceive and distinguish, with distinction implying simultaneous knowledge and pluralism, yet there is the calling of oneness, which thus means not to persecute one by the other; the heart dreams when sleeping, wanders when free and schemes when ordered, so the heart has never been motionless, yet there is the calling of tranquility, which thus means not to be disturbed by the dreams, schemes, and so on.
>
> (人何以知道？曰：心。心何以知？曰：虛壹而静。心未尝不臧也，然而有所谓虚；心未尝不两也，然而有所谓一；心未尝不动也，然而有所谓静。人生而有知，知而有志。志也者，臧也。然而有所谓虚，不以所已臧害所将受谓之虚。心生而有知，知而有异。异也者，同时兼知之。同时兼知之，两也，然而有所谓一，不以夫一害此一谓之壹。心卧则梦，偷则自行，使之则谋。故心未尝不动也，然而有所谓静。不以梦剧乱知谓之静)(《荀子-解蔽篇》).
>
> ("Jiebi" chapter of *Xunzi*)

In Chapter 4, we will mainly engage Traditional Confucian Constitutionalism, especially the arguments of three approaches, namely the institutional, ritualistic, and religious approaches, as well as the main problems and prospects of them.

Chapter 5 will seek to describe the emerging background, the contents, as well as the possible philosophical foundation of Sinicized Marxist Constitutionalism in China. The major parts of this chapter will be focused on the three approaches under the general canopy of Sinicized Marxist Constitutionalism, including their nuanced differences.

After sorting out the three constitutional paradigms, Chapter 6 will seek to compare their respective strengths and weaknesses, analyze the current strategic configurations as well as their developmental trends, and provide some forecasts about the possible results of this new "romance of three kingdoms."

Finally, as the issue of constitutional legitimacy and the ideologies for authentic constitutionalism has acquired a global dimension over the last several decades, Chapter 7 will discuss the global significance of the recent developments of constitutionalism discourse in China at the theoretical level as well as China's constitutionalism choice at the practical level.

2 Conceptual frameworks towards constitutionalism in China

Key concepts clarified

Before getting into specific constitutional paradigms, it is helpful to have a clarification on the key concepts closely related. Here we will review the two concepts of constitution and constitutionalism in both Western and Chinese contexts respectively. In the Western contexts, there are many different definitions of the term "constitution" depending on the perspective one takes, such as philosophical, legal, political, and so on. One popular perspective is to define the notion of constitution in both its abstract and concrete senses. In its abstract sense, a constitution refers to "the system of laws, customs, and conventions which define the composition and powers of organs of state, and regulate the relations of the various state organs to one another and to the private citizen"; in its concrete sense, a constitution "refers to the document in which the most important laws of the constitution are authoritatively ordained" (Lin, 2000, pp. 2–3). This is similar to A. V. Dicey's distinction between "constitutional convention" and "constitutional law," which seem to correspond well to the abstract and concrete senses respectively (Waluchow, 2007). For critical legal theorists such as Scott Newton (2006), besides the dimension of a constitution as a kind of final product well captured in Lin's definition, a constitution also has a process dimension, which in the general sense refers to the "distinctively human work of constituting, of making or fashioning or constructing the human (social, cultural, political) world," and consequently "political society itself and the institutions of which it is made up, the enabling framework for all these varied forms of life and collective human activity in general, are constituted" (p. 328).

Despite the widely shared ideal type kind of definition of constitution as we just reviewed, we should also be aware of its mottled conceptual history as Maddox (1989) has noted.[1] Etymologically, the term "constitution" originates from the Latin *constitutio*, which means ordinance, organization, and charter, and so on. It is perhaps first used by Cicero as a political concept to denote the Greek concept of *politeia*, a descriptive term of the political community "as it actually is" (Maddox, p. 51). According to Maddox, through adding the Latin connotation of "establishment" to the *polis*-ness of *politeia*, Cicero seems to offer a new conception of the political community that is "republican specific" and refers to "institutional arrangements that would ensure stability, freedom, and above all justice" (p. 51). For Maddox, this limited or "republican-specific" notion of government did not last long, and the term was

1 This awareness is important especially in regard to the need of being able to critically evaluate the scholars' references to historical sources, and consequently the credibility of their arguments.

appropriated by later emperors to denote their edicts and decrees throughout medieval history until the 16th and 17th centuries when Cicero's sense was re-invoked (p. 52). Interestingly, while perhaps not as explicit as Cicero, Aristotle also uses the value-free word *politeia* to refer to the best kind of regime, which is a mixed republic. In fact, many modern scholars still translate Aristotle's *politeia* as "constitution," and his ideal regime as a "constitutional regime"; it is thus no wonder to see the common practice of tracing the origin of Western constitutionalism back to the ancient Greeks, especially to the writings of Aristotle ("Constitution," 2009; Gordon, 1999; Maddox, 1989). This is what we will clarify next.

Compared to "constitution," the term "constitutionalism" has a fairly recent origin, even though the idea is widely held to have its provenance in classical antiquity. According to the *Oxford English Dictionary*, it first appeared in 1832, but some have contended that the term was coined in America during the Revolutionary period (Gordon, 1999, p. 5). Within contemporary Western discourse, constitutionalism is usually equated with liberal constitutionalism, which

> is the idea, often associated with the political theories of John Locke and the "founders" of the American republic, that government can and should be *legally* limited in its powers, and that its authority depends on its observing these limitations.
>
> (Waluchow, 2007, italics added by author for emphasis)

However, this dominant definition is largely influenced by the US experience, since as Gordon points out, the emphasis of legal restraints on government power does not apply well to the cases of the UK and other countries that follow constitutional conventions rather than constitutional laws (p. 5). So as a result, Gordon (1999) argues that a better understanding of constitutionalism is that the coercive power of government should be constrained, and accordingly, the popular political slogan of "a government of laws and not of men" endlessly stated since the ancient Greeks "makes better sound than sense" (pp. 5–6). While agreeing with Gordon's observation here, I think the problem is more with conceptual changes regarding the notion of the "law." The ancient notion of law is certainly very different from that of the modern sense, and we could actually find similar parallel of conceptual changes in the Chinese tradition as well. Bearing these shortcomings in mind, I prefer to adopt Larry Backer's (2009a) definition that constitutionalism is "a means of evaluating the form, substance and legitimacy" of the constitutions (pp. 106–107), which has the key characteristics of "originating as a system of taxonomy and legitimation that is grounded in a set of normative assumptions about the meaning and purpose of government" (p. 110).

After this brief overview of the notions of constitution and constitutionalism in the Western context, it is useful to have a brief look at these concepts within the Chinese discourse as well. Linguistically, a constitution is usually translated as "*xianfa*" (宪法) in Chinese, which is defined from two different angles. The first is only from its legal status in the Chinese domestic legal system, where it is usually defined as "the supreme law of the state or fundamental law of the state" (*guojiazuigaofa huo genbendafa* 国家最高法或根本大法) (Lin, 2000, p. 4). The second is to combine the legal status of a constitution with several other characteristics, such as having a class nature, being the fundamental document of the state guaranteeing basic individual rights, and so on (Lin, pp. 4–6). Following the second approach, Lin defines a Chinese constitution as

> a fundamental law of the state, which enjoys supremacy, lays down the essential constitutional principles and the tasks of the state, establishes and defines the composition

> and powers of organs of the state, and regulates the relationships among these organs to one another and to the private citizens.
>
> (p. 7)[2]

Constitutionalism, linguistically, is translated as ***lixian*** 立宪 (setting up a constitution), ***xianfazhuyi*** 宪法主义 (the "ism" of a constitution), or ***xianzheng*** 宪政 (government by constitution), with the last two most widely used by contemporary scholars (Lin, 2000, p. 8). According to Lin and Zhu (2009), definitions of constitutionalism in China have pluralized since the 1990s, but most of them have been deeply influenced by Mao Zedong's ideal type definition of constitutionalism as the "politics of democracy" (***minzhudezhengzhi*** 民主的政治) even today (p. 38), so a widely shared common denominator is that constitutionalism should serve to promote democracy[3]; in other words, they are following the approach of democratic constitutionalism rather than liberal constitutionalism as taken for granted in the West (Lin, p. 10). However, as Lin and Zhu argue, Mao's ideal type definition is not only deeply rooted in the conceptual history of constitutionalism in China as articulated by Liang Qichao (梁启超), Yan Fu (严复), Sun Zhongshan (孙中山), and so on, which associates constitutionalism with democracy closely, but also emerges within a specific context of the dominance of the Nationalist Party in China (p. 38). While the content of democracy during the period of civil war in China is certainly different from that of today, Mao's ideal type definition is still quite influential. Nevertheless, as Chinese intellectuals have learned more about Western Liberal Constitutionalism, the understanding of constitutionalism in China has also been deeply influenced by liberal constitutionalism, and that is why some mainland pro-government political theorists are calling for the abolition of the concept of constitutionalism altogether (Lin & Zhu, p. 38). Now, after a general clarification of the key concepts, let's have a look at the general approaches that have been used to study these topics.

Previous conceptual frameworks

As Lin and Zhu (2009) point out, in the 1990s, Chinese constitutional scholars were focusing on translating/introducing Western constitutional works and sorting out the constitutional history of China in the past century, with little work dedicated to analyzing constitutionalism in contemporary China (p. 40). However, in the past decade, the literature on China's constitutionalism has proliferated, largely due to the Chinese government's call for building a state based upon the rule of law and entrenching this into the People's Republic of China (PRC) Constitution in 1999. Balme and Dowdle (2009) categorize four ways for approaching the topic of constitutionalism in present-day China, namely through the "judicial power" perspective, "political jurisprudence" perspective, "popular constitutionalism" perspective, and "envisioning the state" perspective.

The "judicial power" perspective is particularly prevalent among legal scholars, who often associate (and even conflate) constitutionalism with the judiciary's power and its

2 According to Lin, laying down the fundamental tasks of the state, which change with time, is a unique feature of the Chinese constitution not seen in the West due to its very different political culture and system (p. 4).

3 It is worth pointing out that the understandings of democracy in China and the West are certainly very different. For a good historical account of the Chinese conception of democracy, see Jin, Liu, and Lam (2005); for a good contemporary account, see Chu, Diamond, and Nathan (2008).

effectiveness in enforcing constitutional rules (Balme & Dowdle, 2009, p. 2). These scholars largely view a constitution in the concrete sense as the document of the supreme law of the state, so their logic follows as a general syllogism: "constitutions are phenomena that are comprised of laws and laws are phenomena that are enforceable by courts; therefore, constitutions are phenomena that are enforced by courts; and therefore, constitutionalism is principally a product of judicial power" (Balme & Dowdle, p. 2). These scholars hence emphasize the rule of law and judicial independence. However, as Balme and Dowdle contend, "this court-led model of constitutional development is actually incomplete" for studying China's transitional constitutionalism, because it presumes a relatively mature constitutional system with the notion of rule of law firmly embedded in a stable constitutional culture that gives "special and deontological status to both 'the law' and the courts' particular and unilateral explications of that law" (p. 2).[4] For this reason, Balme and Dowdle point out two important caveats for understanding the relationship between constitutionalism and judicial power. First of all, the definition of constitution certainly should go beyond its concrete sense, since in even the most effective constitutional systems in the world, significant aspects of the constitutional structure are largely nonjusticiable [sic], with the UK's "unwritten constitution" as a paradigmatic example (Balme & Dowdle, p. 2).[5] Second, the notion of judicial independence is also not only problematic but also misleading, since "the metaphor of 'independence' cloaks the cooperative dynamics upon which a Constitution vitally depends for its effectiveness" (Balme & Dowdle, p. 4). In fact, without the voluntary cooperation of other constitutional actors or society as a whole, it is unclear how the inherent status of the judiciary as the constitution's least dangerous branch could render it possible to enforce the constitutional norms against other non-cooperative constitutional actors (Balme & Dowdle, p. 4).[6] Furthermore, for emerging democracies, a crucial theoretical question remains why an inherently undemocratic institution like the judiciary should have the final say over the most authoritative matters of the state (Balme & Dowdle, p. 5). For these reasons, the legal "judicial power" paradigm of studying constitutionalism has been challenged by various scholars, and consequently a "political jurisprudence" perspective has been advocated by some, which we will review next.

The "political jurisprudence" perspective seeks to understand China's emerging constitutionalism by focusing on its political feature, which relates constitutionalism to democracy. As Balme and Dowdle (2009) point out, in contrast to the conventional wisdom of conflating constitutionalism with democracy, Anglo-American constitutionalists tend to view constitutionalism as an alternative or necessary supplement to democracy, in the face of the possible danger and harm of the "tyranny of the majority," latent in the actual working of purely democratic mechanisms, and "it is in this tension between constitutionalism and democracy in which the distinctive relevance and importance of the courts and

4 One perhaps should remember that it took quite some time for constitutionalism to mature in the US, France, and so on (Balme & Dowdle, p. 3).

5 Balme and Dowdle further point out the Netherlands, Sweden, Italy, Japan, and India as examples in which there is either no judicial review, little application of the power, or little effect even after using the power (p. 3); furthermore, in emergent constitutional systems, the intervention of judicial review by the courts have often led to constitutional crises rather than positive progresses, as shown in the cases of South Africa in the 1950s, India and Korea in the 1970s, Russia and Peru in the 1990s, and Philippines and Thailand in the recent decade (p. 3).

6 A good anecdote for this is President Andrew Jackson's purported statement in 1832 that "Mr. [Chief Justice John] Marshall has made his decision, now let him enforce it" (Balme & Dowdle, 2009, p. 4).

their judicial power to constitutionalism lies" (p. 6).[7] In other words, "one of the defining constitutional roles of the courts lay in their distinctive ability to protect 'discrete and insular minorities' from majoritarian tyranny," due to their "insulation from majoritarian, populist, and democratic politics" (Balme & Dowdle, p. 6). This perspective renders greater insights concerning China's constitutional development as it locates constitutionalism in the broader context of China's political reform (Balme & Dowdle, p. 6). Amid urgent need for political reform to deal with the rampant corruption and abuse of power in China, the leadership in China has opted for the courts and law as the principal vehicles for political reform, due to its deep suspicion about Western competition-electoral style democracy and the obvious high cost of initiating a Maoist Cultural Revolution style democracy.[8]

Because of these insights, Balme and Dowdle (2009) argue that China presents an interesting twist to the relationship between constitutionalism and "judicial power," since, on the one hand, the courts have been given a defining role in the emerging constitutionalism consistent with the "judicial power" vision, but on the other hand, they are not rendered independent from outside interference, as demanded by the "judicial power" school (p. 7). Despite this crucial twist, Balme and Dowdle observe that the courts "nevertheless feature as the constitutional forum of first resort to persons advancing political reform," and they suggest that the reason for this has to do with the expressive aspect of the courts' contribution to the emerging constitutionalism in China today (p. 7). For Balme and Dowdle, the "litigants and constitutional activists are using the distinctive discursive dynamics of litigatory interaction, not so much to win cases, but to advance a kind of 'jurisprudence' for constitutional-political reform" (p. 7). By "jurisprudence" in this context, the authors mean the "complex web of interconnected normative ideas and social expectations that give meaning, identity, and legitimacy to a nation's political-legal, and in this case constitutional, environment" (Balme & Dowdle, p. 7). In fact, this is the subtle message Balme and Dowdle want to express through the usage of "political jurisprudence," which recognizes the interdependent nature of constitutionalism that binds jurisprudence to the norms and expectations of various political actors (p. 7).

If the second perspective could be regarded as largely a top-down approach for political control, then "popular" constitutionalism seeks to locate China's emerging constitutionalism in the larger context of society, particularly regarding its possible perceptions as well as potential consequences. For Balme and Dowdle (2009), "popular constitutionalism" emerges when the "perhaps initially conceived of by China's leadership as a top-down exercise in social management, legal reform is now interacting with the public and the grassroots in ways that are outside of such political control" (p. 9). According to them, no matter what the real intentions behind the moves, "the simple fact that China is appealing to a rhetoric of 'rule of law' (whether *fazhi* [法治] or *yifazhiguo* [依法治国]) clearly affects social understandings and expectations," and "provides a new set of social meanings against which governmental and political behavior is judged by the society as a whole" (Balme &

7 The continental tradition differs a little on this as the courts of continental European countries seem to play a lesser role in constitutionalism due to the "more pronounced preference for a political (as opposed to juridical) form of dispute resolution" (Balme & Dowdle, p. 6).

8 In fact, Andrew Nathan already forecasted in 1996 the promising future of a "constitutional option" for China's political development, largely because of the improbability of the alternatives (as cited in Balme & Dowdle, p. 1).

Dowdle, p. 8). The *de facto* effects of the constitutional moves are that the citizenry has been empowered by at least providing them

> a means of expressing their political desires and concerns that cannot be completely ignored or shut off by the party-state, to the extent that that state itself wants to maintain at least the appearance of some degree of social credibility.
>
> (Balme & Dowdle, p. 8).

It is primarily for this reason that Balme and Dowdle contend China's "constitutional option" is not an option at all, but already a *fait accompli* (p. 9). In fact, it is quite understandable to regard China's current constitutional moves as a bottom-up process that is driven by the social forces released by Deng's reform and opening-up, which has nevertheless survived the elite crackdown in 1989 and the elite political paranoia during the 2008 Olympics (Balme & Dowdle, p. 9). Nevertheless, as we all know, there are also occasional reports that some "right-protection activists" (*wei quan ren shi* 维权人士) are arrested or taken under house detention, despite the various positive moves of legal reform and human rights protection. This phenomenon of mixed actions and messages may actually betray the limitation of the "top-down" and "popular" constitutionalism dichotomy, since what is truly underlying the phenomenon as well as the twist discussed earlier may be a dilemma faced by the Chinese leadership: how to encourage the positive function of constitutional moves while curbing the potential excesses of social forces that could slip out of its control. In fact, one perhaps could argue that the Communist Party of China's current strategy is similar to the statecraft of Emperor Shun, which is "to hold the two extremes and apply the middle to the people" (*zhiqiliangduan, yongqizhongyumin* 执其两端, 用其中于民) (*The Doctrine of the Mean* 《中庸》).

If these perspectives are moving in the direction of greater outlook, the fourth analytical framework then goes even further, since it delves into the mental realm of the people's envisioning of the state. For this perspective, a constitution is rather a particular conceptualization of the nature of the state, and constitutionalism is "not a gift from the elite to the masses" but rather "a way of giving social meaning to the metaphor of 'the state'" (Balme & Dowdle, p. 9). Balme and Dowdle use the different visions of state in the US and France, namely one as a government to be limited and feared, and the other as a reified political will, as examples (pp. 9–10). For Balme and Dowdle, constitutional thinking in China is perhaps even more sensitive to the symbiotic relationship between "constitutionalism" and one's envisioning of the state, as captured in the concept of *fatong* (法统), which is a republican derivative of the *daotong* (道统) in the Confucian tradition (p. 12). As Xiao-Planes (2009) shows in her article "Constitutions and Constitutionalism: Trying to Build a New Political Order (1908–1949)," viewed from the lens of *fatong*, the seemingly incoherent and intermittent constitutional history of the Republican period is "a history, not so much of institutions and doctrines, but of searching for what the Chinese 'state' was all about in the absence of a defining monarch and in the presence of almost perpetual and politically-existential crisis" (Balme & Dowdle, p. 11).

My conceptual frameworks and findings

As we can see, the four analytical lenses seem to move in the direction of greater depth and complexity, with each providing some new insights into the study of constitutionalism in China. It is worth pointing out, though, just as Balme and Dowdle (2009) point out, that "these lenses should not be viewed, as they too often are, as stand-alone analytic constructs, but as interrelated conceptual frameworks whose power lies in their collective interplay" (p. 2). Nevertheless, one crucial aspect seems missing in the picture presented so far, namely the value framework from which legitimacy, a key notion of constitutionalism, is based. Modern scholars seem to have forgotten the ancient sages' insight that different types of regimes would engender different kinds of persons, with different dispositions, thinking modes as well as actions. In fact, for some, if in the 20th century all subjects needed to defend themselves in front of the court of reason for their existence, the 21st century will be the century in which all subjects and theories, including legal studies, will have to defend their existence in front of "humanistic studies" (*renxue* 人学), which essentially concerns the inner welfare of the people (Li, 2005).[9] It is from this concern that my conceptual framework for understanding constitutionalism in China will thus go beyond these four perspectives and will seek to combine Larry Backer's (2009a) ideological framework,[10] which regards constitutionalism as a *weltanschauung* containing within it its own ontology, explanations, objectives, methodology, epistemology, and etiology, and the critical legal theorist Scott Newton's (2006) constitutionalism *sub specie Spinozae*, while incorporating the insights of the four analytical lens reviewed earlier. Next, I will briefly introduce Backer and Scott's frameworks.

For Backer (2009a), a distinctive feature of the constitutionalism discourse since World War II (WWII) is the increasing primacy of value frameworks. According to him, the old consensus of constitutionalism prior to WWII, which was largely grounded in domestic law and the peculiar will of the territorially defined demos, has been replaced by a new consensus, which grounds constitutional legitimacy on its conformity to a higher norm shared by the community of nations (p. 101). He identifies five main types of constitutionalism, namely nationalist, transnational, natural law, theocratic, and Marxist-Leninist, based on their respective ideological presumptions (Backer, 2009a, p. 111).[11] These normative frameworks are largely incompatible and to some extent aggressively competitive, which is why Backer points out that "constitutionalism has become another *means* of organizing the great competition between communities of believers for control of legitimating discourse of political organization" (p. 112), a kind of traditional form of competition that once was reserved for religions (p. 175).

Besides those ideological frameworks that underpin the particular values variants of constitutionalism, however, Backer (2009a) also identifies a broader and more basic animating ideology that underlies constitutionalism as a whole (p. 161). This meta-ideology, according to Backer, is a kind of *weltanschauung* that contains within it its own ontology, explanations, objectives, methodology, epistemology, and etiology (p. 162). This worldview contains an ordering or taxonomic element, normative element, and

9 "Humanistic studies" seem to be an increasingly hot subject in China, and Confucius perhaps has added a good footnote to it over 2,500 years ago: "if the people are sustained, the governance will prosper; if the people are not sustained, the governance will die away" (其人存，则其政举，其人亡，则其政息) (*The Doctrine of the Mean* 《中庸》).

10 Backer's "ideology" does not have a conventional negative connotation but means "an overarching set of beliefs and values" (2009a, p. 161).

11 It seems that Backer does not make a qualitative distinction between the first two types and the last three types; nevertheless, the former might be regarded as vertical and the latter horizontal, with both groups overlapping to some extent.

implementation element (pp. 163–167), and accordingly, Backer develops a five-element definition of constitutionalism:

> (1) a system of classification, (2) the core object of which is to define the characteristics of constitutions (those documents organizing political power within an institutional apparatus), (3) to be used to determine the legitimacy of the constitutional system as conceived or as implemented, (4) based on rule of law as the fundamental postulate of government (that government be established and operated in a way that limits the ability of individuals to use government power for personal welfare maximizing ends),[12] and (5) grounded on a metric of substantive values derived from a source beyond the control of any individual.
>
> (p. 679)

This feature of constitutionalism as a *weltanschauung* is also the primary difference with institutionalism, since the former is not only an architectural project but also a "program of moral and political regeneration," to use Backer's words (p. 121). This is also why Backer contends that constitutionalism invokes both evocative symbolism as well as instrumentalism (p. 163). As we will see, this is in fact where Backer's framework connects with critical legal theory perspectives such as that of Scott Newton's constitutionalism *sub specie Spinozae*, which I will briefly review next.

According to Newton (2006), Spinoza regards constitutions as both necessary and dangerous and also draws a parallel and analogy between the working mechanisms of constitutionalism and imperialism. Constitutions are necessary and dangerous, because Spinoza on the one hand appreciates "the affective and rational necessity of juridical institutions, as indispensable building materials of political imagination and reason, as the forms through and across which *potentia* must work," and on the other hand cautions

> of their false transcendence, their capacity to bewitch the multitude and lull the learned (and maybe the vice-versa), to appear on high or over against us, in the awe-inspiring but imaginary majesty of *potestas*, with its residual aura of divinity.
>
> (p. 331)

For Spinoza, the danger is particularly manifested through "the doctrine and practice of *constitutionalism*, which runs the risk of the fetishisation and reification of constitutions" (Newton, p. 334). For example, Newton points out that the mystification of "separation of powers" has obscured and excluded considerations of other democratic arrangements that do not involve this mystical doctrine of "division-in-unity" (p. 335).[13] From this perspective, the electoral formulas of contemporary democracies, which "lie at the very heart of the operational legitimacy of the constitutional order," have been "strangely neglected and ignored" and are also "extraordinarily 'unscientific' and crude, and susceptible to

12 While Backer uses the notion "rule of law" in the conventional sense referring to the rule of positive laws, his explication in the bracket seems not to exclude moral laws or natural laws as long as they could be successfully internalized, so my approach will have a broad definition of rule of law in order not to exclude any constitutional blueprints *a priori*.

13 For some good explorations of alternatives to the liberal constitutionalism, see Ackerly (2005) and Angle (2005).

manipulation" (Newton, pp. 335–336).[14] Understanding Spinoza's critique here, we could then see why Newton directs our attention to Habermas' notion of "constitutional patriotism," as he points out, "A cultivated identification, invested with an aura of emotional attachment suggested by the term patriotism – invested with love, in the Spinozan affective vocabulary – runs a constant risk of mystification, of heightening rather overcoming alienation" (p. 338). This actually relates to Spinoza's insight about the parallel between liberal constitutionalism and imperialism, which we will briefly review next.

According to Newton (2006), the Spinozan perspective sees liberal constitutionalism and imperialism as "deeply implicit and interlinked" because "They are obedient to the same logic of the alienation of power and the fixation of structures of rule" (p. 326). It is beyond the scope here to elaborate the similar mechanisms they shape institutions as well as subjectivities. What is worth pointing out is the fact that they both emerge from the multitude, the expansion of which has no boundaries. As Newton points out,

> Nothing theoretically limits the magnitude of the multitude. This capacity of indefinite enlargement is one of the most compelling and politically useful aspects of Spinoza's concept. It is a capacity that is inherent in the sheer force, the potential itself of the multitude. . . . Thus, viewed in relation to the multitude's *potentiae*, the demarcation of territory is always just artificial or conventional.
>
> (p. 350)

For Newton, similar logics still apply in contemporary globalized world, even though it is under the disguise of empire rather than imperialism. Just as he observes,

> If Imperialism in the late and post-colonial phase had become a motor for the propagation of individual, local "constitutionalisms" rather than one grand metropolitan version, the arrival of Empire witnesses an unprecedented renewal of pressures on "local constitutionalisms" for convergence on a very limited set of institutional models.
>
> (Newton, 2006, p. 354)

It is for this reason that Newton (2006) ends his article with the following statement:

> Constitutionalism lives and thrives as never before, for better and worse. The force of juridification, the fetishisation and reification of particular institutional arrangements, endure. *Sub Specie Spinozae*, the structural perils of alienation, uniformity, and frustration of change (the blockage of recuperation of *potentia*) persist, as does the connection to Imperialism, now in the form of Empire. At the deepest level of Spinozan critique, the chief peril of constitutionalism, one not recognized as such by Hardt and Negri, and its most poisoned genetic transmission to the derived and evolved and expanded constitutionalism which is imperialism, now Empire, may lie in the distortions it operates and the institutional constraints it places on the spontaneous development of political subjectivity itself, the flourishing of the multitude, the increase in its powers through expansion and combination.
>
> (p. 355)

14 For an excellent analysis of manipulations in democracies, see Cheminant and Parrish's (2011) latest edited book *Manipulating Democracy: Democratic Theory, Political Psychology, and Mass Media*.

This Spinozan ethico-political perspective, which centers on the relationship between power and authority (*potestas* and *potentia*), the nature of the multitude (*multitudo*), the play of reason and passion (*ratio* and *affectus*), and the eternal driving force of desire (*cupiditas*) (p. 326), seems to broaden our vision on constitutionalism significantly. This is also where the constitutionalism *sub specie Spinozae* transcends normative politics, since it is largely an analysis of the social-psychological and religious origins and effects of constitutions and a description of social erotics (p. 330).

My understanding of constitutionalism relies primarily on the last two frameworks while not ignoring the insights of the first four as reviewed earlier, largely because the last two hold deeper insights and more comprehensive visions about the topic. In fact, the crucial need to be delicate and comprehensive is determined by the nature of the research topic. With constitution incorporating the fundamental organizing principles of a state, and significant symbolic power over society, the topic should be approached with the greatest caution since one minor error might lead to tragedy, just as the Chinese idiom "a minute discrepancy can lead one thousands of miles astray" (*shizhihaoli miuyiqianli* 失之毫厘，谬以千里) vividly expresses. In fact, one perhaps could conceive contemporary Constitution as the substitute for the Throne in the past, which for the ancient Chinese serves as the trigger of the whole state, so some of the subtle ancient teachings and warnings for the Throne could well apply to today's constitutions.[15] Understanding this, perhaps we can better comprehend Confucius' teaching that only the Son of Heaven is capable of determining the rituals, setting up institutions and examining literatures (非天子不议礼，不制度，不考文) (*The Doctrine of the Mean* 《中庸》). In its traditional pictographic form, the Chinese character for "constitution" (*xian* 宪/憲) is made up of three parts: danger (*hai* 害), eye (*mu* 目), and heart (*xin* 心). One interpretation is that the ancient sage who invented the character intended the word to convey the need for an enlightened heart with clairvoyance to perceive dangers. "This actually echoes Confucius' requirements that the officials must have foreknowledge of the decline of states from all directions to qualify as parent-like officials of the people" (四方有败，必先知之，其可谓民之父母矣) ("Confucius at home at leisure" of *Li Ji* 《礼记-孔子闲居》).

With the more comprehensive conceptual frameworks born in mind, the defining features of the three constitutional discourses in China are also clear. If we concede that all three constitutionalism frameworks seek to constrain the state and society at large, we could then see that they have very different targets as well as strategies. For Western Liberal Constitutionalism, its primary target is the public power and the officials who utilize it, or what is traditionally called the rulers. Its primary strategy is through rule of positive law, which applies to the officials and the common people alike, though tilting towards the protection of the individual who is usually on the weaker side. Consequently, the court plays a paramount role in the constitutional order. For Traditional Confucian Constitutionalism, its primary target is the common people, or the ruled, because they, being more susceptible to strikes of passion, have the tendency to get rid of even legitimate rulers and together they are always superior in strength than the latter. This echoes Aristotle's insight that it is difficult for the many to be outstanding in virtue by nature, but proficient "particularly regarding military virtue, as this arises in a multitude" (*Politics*, 3.7.4). Traditional Confucian Constitutionalism's primary strategy is through rule of rituals, which applies to the officials

15 See "On the Way of the Throne" in *Huainanzi* (《淮南子-主术篇》) for example.

and the common people alike, though tilting towards the protection of the officials who are usually on the weaker side from this perspective. Accordingly, the Confucians who have the exclusive privilege of interpreting the rituals play a paramount role in the constitutional order, though their endeavor has been to primarily entrench the authority of the rulers for cultivating moderate characters of the common people. For Sinicized Marxist Constitutionalism, it is a mixture of Western Liberal Constitutionalism and Traditional Confucian Constitutionalism. It has borrowed the element of "rule of law" from Western Liberal Constitutionalism to provide a firmer protection of the individual rights, but at the same time, it has also sought to entrench the authority of the Communist Party of China in the current Chinese context, retaining the civilizing function traditionally occupied by the Confucians and is vulnerable to the rebellions of the people. Accordingly, both the court and the ruling party play very important roles in this constitutional order, but as the interest of the whole in the long term is greater than the individuals in the short term, the Communist Party of China still preoccupies a more paramount position than the court in the Sinicized Marxist Constitutional order.

As we can see, there are actually striking parallels between the three constitutional frameworks even though with some crucial distinctions. For example, none of the most autonomous bodies of the three constitutional frameworks, namely the court, the Confucian college (*taixue* 太学), and the Communist Party of China, are directly elected, but they nevertheless assume the crucial role of supervising the state and society at large.[16] To some extent, they could be well regarded as the vanguard part of society, or otherwise they should have not been rendered such privileges. They in fact also assume the function of defining and shaping the norms of the state and society as well. Here in fact come their crucial differences. From the perspective of Traditional Confucian Constitutionalism and Sinicized Marxist Constitutionalism, the vanguard part of Western Liberal Constitutionalism is actually quite myopic, because it is mainly preoccupied with codified laws and individual rights only. Nevertheless, it resonates well with the masses who are preoccupied with these things as well. There is no need to repeat Western Liberal Constitutionalism's critiques of the Confucians and Communist Party of China, such as their irresponsiveness to the demands of individuals, since they are quite familiar to us. Nevertheless, the Confucians and the Communist Party of China may well regard their distance and autonomy from the masses as a direct result of their vanguard nature. For the Confucians and the Communist Party of China, while they do have quite some similarities, the defining distinction between them may well be their prescriptions for coping with contemporary problems. It is in this regard that the Communist Party of China regards itself more advanced than the Confucians as they have been successful in addressing the problems China has been facing since its recent history.

However, these defining features would also have profound implications. As we can see, while Western Liberal Constitutionalism has been quite subtle and successful in curbing the potential abuse of the public power by the rulers, it ignores the threat of the abusive usage of power by the masses as a whole themselves. Theoretically there is nothing that could limit the masses, who could even change the constitution with a supermajority vote. The reliance on the rule of law would not cultivate people's moderation and shape their characters and

16 The degree of supervision varies among the three, with perhaps the court of Western Liberal Constitutionalism most passive and the Communist Party of China of Sinicized Marxist Constitutionalism most active.

may actually inflate them with certain arrogance and fanaticism.[17] These latter characteristics are not easy to perceive during peaceful times when everything goes well, but may erupt when things dear to them are at stake, and is particularly shown in their attitudes towards outsiders who do not seem to enjoy the same protection of rule of law as insiders. One example might be the hard-core liberal's difficulty in tolerating violations of their norms such as human rights abuses both at home and abroad. As for Traditional Confucian Constitutionalism and Sinicized Marxist Constitutionalism, despite all their harshness and idiocy, their vanguard parts do serve as a constraint on the masses, who out of habituation may become more "submissive" but nevertheless less arrogant and fanatic. Just as Newton has analyzed through constitutionalism *sub specie Spinozae*, Western Liberal Constitutionalism basically operates in similar logic as imperialism, so its expansion is unstoppable. In Jiang Qing's words, the biggest problem with Western Liberal Constitutionalism is the predominance of the legitimacy of the masses (*minyihefaxingyichongduda* 民意合法性一重独大). Bearing this in mind, we could then better comprehend the perspectives of Traditional Confucian Constitutionalism and Sinicized Marxist Constitutionalism, as well as attain a more informed forecast of the final result of constitutional game in China, which will be further discussed in the conclusion chapter.

To sum up, we have reviewed the definitions of the key concepts of "constitution" and "constitutionalism" in both the Western and the Chinese contexts, the conceptual frameworks used by others for studying the emerging constitutionalism in China, and my own more comprehensive framework as well as the findings on the three constitutionalism discourses through this lens. In the following three chapters, I will review the three constitutional discourses, starting with the Western Liberal Constitutionalist discourse as it is the most dominant and perhaps also the most taken for granted.

17 This is from the perspectives of Traditional Confucian Constitutionalism and Sinicized Marxist Constitutionalism, and the advocates of Western Liberal Constitutionalism may strongly disagree on this.

3 Western Liberal Constitutionalism in China

Its history, core claims, and challenges

Introduction

Since the Western idea of constitutionalism first entered into China about one and a half centuries ago, it has generated significant impacts on the history of China. Its main advocates engaged in a profound polemic with various schools regarding China's salvation as well as future during the late Qing and early Republican periods. With the Confucian school more or less knocked out of play by the end of the post-imperial period, liberal and Marxist ideologies then equipped two opposing sides and engaged in a civil war that ended with the Communist's triumph in mainland China and the Kuomintang's retreat to Taiwan in 1949.[1] To consolidate its power, the Communist Party in China has sought painstakingly to eradicate liberal and feudalistic thought through harsh campaigns such as the 1957 Anti-Rightist Movement and the later Cultural Revolution. However, despite the Communist Party of China's efforts to not only "cut the weeds" but also "dig up the roots" of liberal thought, the latter gradually resurfaced in China in the wake of China's reform and opening-up and have posed challenges to the orthodox ideology of the Chinese government. One major blow to the regime is the Tiananmen Square protest of 1989, which ended with bloody suppression by the authorities. In spite of the relatively quiet period of ideological contention that immediately followed, the liberal camp persisted, and its voice gradually re-emerged in China again, especially in the late 1990s and more recently with the issuing of *Charter 08* by some liberal dissidents in China. The Chinese government has sentenced the main drafter of *Charter 08*, Liu Xiaobo (刘晓波), to 11 years in prison on charges of inciting subversion of the state. Nevertheless, Liu was awarded the Nobel Peace Prize of 2010, which consequently pushed the Chinese government and the issue of constitutionalism back into the spotlight of the world community. Recently, in the wake of the Middle East and North Africa uprisings, the Chinese government has seemingly strengthened its suppression of the liberal dissidents, and there are mixed messages regarding China's political reforms in light of the actions of the new administration. Thus, how the new stage of the game will play out is an important question for all people who are concerned about the future of China as well as the world order. To have a more informed understanding of current strategic configurations and better forecast of the future of constitutionalism in China, this chapter will seek to review the expansionist history of Western Liberal Constitutionalism in China, its core claims, and the main challenges it faces today.

1 This dichotomy is surely neither absolute nor precise, since both sides certainly contain some Confucian elements and the Nationalists are influenced by Marx-Leninism as well, so the dichotomy is for general comparative purpose here.

Western Liberal Constitutionalism in China[2]

The expansionist history of Western Liberal Constitutionalism in China

There are two main waves of Western Liberal Constitutionalism in China. The first broke upon Chinese shores in the late Qing to early Republican period, and the second landed in the period since PRC's reform and opening-up. In mainland academia, many works have been written on the constitutional history of China in the last century, such as Hou Yijie's (侯宜杰) *The Political Reform in Early 20th Century China: The History of the Late Qing Constitutional Movement* (《二十世纪初中国政治改革风潮：清末立宪运动史》) (2009); Chen Feng's (陈峰) *The Research Outline of Chinese Constitutional History* (《中国宪政史研究纲要》) (2003); and Deng Lilan's (邓丽兰) book *Western Thoughts and the Evolution of Republican Constitutional Movements* (《西方思潮与民国宪政运动的演进》) (2010), to name just a few. Next, I will provide a brief review of the expansionist history as manifested in each period.

The first wave during the late Qing and early Republican periods

The origin of Western Liberal Constitutionalism in China is widely traced back to the early years following the Opium War with Britain in 1840.[3] Shortly after China's defeat in the war and the consequent humiliation suffered thereafter, some officials and elites of the imperial Qing, such as Lin Zexu (林则徐), Xu Jishe (徐继畬), Weiyuan (魏源), and so on, began to introduce the outside world to the "arrogant" "Middle Kingdom." The two most famous works of the time, *A Brief Introduction of the Globe* (《瀛寰志略》) and *An Introduction to the Overseas States* (《海国图志》), for example, not only describe the geography, customs, and mores of various countries, but also introduce and praise the political system of Western nations. While they do not use the term "constitutionalism" to describe the Western political paradigm, they nevertheless expose the Chinese to certain institutions as well as principles of Western Liberal Constitutionalism for the first time. However, just as scholars widely acknowledge, due to the Qing court's deep-rooted arrogance as well as close-mindedness about the superiority of its institutions and culture, it attributed the defeat at the hands of the British to poor weapons and inadequate knowledge of Western countries; as a consequence, Western Liberal Constitutionalism was not taken seriously, let alone put into practice (Ma, 2006; Zhang, 2008). What the Qing court did instead was to learn from Western technology and science through the Self-Strengthening Movement (*yangwuyundong* 洋务运动), with the hope of resisting the colonial powers. The Westernization Movement did achieve some success in modernizing China's backward industries as well as weapons. However, the court soon discovered that it was not possible to learn from the West only its material and technological knowledge while keeping China's institutions and cultural core intact. The turning point was the utter defeat of the Qing's modernized Northern Fleet by the Japanese navy during the Sino-Japanese War in 1894–1895, which astonished the Qing court and intellectuals and

2 The contents of Western Liberal Constitutionalism will be clearer later and for most scholars it includes at least the dimensions of democracy, rule of law and human rights protection.

3 Before the Opium War, it is recorded that some Western missionaries, such as K. F. A. Gutzlaff, had started to introduce Western constitutional ideas into China (Tong, 2009, pp. 99–100), but as their influence is very minimal it is largely negligible here.

consequently pushed constitutional thought into a sweeping movement of institutional reform.

The Sino-Japanese War of 1894–1895 is surely an important landmark and also a catalyst of the spread of Western Liberal Constitutionalism in China. Before that, the Qing court and intellectuals regarded the recent humiliation of the Opium War as something similar to the humiliation imposed by the ethnic minorities during the Yuan and Qing times (Zhang, 2008, p. 43). As Chinese culture has a strong capacity to assimilate foreign invaders and their influences, some still hoped that "the Westerners would be exposed and influenced by the sagely learnings of the Chinese and become persons disposed towards the good in the foreign land" (Liang, as cited in Ma, 2006, p. 31). That is why the Qing court and intellectuals' attitude towards the West in the half century following the Opium War is mainly "to study the barbarians' technologies to counter them" (*shiyichangjiyizhiyi* 师夷长技以制夷), which became the main agenda behind the Self-Strengthening Movement initiated in the 1860s. However, the defeat by the tiny island state of Japan and consequent cession of territory as well as payment of compensation completely shattered the Qing's confidence and complacency. As Japan previously had similar structures and situations with China, the Qing court and intellectuals started to realize the importance and power of constitutionalism, which for them is the main factor leading to the huge power disparities.[4] This then ushered China onto the bumpy road of setting up a constitution.

For some Chinese constitutional scholars, the constitutional journey of China did not start until 1898, when the young emperor *Guangxu* (光绪) accepted the propositions of Kang Youwei (康有为) and launched a political reform in the direction of Western Liberal Constitutionalism. However, the reform lasted only 103 days and was strangled by the conservatives in the court headed by Empress Dowager *Cixi* (慈禧). The result was the confinement of the emperor and the beheading or exile of the reformers. Ironically, the conservative clique changed its stance and started to push for constitutional reform a few years later. In 1906, the Qing court issued an edict declaring that China would have a constitutional polity within 9 years, and in 1908, it issued the first proto-constitution in Chinese history, the "General Principles of the Constitution by Imperial Order" (*qindingxianfadagang* 钦定宪法大纲). The overall plan was to model a Chinese constitution on the Japanese Meiji Constitution, which itself drew from the Prussia Constitution of 1850, with the emperor continuing to embody national sovereignty and hold supreme power (Zhang, 2008, p. 44). However, with the rising tide of anti-Manchu movement led by the "Chinese United League," or the "Chinese Revolutionary Alliance" (*Tongmenghui* 同盟会), and the outbreak of the Wuchang Uprising in 1911, the Qing imperial court hurriedly issued a decree titled the "Nineteen Credos" (*shijiuxintiao* 十九信条), which resembles the British constitutional system and has the imperial prerogatives of the 1908 constitution abolished. For some, the "Nineteen Credos" embodied the view of limited monarchy for the first time in Chinese history, and China may well have evolved along a similar trajectory as Britain had the opposing forces compromised and accepted it (Zhang, 2008, p. 45). Nevertheless, the public rejected it, and consequently, the Qing was finally brought down and replaced by

4 It is worth pointing out that the Meiji Restoration was not a shift to liberal constitutionalism but a commitment to modernization with a monarchical constitution. In this sense, the term "constitutionalism" is closer to its Chinese translation of "constitution setting up" (*lixian* 立宪) here. For a more detailed comparison of the constitutional reform in China and Japan in the 19th century, see Zhang (2008, p. 42) and Ma (2006, p. 35).

the Republic of China (ROC). The attempt to develop a constitutional monarchy was thus aborted, and the constitutional journey evolved into the Republican period.

The constitutional development of the Republican period can be divided into two main periods as well, with the Nationalist Party's transformation into a revolutionary party under the influence of the Soviet Komintern in 1923 as the dividing point. This is also the year in which Sun Yat-sen first advocated his three-step proposal for reaching constitutionalism, namely first through military government (*junzheng* 军政), then tutelage government (*xunzheng* 训政) under the direction of a vanguard party, and finally a constitutional government (*xianzheng* 宪政). During the period of 1912–1923, there are a total of four constitutions or constitutional drafts. The first is the Provisional Constitution of the Republic of China (*zhonghuaminguolinshiyuefa* 中华民国临时约法) issued in March 1912, which incorporated the idea of the sovereignty of the people for the first time and was also modeled after the constitutional system of France's Third Republic, which gives supreme power to the bicameral legislature. This was intentionally designed to curb the ambitions of Yuan Shikai (袁世凯), the former commander of the Beiyang Army of the Qing court and the provisional president of the newly established ROC at that time in exchange for his collaboration in forcing the emperor to abdicate (Xiao-Planes, 2009, pp. 41–42). The ROC conducted its first national election in the winter of 1912–1913, which had a turn-out of 40 million voters, or about 10.5 percent of the population (Xiao-Planes, p. 42) and witnessed the Nationalist Party voted in as the majority in the parliament. The newly elected parliament then called for a constitutional convention in April 1913 and drew up the "Draft Constitution of the ROC," also called the "Tiantan Draft Constitution" (*tiantanxianfacaoan* 天坛宪法草案) for the drafting committee met at the Tiantan or the Temple of Heaven. The Draft is largely a compromise between the Nationalist Party, who naturally wanted to have a dominant legislature and weak executive, and the Progressive Party headed by Liang Qichao, who, now allied with Yuan Shikai, wanted to have a strong executive branch to stop the centrifugal political forces plaguing China at that time and to counter the dominance of the National Party in the parliament (Xiao-Planes, p. 42). Nevertheless, Yuan Shikai, dissatisfied with the results and holding predominant military superiority, dissolved the parliament in early 1914 and replaced the still formally in force Provisional Constitution of 1912 with his "New Constitutional Pact" (*yuanjiyuefa* 袁记约法), which established a "life-long presidency" with virtually omnipotent power. However, perhaps inflated by his ambitions, Yuan Shikai began to advocate for the restoration of monarchy in 1915 and crowned himself in December 1915, despite strong opposition from various quarters. The retrogression immediately provoked insurrections in several southwestern provinces proclaiming the "defense of the Republic" (*huguo* 护国) and resulted in the carving of *de facto* independent kingdoms by some local warlords. Accordingly, following Yuan Shikai's death in 1916, constitutional debates focused on whether to incorporate clauses for the powers of local and provincial government, as well as how much power should be attributed to them (Xiao-Planes, pp. 45–47). The result is the still-born Cao Kun Constitution (*caokunxianfa* 曹锟宪法) of 1923, which is significant for its intention to enlarge the rights of citizens and blend centralization with federalism (Xiao-Planes, p. 48). Nevertheless, as the then President Cao Kun was elected because of his open bribery of a great number of parliament members, public trust in the parliament and the new Constitution virtually collapsed, and the constitutional journey entered the second Republican period (Xiao-Planes, p. 48).

During this period of 1923–1947, the dominant constitutional philosophy was that of Sun Yat-sen, which had the distinctive defining features of incorporating certain indigenous Chinese and Soviet Union elements into its Western parliamentary model. There are three main doctrines underlying Sun Yat-sen's constitutional thought, namely the "three principles of the people" (*sanminzhuyi* 三民主义); the "five-power constitution" (*wuquanxianfa* 五权宪法); and the three-stage transition theory towards a constitutional state, namely military, tutelage, and constitutional stages (*junzheng xunzheng xianzheng* 军政，训政，宪政). The "three principles of the people" consists of their subsistence (*minsheng* 民生), their sovereignty (*minquan* 民权), and their nationalism (*minzu* 民族). The "Five-Power Constitution" refers to the constitutional arrangement of executive, legislative, judiciary, examination, and control powers of the central government, which was supposed to have unlimited capacity (*neng* 能), while the people was supposed to hold unlimited sovereign rights (*quan* 权). The influence of three primary sources on Sun Yat-sen's constitutional thought is quite widely acknowledged within academia: the examination and control powers of Sun's "Five-Power Constitution" were largely an adoption of indigenous Chinese institutions; the division of the executive, the legislative, and the judicial powers was learned from Western parliamentary democracy; and the three-stage transition theory towards a constitutional state as well as the party-state model was inspired by the Soviet Union's experiences (Xiao-Planes, 2009, p. 48). Accordingly, the five constitutions drawn up during this period are all consistent with Sun Yat-sen's constitutional thought. The most outstanding feature is Sun's inspiration from the Soviet party-state model, which is also the main idea behind the 1931 "tutelage constitution." It is mainly for this reason that 1923 is the dividing point of the republican constitutional development, as it is in this year that the Nationalist Party was transformed into a revolutionary vanguard party modeled on that of the Soviet Union (Xiao-Planes, p. 50). When the "political tutelage" phase was completed, the new Constitution of the Republic of China was proposed in 1946 and put into practice since 1947 until today in Taiwan. The new Constitution is derived from an initial draft written by the well-known liberal intellectual Zhang Junmai (张君劢), which is basically faithful to Sun's "three principles of the people" but adds the fourth principle of "direct guarantee" (*zhijiebaozhang* 直接保障) of citizen's rights by the constitution (Xiao-Planes, p. 55).

As we can see, the constitutional journey of this period is not predominantly influenced by Western Liberal Constitutionalism, but nevertheless, the constitutions of the Nationalist Government are more inspired by Western Liberal Constitutionalism than the alternative constitutional trajectory under the leadership of the Communist Party of China, practiced in the Communist Party of China-controlled areas during the Republican period and in the PRC thereafter. It is for this reason that I have included the constitutional development of the Republican period here as part of the expansionist history of Western Liberal Constitutionalism. Since then, however, Western Liberal Constitutionalism virtually disappeared in the mainland, and we need to jump to the PRC's reform and opening-up period to continue our review of the history of Western Liberal Constitutionalism in China, which we will do next.

The second wave of Western Liberal Constitutionalism in China during the reform era

As Zhang Qianfan (2008) points out, the journey of Western Liberal Constitutionalism in China as shown in the first wave took three steps: first of all, the ideas of Western Liberal Constitutionalism were introduced and accepted by intellectuals; second, those intellectuals started to influence officials and the populace's perceptions of these ideas; third, some "enlightened" officials pushed for institutional reform in light of these new ideas with the aid of the reform-oriented intellectuals as well as the populace; the end result depended upon the interactions between reform-oriented forces and conservative forces that have a vested interest in the status quo. While the Qing constitutional reform largely failed because of the strong opposition of the conservative forces in the court as well as the failure of Western Liberal Constitutionalism to take root among the populace, the three-step expansionist roadmap seemed to be a good one, and here, I will review the second wave of the spread of Western Liberal Constitutionalism in China through a similar lens as well, though with some important differences due to the very different settings. Particularly, as the institutional dimension of this period is not so prominent, I will spend more time on the penetration of Western Liberal Constitutionalism ideas over the institutional reforms than I did in the last section.

First, let's have a close look at the spread of Western Liberal Constitutionalism among Chinese intellectuals during the reform era. The spread of Western Liberal Constitutionalism is certainly all-encompassing in the public realm since China's opening up to the outside world, but an adequate discussion of this issue is beyond the scope of this book and diverges from the main concerns of this study, so I will mainly review Western Liberal Constitutionalism's penetration into the field of constitutional studies. Constitutional studies is a good choice, because it is not only the subject where most advocates of Western Liberal Constitutionalism are located today,[5] but also the area that has experienced the most rampant spread of Western Liberal Constitutionalism within Chinese academia. In Pan Wei's words, this is the area "hardest hit" by Western ideological imperialism (personal communication, May 20, 2010). Riding the tide of the dramatic increase of legal studies in China since the reform era, constitutional studies have also witnessed rapid increases.[6] For example, the number of students enrolled in graduate programs of constitutional law has expanded from a dozen per year in the early 1980s to almost 300 per year in 2000 (Tong, 2009, p. 102). During the same period of time, there were over 70 books or other major constitutional education material published in China and 2,900 journal articles on constitutional law published nationwide (Tong, pp. 102–103). As constitutional law is mainly a discipline imported from the West, the penetration of Western Liberal Constitutionalism is thus inevitable and also remarkable.

The penetration of the Western liberal constitutional discourse into China is well explored by Yu Xingzhong (2009) in his article "Western Constitutional Ideas and Constitutional Discourse in China, 1978–2005." In this article, based on his comprehensive review of the influence of Western constitutional theories on Chinese constitutional scholarship in the reform era, Yu contends that "Chinese constitutional discourse has been significantly

5 On this, some liberal intellectuals in China such as Liu Junning and Wang Juntao might hold a different view, as they think that the forces advocating Western Liberal Constitutionalism in China mainly includes liberal intellectuals, dissidents, emerging business communities who want to protect private property, reformists within the establishment (*tizhinei* 体制内), international players such as the US foundations and civil society organizations, and some local governments, as well as some young journalists (Gunde, 2003).

6 Records show that in 1977 a few law departments and faculties were reopened or established with 223 undergraduate students admitted; in 1978, the total number increased to 729 among more universities; and by 1980, there were fourteen universities that had legal studies programs with 2,828 students enrolled (Tong, 2009, pp. 100–101). In 2008, the number of students enrolled in law programs had increased to near 700,000 (China Yearbook, 2008). As for constitutional studies, before 1949, there were some courses in constitutional law taught in the political science curriculum, but they shortly disappeared from the Chinese curriculum in the newly founded PRC; nevertheless, constitutional education and research were restored in 1977–1978 (Tong, p. 100).

'Westernized'" (Yu, p. 114). First of all, the author points out that, due to various factors, the constitutional literature in China has proliferated in recent years, as shown in the enormous numbers of books, articles, and conferences, as well as websites written on constitutional law and constitutionalism; most Chinese constitutional scholars have conscientiously looked to Anglo-American and continental European constitutional ideas for inspiration in these discussions and debates (Yu, p. 114). Most important works on Western Liberal Constitutionalism, such as Bruce Ackerman's *We the People*, Ronald Dworkin's *Taking Rights Seriously*, and *Law's Empire*, Friedrich Hayek's *The Constitution of Liberty*, as well as those of Cass Sunstein and Richard Posner, have not only been translated and introduced to Chinese academia but are taken as the "foundational references" for both Chinese students and scholars working in the areas of legal theory and constitutional law (Yu, p. 114). Yu further supports his arguments with some specific cases. For example, he elaborates how Albert Venn Dicey's and Friedrich Hayek's understandings of rule of law have been widely accepted in Chinese legal studies, with Professor Deng Zhenglai (邓正来), a well-known Hayekian scholar in China, as a good example (Yu, pp. 115–117). The emerging "rights talk" fashionable in China in recent years is also deeply influenced by Ronald Dworkin's philosophy of "rights," which is well introduced and spread through the efforts of some influential scholars such as Zhang Wenxian (张文显), a constitutional scholar based in Jilin University, who also served as the President of the Supreme Court of the Jilin Province (Yu, p. 118). Yu also discusses the influence of Benjamin Constant's account of the nature of popular sovereignty on Chinese scholars such as Professor Li Qiang (李强) at Beijing University, the practice of judicial review from the US constitutional experience on the "judicial activism" of China, especially since the *Qi Yuling* case in 1999, which is regarded by some as the "first constitutional case" in the history of China, and Tocqueville's insights about the "tyranny of the majority" as well as democratic development.[7]

Through the medium of these intellectuals, the influence of Western Liberal Constitutionalism has also spread to many officials, which is perhaps well manifested in the ideological changes of the government as well as its constitutional amendments, especially the entrenchment of the "human rights" clause in the Constitution. It is beyond the scope of this chapter to give a careful review of these ideological changes, which will be elaborated in Chapter 5 on Sinicized Marxist Constitutionalism, so instead I will just mention a few key events that are relevant. First of all, the five constitutional amendments to the Chinese constitution during the reform era were clearly moving in the direction of getting closer to the aspirations of Western Liberal Constitutionalism. For example, the 1988 amendments intended to legitimize the existence of a private economy and the transfer of land-use rights; the 1993 amendments sought to attune the constitution to the changing political-economic situation as well as to the need for further reform and opening-up; the 1999 amendments entrenched the goal of "governing the country in accordance with law and building a socialist rule of law state" into the constitution; the 2004 amendments elevated the respect and protection of "human rights" to the national constitutional level. In practice, the government's institutional reforms have also come closer to the prescriptions of Western Liberal Constitutionalism, as shown in their reform efforts along the dimensions of democracy, rule of law, human rights, and central-local relations. The promotion of some Western Liberal Constitutionalism influenced scholars, such as Xia Yong (夏勇), a former constitutional

7 It is worth pointing out that Donald J. Maletz's (2002) article "Tocqueville's Tyranny of the Majority Reconsidered" especially targets this widely held misreading and misconception.

scholar; Xin Chunying (信春鹰), a legal scholar; Zhang Wenxian previously mentioned; and Yu Keping (俞可平), a political scholar well known for his thesis "democracy is a good thing," and so on, to certain core positions of the government also renders support to this reading.[8] One could point to the former Chinese Premier Wen Jiabao, the highest liberal-oriented leader in China, as an example as well, who has publicly called for political reforms several times and also criticized feudalistic and the Maoist forces as barriers for such moves (Jiang, 2011). In fact, it is these developments that provoke cultural conservatives such as Jiang Qing (2009) to bemoan the fact that China has not turned from its path of diverging from its indigenous tradition and is instead moving closer to the West, which in his view is a pathologically dangerous path that has been taken since China's New Culture Movement in the early 20th century.

Nevertheless, despite the penetration and impacts of Western Liberal Constitutionalism institutions and values in China, the government seems to still keep under control and seeks to confine and guide the spread of the latter. This is manifested in many actions and policies, and here I will just mention a few. First of all, compared with the progress of legal studies, the development of constitutional studies in Chinese academia is still constrained and limited. For example, while Chinese constitutional law is one of the 14 core courses of the undergraduate legal curriculum as established by the Ministry of Education, it is only allocated one semester, and the classes scheduled each week are minimal compared to other courses (Tong, 2009, p. 101). Within the limited time allocated to the course, the focus of teaching is also tilted toward the "Chinese Constitution" part rather than its Western counterparts or comparative dimensions (Tong, p. 101). This is also well shown in the number of articles published on constitutionalism and other topics. In the past four decades, there are over 12,000 articles with the keyword "rule of law." This is a significant contrast to that of "constitutionalism," which has 2,222 articles with this term as the keyword, and "liberal constitutionalism," which has only 3 articles.[9] Second, the room left for law and courts to play greater roles is also confined. This dimension has been well captured and analyzed by many works, such as Lubman's (2000) book *Bird in a Cage: Legal Reform in China after Mao*, so I will not review this issue here. The third aspect is shown in the government's firm stance towards liberal radicals, such as its harsh suppression of the protesting students in the Tiananmen Square in the summer of 1989 as well as the severe punishment on the main drafter of *Charter 08*, Liu Xiaobo, and so on. To some extent, *Charter 08* provides a good synopsis of the core tenets of Western Liberal Constitutionalism, which we will review next.

Before turning to the normative claims of Western Liberal Constitutionalism, however, we need to note that although the two waves of the spread of Western Liberal Constitutionalism in China share some resemblances, they also differ in some important respects. For example, the rational to advocate Western Liberal Constitutionalism has changed

8 The current or past positions of these scholars are or were the Director of the National Administration for Protection of State Secrets, the Deputy Secretary of the NPC, the President of the Supreme Court of Jilin Province, and the Deputy Director of the Compilation and Translation Bureau of the Communist Party of China respectively.

9 The statistics is based on a search of the keywords of "rule of law" (fazhi 法治), "constitutionalism" (xianzheng 宪政), and "liberal constitutionalism" (ziyouzhuyi xianzheng 自由主义宪政) respectively in the China academic journals full-text database of the China National Knowledge Infrastructure (CNKI) on June 6, 2018. There is a seemingly decrease of entries on "liberal constitutionalism" in the database, perhaps due to the stricter scrutiny and filtering of the sensitive terms in the past few years.

dramatically. During the late Qing and early Republican period, Western Liberal Constitutionalism was largely taken up with very pragmatic purposes: to strengthen the state and save China from various problems, not least the external threat; at that time Western Liberal Constitutionalism available for imitation is also not as liberal as today's. During the reform period, however, advocates of Western Liberal Constitutionalism wanted to endorse certain liberal principles to increase individual freedom and improve the individual lives. The social and intellectual contexts have also changed dramatically. In today's China, the means of spreading Western Liberal Constitutionalism tenets have become much more diversified and complicated, but at the same time, the liberal intellectuals' influence has also decreased due to the changing circumstances, especially that brought by the rapid marketization process in the 1990s.

Normative claims of Western Liberal Constitutionalism

A manifesto synopsis of Western Liberal Constitutionalism in Charter 08

The normative claims of Western Liberal Constitutionalism are well summarized in *Charter 08*, which I will present a review in this section. *Charter 08* is a manifesto published on December 10, 2008, the 60th anniversary of the Universal Declaration of Human Rights, by some liberal intellectuals and human rights activists in China. It imitates the anti-Soviet *Charter 77* issued by dissidents in Czechoslovakia in both form and content. Since its release, it has reportedly gathered many signatures from people both inside and outside of China endorsing it. One of the main authors of *Charter 08*, Liu Xiaobo, was sentenced to 11 years' prison for the charge of "inciting subversion of state power" but was nevertheless awarded the Nobel Peace Prize for the year 2010. The Charter basically summarizes all the core claims of Western Liberal Constitutionalism in China and calls for 19 specific reforms of current Chinese political regime to endorse the "universal values" (*pushijiazhi* 普世价值) of "mainstream civilization" as manifested in the Western world. The core tenets included in the Charter are six vague declarative values: freedom, human rights, equality, republicanism, democracy, and constitutionalism. The specific reform proposals are:

constitutional revision in accord with the previous core tenets, separation of powers and checks and balances
legislative democracy in the sense that legislatures at all levels are directly elected by the people
judicial independence
public use of public instruments in the sense that all armed forces and civil servants should be politically neutral and loyal to the state only
human rights protection
election of public officials with the principle of "one person, one vote"
urban-rural equality through abolition of the current urban-rural two-tier household registration system
freedom of association, assembly, expression, and religion
replacement of civic education for the current political education that has a strong ideological and partisan nature
private property protection

fiscal reform to democratize public finances and guarantee taxpayers' rights
social security
environmental protection
a federal republic
transitional justice by restoring the reputation of and giving compensation to individuals and families that previously have suffered (*Charter 08*, 2008).

A four-pillar explication of Western Liberal Constitutionalism by constitutional scholars in China

Given its nature as a manifesto, the Charter only briefly explains the proposals and does not offer an account of the theoretical rationale behind them; nevertheless, the constitutional study community in China seems to have taken the claims of the Charter for granted, and their intellectual findings have offered theoretical support to these claims. Next, I will thus review the core arguments of the constitutional study community in Chinese academia as articulated by Li Buyun. Li is widely regarded as a leading scholar on Western Liberal Constitutionalism in China today, and his arguments are also quite representative of the community.[10] Despite the fact that different scholars give different definitions to the notion of constitutionalism, the majority of constitutional scholars in China regard constitutionalism as the ideal political system of modern civilization and agree that constitutionalism includes three core components, namely democracy, rule of law, and human rights. This is originally advocated by Li Buyun in 1991, as he uses it to summarize the various interpretations of constitutionalism and defines it as

> a political system which regards the realization of a series of democratic principles and system as its main content, rule of law as its basic guarantee, and the fulfillment of the most extensive set of human rights as its goal.
>
> (2006, p. 3)

After two decades' further research and dialogues, Li Buyun has decided to add one more element to his "three-element definition," namely the "supremacy of the constitution" (*xianfazhishang* 宪法至上), which he did at a recent conference on "Socialist Constitutionalism with Chinese Characteristics." For Li (2006), "democracy, rule of law, and human rights" are the substantive core of constitutionalism, and "the supremacy of constitution" is its required external form (p. 2). Next, we will review the four core elements in turn, which, as we shall see, also cover almost all the proposals listed in *Charter 08*.

Democracy pillar

According to Li (2006), popular sovereignty is the essence of democracy, which means that all state power belongs to the people who are the masters, and the government as the servant should work for the happiness of the people in all of its activities (p. 4). Accordingly,

10 Li Buyun is one of the most well-known and respected legal philosophers in China today. He has published extensively in the fields of legal theory, particularly theory of rights, human rights and rule of law, constitutional law, and the legislative system. He is also one of the speakers invited to present lectures to China's top leaders on law-related topics.

there are four institutional components: first, free and fair general elections; second, actual possession by all elected power organs of their mandated powers without being superseded by any other unelected individuals or organizations; third, separation of powers and checking mechanisms to prevent corruption as a result of unbalanced power; and fourth, the right to information, participation, discussion of political issues, and supervision of government on the part of citizens as well as their representatives in the congress (Li, p. 4). For Li, while China did stipulate its first electoral law in 1953 with universal franchise and issued a new election law in 1979, the malpractices of previous eras summed up as the "higher level decides the list and the lower level agrees" have not been fundamentally changed (p. 6). Li seems to be referring to the fundamental conflicts that exist between the universal election principle of democracy and the Communist Party of China's principle of "the Party is in charge of cadre management" (*dangguanganbu* 党管干部).[11] Regarding general elections, Li contends that the masses should be "fully trusted" and "competitive mechanisms must be fully introduced into elections," so that the Communist Party of China and its members could "maintain youthful vigor" and avoid "stagnation, retrogression, and corruption" (p. 6). As for the second institutional component of democracy, Li argues that, in the Chinese context, the NPC should not be directed by any unelected dictators, army, or any other organizations such as parties (p. 6). Regarding the separation of powers and checks and balances, Li points out that this institutional component would help to maintain political stability, assure correctness of national policy and law, as well as facilitate the initiative and enthusiasm of central and local government organs (p. 7). In Li's view, in most cases, China has not handled well central-local relations and market reform should lead to greater local autonomy (p. 9). Finally, for the fourth component, Li thinks that the people, as masters, should have full rights to information, participation, and discussion in order to exercise the authority of supervising the government (p. 10).

Rule of law pillar

The second core element of constitutionalism is rule of law. Li (2006) attributes five principles to the rule of law: first, a complete set of laws based on and also consistent with the spirit of constitutionalism should be stipulated by the state; second, all state organizations, parties, and leaders should act in accordance with the law with no privileges whatsoever that over-ride the constitution and laws; third, the making and implementation of the constitution and laws should follow democratic procedures; and fourth, all citizens should be equal before the law; fifth, the judiciary should be independent (p. 11). For Li, rule of law, as opposed to rule of men, is not only the result of modern civilization, but also its very expression (p. 12). Accordingly, Li contends that to entrench the rule of law, institutions of constitutional supervision and judicial independence are necessary (p. 14). In Li's view, the system of constitutional supervision takes judicial review as the key link but covers more than the latter, as it would also include impeachment of leaders, recall of the people's representatives, and the power to interpret the constitution and protect rights, and so on (p. 14). In the Chinese case, the NPC as well as its standing committee actually assumes the function of this constitutional supervision, but Li contends that the articles in the Constitution stipulating it are empty, as there is no special organ or procedure to have this function

11 For an interesting and insightful comparison of the two representative theories, namely the Western liberal version and the Communist Party of China's "vanguard" version, see Jing Yuejing (2007).

carried out (p. 14). Many constitutional scholars have devoted their attention to this issue, and one of the hottest topics of debates in contemporary Chinese legal studies is whether China should increase the power of the People's Supreme Court to the level of its counterpart in the US system or establish a Constitutional Court as Germany has, or a supreme Constitutional Committee within the NPC (Backer 2010). Recently, Larry Backer from the US has advocated the alternative of setting up a Constitutional Committee within the Communist Party of China.

Human rights pillar

The third core component is human rights protection. For Li (2006), "democracy and rule of law are means to realize human rights because the citizen's political rights and justice are among the ends of the government," and human rights are among "the highest material and spiritual needs of mankind" (p. 20). Accordingly, securing human rights is one of two fundamental functions of modern constitutions, with the other being the stipulation of the forms, authorities, procedures, and relationships of state powers (Li, p. 20). In Li's view, there are two sources of human rights corresponding to the natural attributes and social essence of a human being. In other words, the natural attributes of a human being render a person the rights to life, security, freedom of thought, and so on, all of which are related to the inherent dignity of a person as a human being, while the social essence of a human being dictates that political, social, economic, and cultural levels of development in a country affect the existence as well as enjoyment of human rights (Li, p. 21). Overemphasis on one origin would lead to partial understandings as well as biases towards the development and protection of human rights (Li, p. 22). Correspondingly, Li argues that the fulfillment of human rights also needs a balanced view on the relationship between political and civil rights on one hand, and social, political, and cultural rights on the other hand, as well as the relationship between individual rights and collective rights (p. 22–23).[12]

Supremacy of constitution pillar

Besides the three core substantive components of Western Liberal Constitutionalism as reviewed earlier, Li Buyun recently has added a fourth core component, which is the "supremacy of the Constitution." According to Li (2006), adding in this fourth element highlights the supreme status as well as function of the constitution in the political, legal life of a country. The "four elements" definition also summarizes more comprehensively the intensions as well as extensions of constitutionalism, and denotes the scientific content of the notion of "political civilization" (Li, pp. 4–5). This fourth element has been advocated by various scholars as well, such as the well-known legal scholars Guo Daohui (郭道辉) and Li Long (李龙), and so on (Li, p. 4). Another reason for Li's addition of this element is perhaps his agenda of echoing and riding on the repeated calls of the Chinese leadership for "governance in accordance with the Constitution" (*yixianzhiguo* 依宪治国) in recent years (Li, p. 6). Li, however, seems to be intentionally blurring the two concepts, and this

12 Theoretically no liberal scholar would deny the need for balance, but they differ on the balancing point among themselves. Most hard-core liberals, who advocate classical liberalism, emphasize more political and civil rights. In this regard, Li Buyun seems more moderate than them, but does not provide a clear account of his balancing point.

may well be another evidence for the established political scholars that the constitutional scholars in China are usurping the title of constitutionalism, including the "red" title of "Socialist Constitutionalism with Chinese Characteristics" to secretly assume a leading role in directing China's political reform in the future (Chen Hongtai, personal communication, June 10, 2011).

This is then a brief review of the core claims of Western Liberal Constitutionalism as perceived by constitutional scholars in contemporary China. There are surely many different understandings of constitutionalism in China. Some scholars take a narrower vision by equating constitutionalism with rule of constitution and laws; some use it to denote limited government, while others have regarded the essence of constitutionalism as residing in polyarchy as opposed to the concentration of powers, for without a dispersion of power the agreed "entrenched" rules could be annulled by dominant actors at their will (Tang Shiqi, personal communication, May 21, 2010; Zhou, 2005). Nevertheless, Li's explication is comprehensive and also quite representative. Some other liberal scholars, such as those who attended the conference on "Constitutionalism and China" in 2004 in Sydney, do not differ on the core explications but simply emphasize the parallel and close inter-linkages between liberalism and constitutionalism in China as well as the historical reasons for its failure in recent history (Cheng, 2008, p. 392). In fact, the liberal-oriented community has successfully monopolized the term "constitutionalism" to refer to its understanding of Western Liberal Constitutionalism and consequently induced and forced established political scholars as well as officials to evade the notion. However, generally speaking, most constitutional scholars in China have not developed as sophisticated an understanding of the philosophical foundations of constitutionalism as Western scholars have. This may have contributed to the predicament Western Liberal Constitutionalism faces in China today, which we will have a brief review next.

Criticisms of Western Liberal Constitutionalism in China

We could categorize the criticisms of Western Liberal Constitutionalism in China into three main strands depending on their respective stances as well as arguments. The three strands are moving in the direction of becoming more vehement and profound. The first strand is perhaps most sympathetic to advocates of Western Liberal Constitutionalism in China, as it only challenges its practicality, or its prospects of getting transplanted in Chinese soil. The second strand goes one step further by challenging the advocates of Western Liberal Constitutionalism for their ahistorical and sectarian approach. The third strand contends that the core pillars of Western Liberal Constitutionalism are ungrounded and consequently have been "hollowed" out or "eroded" by all kinds of insights from post-modern and deconstructive discourses. This categorization certainly is neither absolute nor exhaustive, but it represents well the challenges Western Liberal Constitutionalism in China faces at the moment. Next, we will have a brief look at each of the three strands.

The problem of getting transplanted and acclimatized

This strand of criticism is relatively moderate, as it does not challenge the core tenets of Western Liberal Constitutionalism; instead it simply raises questions about the compatibility between Western Liberal Constitutionalism and the Chinese cultural ethos as well as the practicability of transplanting it into China in the face of the resistance of the current party-state regime. Arguments falling within this strand also could be divided into two groups.

The first group realizes the importance of a supporting cultural ethos for institutional grafting and the potential harm of forcing Western Liberal Constitutionalism to take root in some "inhospitable soil." For example, through a review of the historicity of liberalism in both the West and China respectively, including the distinctions between classical liberalism, neo-liberalism, and pragmatic neo-liberalism and the possible theories for the transplanting of Western Liberal Constitutionalism in China, namely natural law and positivism as well as historical jurisprudence, M. Ulric Killion (2003) concludes that the neo-liberal constitutionalism modeled on the US's separation of powers and independent judicial review is a denial of both the historicity of Western liberalism and China's ontological base in the Confucian tradition. For Killion (2003), it is odd that advocates of Western Liberal Constitutionalism in China dismiss the importance of the historical particularity of China even though Western Liberal Constitutionalism itself has a particular contingent provenance (pp. 20–21). This is supported by Tong Zhiwei (2009), a well-known legal scholar in China, as he also criticizes Chinese constitutional scholars for ignoring "the actual historical and cultural processes of constitutional development" and for "simply import[ing] alien institutions into China's constitutional system in an ahistorical way" (p. 106). Furthermore, concerned about the dynamics of the "transplant effect," Killion (2003) examines three main possible theories of law for providing a mechanism to transplant Western Liberal Constitutionalism into China, namely naturalist, positivist, and historical jurisprudence theories; the result is that historical jurisprudence theory is the most promising among the three, but this theory points to the importance of the Chinese indigenous cultural tradition that is based on Confucianism (pp. 18, 26–29).[13] For Killion (2003), the historic excesses and abuses of liberalism as manifested in Western history for its contribution to various revolutions, the rejection of legitimate authority, anti-clericalism, and other such tragedies would further frustrate the endeavor to transplant Western Liberal Constitutionalism in China. However, Killion (2003) does not offer a refined definition of China's ontological base in Confucianism, but simply uses it to denote the tradition that has led to "a distinctively Sinic infrastructure; for example polity, socioeconomic, and legal, that perhaps constitutes a blend of both Non-Western and Western models and taxonomies, if not simply distinctive Chinese models and taxonomies" (p. 19). This seems to be a fatal weakness of Killion's arguments, as he certainly needs more sophisticated arguments to be able to respond to the counter examples of Taiwan and Korea, which have presumably Confucian tradition but have successfully embraced Western Liberal Constitutionalism. This is in fact an example of the general weakness of this group of arguments from a cultural perspective.

The second group of arguments concerns Western Liberal Constitutionalism's compatibility with current political environment in China as well as its evolutionary logic. As Killion (2003) notes, given that Western Liberal Constitutionalism is positioned far to the left of even the "new left" or radicals in the ideological spectrum of the Communist Party of China's supervision radar and is perceived by the political authority as a threat to its internal security, it is hard to know how Western Liberal Constitutionalism could be transplanted into China. Some advocates of Western Liberal Constitutionalism may justify non-peaceful means, but for most people, this is morally dubious and practically dangerous and may

13 The main weakness of naturalist theory of law as a way to graft Western Liberal Constitutionalism onto China is that "the actions of a Chinese polity, and ontological tradition (Confucianism), challenges and contradicts Western fundamental principles of justice," while "legal positivism engenders the criticism of being anti-democratic" (Killion, 2003, p. 18–19).

remind us of Lu Xun's (鲁迅) polemics against the advocates of "wholesale Westernization" for being the accomplice of imperialism in China's recent history. Nevertheless, it is the relatively more "radical" or "impatient" nature of advocates of Western Liberal Constitutionalism that makes them different from other more moderate liberals in China today and leads some of them to criticize Chinese liberals from Hu Shi to Li Shenzhi for being too idealist and not realistic enough for their endeavors (Cheng, 2008, p. 392). This is also the reason why Liu Xiaobo supports the US war in Iraq and Afghanistan, and proclaims that, given its vast size, China should go through 300 years of colonial rule in order to reach the "civilized" level of Hong Kong today (Lu, 2010). It is in this sense that Western Liberal Constitutionalism belongs to the category of "subversive force" in Liu Jianjun's typology. Based on their different normative orientations, problems concerned, and solution prescribed, Liu (2009) categorizes three types of "forces" among the various political thoughts in contemporary China, namely "subversive force" (***dianfuliliang*** 颠覆力量), "reconstructive force" (***chonggouliliang*** 重构力量), and "curative force" (***zhiliaoliliang*** 治疗力量) (pp. 93–94). Liu uses the examples of Westernization camp (***xihuapai*** 西化派) as the representative of the "subversive forces," and "humanitarianism, civil society theory, and governance theory" and so on as the "reconstructive forces," while New Authoritarianism and Elitism as the representative of "curative forces." While the categorization is certainly far from absolute and precise, it is nevertheless a useful heuristic for our understanding of the various thoughts in contemporary China. This also helps us to distinguish Western Liberal Constitutionalism and the liberal-oriented pro-government scholars mentioned earlier, such as Zhang Wenxiang, Yu Keping, and so on.

As we can see, this strand of criticism is relatively moderate, and it is still largely operating within the liberal paradigm, as their only objection is the difficulty of implementation in China, but they still regard Western Liberal Constitutionalism as the best form of government containing some "universal values" of modern civilization. Accordingly, the force of their criticism is not particularly strong, because once the desirability of Western Liberal Constitutionalism is granted, the focus of debate then becomes its practicability, which is a kind of technical issue that subjects to different cost-benefit calculations. Nevertheless, as we will see, whether or not to accept the universal status of Western Liberal Constitutionalism is the main factor distinguishing this strand of criticism from the second strand next.

The problem of being parochial and sectarian

The second strand of criticisms goes one step further from the first strand, as it denies the universal status of Western Liberal Constitutionalism and challenges Western Liberal Constitutionalism's parochial and sectarian nature. These arguments could be divided into two main orders based on their primary targets, namely obsession with US constitutional model and over-reliance on classical liberalism as the philosophical foundation. Regarding the first order, we can see that advocates of Western Liberal Constitutionalism in China all seem to have the US model in their eyes without realizing or taking seriously other Western models, as shown in their obsession with the constitutional principles of checks and balances, and judicial review. However, just as Balme and Dowdle (2009) point out, if we take the perspective of regarding constitutionalism as the envisioning of the state, we should realize that there is not *a* constitutionalism but a diversity of *constitutionalisms*; for example, even within the West, the French vision of their state is very different from that of the Americans. The obsession with judicial review is also particularly parochial, as even in the most effective constitutional systems in the world, such as the UK, significant aspects of the constitutional structure are largely "nonjusticiable" [sic] (Balme & Dowdle, 2009, pp. 2–3). In fact, there are also quite a number of countries such as the Netherlands, Sweden, Italy, Japan, India, and so on where there is either no judicial review, little application of the power, or little effect even after using the power (Balme & Dowdle, 2009, p. 3), yet operating as well as the US.[14]

Regarding the second order of critique, the critics point out that the over-reliance on classical liberalism as the philosophical foundation of Western Liberal Constitutionalism in China grossly ignores the different versions of liberalism available in the Western history. For example, responding to criticism from advocates of Western Liberal Constitutionalism of modern Chinese liberals for not being "real liberals," Edmund Fung (2008–2009) argues that the Chinese understanding of liberalism, as shown in Yan Fu (严复) for example, is quite sophisticated, and the particular form Chinese liberalism took in recent history actually quite resembles the liberal trend in Western Europe during the first half of the 20th century.[15] As a result, Fung (2008–2009) argues that the key to understand this is an awareness of the historicity of liberalism and its historical contingencies, as well as an appreciation of the different strands of liberal thought in the West (p. 558). This is supported by quite a number of scholars as well. For example, Jiang Yihua (2007), an intellectual historian from Taiwan, points out at a symposium on contemporary Chinese political philosophy held at Zhejiang University that the Western ideas of separation of church and state, checks and balances, supremacy of law, due process, and so on all have their specific stories as well as origins.

As we can see, the force of this strand of criticism is stronger than that of the first strand. The official line and established scholars largely fall within this strand, with their polemic against the so-called "universal values" (*pushijiazhi* 普世价值) embodied in the US model as a good example. However, a weakness in this strand is a lack of very advanced theories to dissociate the normative aspirations of Western Liberal Constitutionalism which is widely taken to be universal and the particular institutional forms imported from the West that are parochial. Without such subtle theories, the force of the arguments may be undermined. Yet, the biggest challenge is that advocates of Western Liberal Constitutionalism in the West have developed very sophisticated and seemingly impeccable theories for establishing a symbiotic relationship between the particular forms Western Liberal Constitutionalism takes and the universal values it aspires for. Nevertheless, these irreproachable theories have been gradually challenged by various "post-" discourses emerged in the West that are equally subtle and sophisticated. These schools have consequently provides resources for the critics of Western Liberal Constitutionalism in China, which we will review next.

The problem of being flawed and ungrounded

If the second strand of critiques of Western Liberal Constitutionalism in China marks a further big step than the first strand, the third strand reaches the core of Western Liberal

14 In their latest article "Political Theory Put to the Test: Comparative Law and the Origins of Judicial Constitutional Review," Maurice Adams and Gerhard van der Schyff (2010) also criticize conventional readings of the provenance of judicial constitutional review in the world, and provide an alternative plausible proposal.

15 For Fung (2008–2009), the Chinese liberals are "legitimate" "statist [liberals] with democratic socialist leanings" even though not the Hayekian classical liberals (p. 558).

Constitutionalism and seeks to shake its foundations. These criticisms come not only from the "New Left" which emerged in the late 1990s, but also from scholars of communitarianism, post-modernism, feminism, post-colonialism, as well as the newly emerging neo-classical schools, including both Neo-Confucians and Leo-Straussians (Jiang, 2007; Xu, 2007).[16] As a result, some intellectual historians in China point out that liberalism has largely exited the central stage of the current public sphere (Jiang, 2007; Qian, 2007; Xu, 2007). For them, besides the competition of the various schools mentioned earlier, another important reason is that Western Liberal Constitutionalism, or what these scholars call political liberalism, does not offer very good answers to many of the most serious problems of contemporary China, such as the wide economic disparity, and prevalent moral nihilism, and so on, which, however, are an inherent part of China's problems any successful ideologies or constitutional discourses need to tackle with.

Regarding the challenge of the philosophical foundation of Western Liberal Constitutionalism, besides Newton's criticism through the insights of Spinoza as reviewed in previous chapter, Mark Warren also provides a subtle and insightful critique of Western Liberal Constitutionalism's dissimulating ideology within the liberal tradition itself. For Warren (1989), even though the republican vision of Western Liberal Constitutionalism deeply influenced by the Greek philosophers does seek to constitute a public space for the individuals to flourish, it fails to identify the social conditions necessary to redeem these promises that have been utilized to justify it. Warren (1989) calls this a "dissimulating ideology" because it justifies "situations by misidentifying them, often by equating a single social relation with an ideal, and then abstracting this from the totality of social relations necessary to its realization" (p. 514). For Warren, the power of liberal constitutionalism particularly relies on its promises of transforming politics from a process of coercion to one of reason, and allowing the individuals to flourish under liberal constitutional protections and guarantees. However, it assumes that individuality and autonomy would flower if only political power was limited, without realizing that the growing "social power," which "operates on the full range of needs, relations, and attributes that constitute persons" could equally "corrupt" or "distort" the natural development of the individuals (p. 523).[17] This is actually why Marx criticizes the liberal constitutionalism for conflating political emancipation with human emancipation (Warren, 1989, p. 523). While Warren still holds some faith in the progressive dimension of the liberal constitutionalism in contrast to Marx, he does acknowledge that at the worst liberal constitutionalism produces "ideological effects that are parasitic on normative ascriptions of subjectivity" (p. 513), and the empirical result might be the opposite to its aspirations (p. 519). While not being fully aware of the latter point's necessity as well as implications, Warren does point to the right directions, which, as we have seen, is well complemented by Newton's insights about its logic as imperialism.

Besides these challenges of Western Liberal Constitutionalism's philosophical foundation, the four pillars of Western Liberal Constitutionalism reviewed earlier are also criticized by arguments from various quarters, which we will review later. Regarding the democracy pillar, not mentioning the rich tradition of anti-democratic thought in the Western history,

16 While this group does not fit together very well, with post-modernism suspect of any foundational theories as a prime example, their criticism of Western Liberal Constitutionalism as well as effect is nevertheless the same.

17 It is perhaps worth pointing out that the Confucians gives the answer by prescribing the rituals, which will be elaborated in the next chapter.

quite a number of works have emerged as a strike to the Western liberal democracy. For example, in his book *Democratic Faith*, Patrick Deneen (2005) provides a trenchant analysis of the democratic faith prevalent in contemporary world and a powerful critique of the underlying assumptions of various democratic theories. We will not have the scope here to go into the details of his argument, but as Deneen points out in his preface:

> This is a study of paradox, an inquiry into how a political system designed to minimize claims of faith itself rests on faith, how a regime embraced for its modernity may be immodest in that embrace, how the rejection of truth in politics has led to the creation of a guiding truth in politics, and how that most anti-utopian regime may become most dangerously utopian at the moment it congratulates itself loudest for its defeat of utopianism in politics.
>
> (p. xvii)

Regarding the rule of law pillar, Jill Frank (2006) challenges the commonly held "truism" in academia that Aristotle is the source of the notion of an opposition between power and lawfulness. Indeed, it is very common to see articles or textbooks tracing the origin of modern rule of law and constitutionalism to Aristotle (Frank, 2006; Xie, 2004, p. 3). Nevertheless, just as Frank (2006) argues, rather than taking the rule of law to exemplify reason's moderation over desire, Aristotle regards the rule of law as a practice of political power, issued from practical wisdom that combines reason and desire (p. 37). I think there is certain validity to Frank's arguments, but the problem is more with the confusing usages of the term law in Aristotle, which due to scope will not be elaborated here. Frank's insight also supports the priority of political authority over legal authority as well, which as we will see in later chapters is a thing taken for granted by both the Confucian and Marxist schools as well.

For the erosion of the human rights pillar, Costas Douzinas (2000) also provides a wonderful genealogical and philosophical account of how "human rights" has triumphed in the world in the sense that it becomes the dominant norm. Another concept closely related to human rights – human dignity – has also been deconstructed by Doron Shultziner (2003). In his article, "Human Dignity – Functions and Meanings," Shultziner shows that

> the meanings of human dignity are socially constructed in accordance with particular cultural and historical contexts. There is no one "true" meaning of human dignity, but rather different levels of "thickness" and "thinness" that are culturally determined in each society.
>
> (p. 1)

These critiques are just some examples that have been advocated in academia, which more or less have been introduced to China by those critics of Western Liberal Constitutionalism, such as Hou Huiqin (侯惠勤),[18] Liu Xiaofeng (刘小枫), Gan Yang (甘阳), Wang Shaoguang (王韶光), Pan Wei (潘维), Jiang Qing (蒋庆), and so on. Nevertheless, as some intellectual historians in China have observed, advocates of Western Liberal Constitutionalism

18 Hou is the party secretary of the Marxist Study Institute at the Chinese Academy of Social Science and has just published an over 700-page book entitled *Marx's Ideological Critique and Contemporary China* (2010) to criticize all non-orthodox ideologies that have emerged in China.

in China have not successfully responded to these criticisms and to some extent are ostrich-like.[19] Even though some more open-minded liberals have sought to return to the more comprehensive liberalism of Mill and Kant to deal with the new challenges of contemporary China as well as the various criticisms as we have reviewed, it seems that most advocates of Western Liberal Constitutionalism are not. This is indeed a major reason for the lack of dialogue among the various schools in Chinese academia today.

Conclusion

In this chapter, we reviewed the expansionist history of Western Liberal Constitutionalism in China, which is divided into the late Qing to early Republican period and the post-reform period. After reviewing the history of Western Liberal Constitutionalism in China, we have seen the core claims of Western Liberal Constitutionalism as explicated in *Charter 08* as well as Li Buyun's works and described the three main strands of criticisms of Western Liberal Constitutionalism in China. To a certain extent, history seems to be repeating itself, because Western Liberal Constitutionalism was ultimately defeated in mainland China in the last century, and today, it is in decline largely due to its inability to respond to many of the current problems China faces as well as to criticisms from various quarters. Even within the constitutional realm, Western Liberal Constitutionalism's "monopoly" status has been broken up, and in recent years, "Sinicized Marxist Constitutionalism" and "traditional Confucian Constitutionalism" have emerged and are being advocated as alternatives. In the following chapters, we will offer a review and discussion of these two alternative constitutional discourses.

19 It is worth pointing out again that advocates of Western Liberal Constitutionalism in the article refer to those who embrace Western liberal political structures centered on multi-party competition and power checks and balances. They are distinct from the liberal-oriented pro-government scholars who selectively adopt certain Western Liberal Constitutionalism principles but nevertheless still uphold the current regime. In this sense, the advocates of Western Liberal Constitutionalism are truly "subversive forces."

4 Traditional Confucian Constitutionalism

Current explorations and its prospects[1]

> It [constitution] is not engraved on marble or bronze, but in the hearts of citizens. It is the true constitution of the state. Everyday it takes on new forces. When other laws grow old and die away, it revives and replaces them, preserves a people in the spirit of its institution and imperceptibly substitutes the force of habit for that of authority. I am speaking of mores, customs, and especially of opinion, a part of the law unknown to our political theorists but one on which depends the success of all the others; a part with which the great legislator secretly occupies himself, though he seems to confine himself to the particular regulations that are merely the arching of the vault, whereas mores, slower to arise, form in the end its immovable keystone.
>
> – Rousseau (1987, p. 172).

Introduction

For a relatively long period of time, it has been widely thought that Confucianism and constitutionalism are incompatible, even antithetical (Chan, 2007; Chaihark, 2003; Zhang, 2001). For example, Confucianism is usually associated with authoritarianism, the rule of man instead of the rule of law, collectivism, hierarchical role-based order, over-emphasis on obligation, and so on, while constitutionalism is founded on the rule of law, individual rights, equality, and so on (Bao, 1998; Chan, 2007; Davis, 1998; Ginsburg, 2002). This view is a prominent feature of Chinese thought from the New Cultural Movement of the early 20th century to the "Asian Values" debates of recent decades. Even today, it still holds some currency among many intellectuals both in and outside China.

However, in recent years, some intellectuals are breaking off the yoke of this dominant view by exploring constitutional resources within Confucianism and challenging previous conceptual frameworks. As we shall see, we can identify three main approaches on the issue of Confucian Constitutionalism in contemporary academia, namely the institutional approach, the ritualistic approach, and the religious approach.[2] What are their respective arguments for Confucian constitutionalism? What are the main problems with the current approaches, and what are the prospects for Traditional Confucian Constitutionalism? These

1 Parts of this chapter have been reproduced with kind permission from the article "Traditional Confucian Constitutionalism: Current Explorations and Prospects," Peng Chengyi, in *Frontiers of Philosophy in China*, 2013: 8,1.

2 This categorization into three groups is certainly not exhaustive and there are surely other voices as well; however, these three approaches seem to represent well the dominant trends of investigations on the issue of Confucian constitutionalism.

are the questions this chapter seeks to explore. I shall argue that these various approaches all make valid discoveries and have unearthed excellent constitutional resources within the Confucian tradition; however, each approach seems to have its respective limitations, and only a combination of them could render a full picture of Traditional Confucian Constitutionalism, which would have some significant implications.

Before delving into a review of the literature on the topic and a discussion of it, a few clarifications regarding the title are needed. I consider these various approaches under the general notion of "Traditional Confucian/Chinese Constitutionalism" (hereafter Traditional Confucian Constitutionalism) for the following reasons. First of all, they are "traditional" because the scholars who advocate these views are all largely exploring the constitutional resources within the history of the Confucian tradition rather than its contemporary manifestations. The religious approach may be the exception, but as their endeavor is very impractical, I do not consider it a plausible way for Traditional Confucian Constitutionalism to adapt to a contemporary context. I keep "Confucian" here largely because these scholars also openly claim to be confining their explorations to the Confucian tradition, which is, though, not rigorously defined. As we will see, this is actually a shortcoming of these approaches, for they do unnecessary injustice to other schools within the Chinese cultural tradition that have deeply influenced both political philosophy and practices throughout the long Chinese history. That is why I have put "Chinese" in the title as well, which is more comprehensive despite its more porous nature. Regarding the concept of "constitutionalism," as we have seen in Chapter 1, there are certainly many different definitions and understandings, so I will not subscribe to a specific definition or perspective here to avoid unnecessary and limiting commitments and will try to clarify the concept whenever the need arises.

Three approaches towards Traditional Confucian Constitutionalism

Institutional approach

As mentioned earlier, based on their stances and perspectives, we can identify three main approaches toward the issue of Confucian constitutionalism.[3] The first is what I call the institutional approach in the narrow sense, because in a broad sense, Confucian *Li* (礼) and Confucianism as a state religion are also institutions. By institutional approach, I mean the approach relying on the checks and balances of power exercised by some substantive power-holding entities. This approach does not challenge the conceptual framework of the liberal constitutional paradigm and instead seeks to demonstrate that the institutions of a Confucian polity actually have mechanisms of checks and balances, which are the core of constitutionalism according to these authors. There are two main dimensions to this approach, with one focusing on the checks and balances along the horizontal line, in other words, among largely equal power-holding entities, and the other along the vertical line, which is between the monarch and his subordinate. We will review these two dimensions next.

3 The identification of the three approaches is not only due to the nature of the literature reviewed, but also out of consideration for constructing an all-encompassing three-layered Traditional Confucian Constitutionalism later. It is worth pointing out, though, that the categorization does not exhaust all the approaches found in the literature, nor does it, in every respect, clearly demarcate the boundaries among them.

The first horizontal dimension is well explored by Jongryn Mo's (2003) case study of the Censorate of the *Chosŏn* Dynasty (*chaoxian wangchao* 朝鲜王朝) in Korean history, in which he shows that Confucianism is actually quite rich in ideas and practices promoting horizontal accountability, many of which even meet the criteria of modern accountability theory. While Mo mainly uses the term "accountability," he treats it as largely equivalent to the notion of "checks and balances," a terminology largely derived from the US context, and also occasionally uses the latter in the article.[4] For Mo (2003), modern accountability theory, as articulated by O'Donnell, stipulates five conditions for the effective operation of an accountability system: 1) existence of vertical accountability,[5] 2) independence of the accounting party, 3) existence of multiple accounting agencies, 4) overlapping jurisdictions of the accounting agencies, and 5) recursive and reciprocal accountability among the accounting agents (p. 57). According to Mo's explication, while the first condition pertains to the mutual reinforcing relationship between vertical and horizontal accountability in a democratic system, the other four requirements deal with two main problems of an accountability system: "how to create accounting agencies that are sufficiently powerful or autonomous to do their job" and "how to hold accounting agencies themselves accountable" (p. 57). For these latter two problems, Mo argues that the *Chosŏn* Censorate had successfully solved them with "an elaborate and surprisingly 'modern' construct" (p. 64). Next, we will briefly review Mo's arguments.

First of all, Mo (2003) contends that the Censorate had a high degree of autonomy with the following designs: it was placed directly under the king, and its members were not allowed to hold concurrent positions in other government branches; the members are exempted from biannual merit reviews like other officials and did not have fixed and guaranteed terms, though they usually were promoted after their tenure ended. Furthermore, the censors were independent from their appointers – the personnel directors, who were usually low-ranking officials of fifth or sixth grade and also most independent from the king and ministers throughout the rest of officialdom (p. 62). Additionally, Mo points out that the state ideology of Confucianism, with its emphasis on moral rectitude and historical examples, provided the *raison d'etre* for the autonomy of the censoring system (p. 62). Regarding the second-order question of holding the accounting agencies themselves accountable, it was solved through the division of the Censorate into three organs, namely the Office of the Inspector-General (OIG) (*sixianfu* 司宪府), the Office of the Censor-General (OCG) (*sijianyuan* 司谏院), and the Office of the Special Counselors (OSC) (*hongwenguan* 弘文馆), the prescription of their overlapping jurisdictions, as well as their reciprocal checks (Mo, p. 62). As a result, Mo points out that a kind of checks and balances emerged in the Confucian polity (p. 63).

For Mo, the most heuristic and also distinctive part of the *Chosŏn* Censorate system was the independence of the individual censors as well as their junior status, which, together with other incentive prescriptions, rendered the Censorate reform-oriented and the internal

4 This is reasonable, because for Mo, "accountability indicates the degree to which power is kept under control, domesticated, or subject to the rule of law" (p. 56). Nevertheless, there might be some subtle semantic gaps between the two, just as that between "checks" and "balances," which Mo does not clarify.

5 The distinction between vertical and horizontal accountability is made by O'Donnell, and is solely based on the power relationships between the accounting and accountable agents. Examples of horizontal accountability include the checks and balances among the three branches of government in the US political system; and those of vertical accountability include the accounting relationships between voters and elected politicians in modern democracies (Mo, p. 57).

agent of change within the bureaucracy (p. 67). In fact, that is what Mo particularly advocates for the institutional reforms in contemporary Korea.

The horizontal "checks and balances" within the Confucian polity unearthed by Mo is in fact well supported by the vast literature devoted to this theme within contemporary Chinese academia.[6] For example, the principles of "mutual surveillance and mutual correction" (***huduhujiu*** 互督互纠), "syncretism of remonstrance and censorship" (***taijianheyi*** 台谏合一), and "using the lower officials to censor the higher" (***yizunlinbei*** 以卑临尊), summarized by a Chinese scholar on the power-checking mechanism of ancient China, clearly render support to Mo's discoveries in the *Chosŏn* case (Ni, 1996, pp. 64–65). Besides these, the Chinese literature broadly covers other institutional aspects such as the emphasis on the codification of power supervision (***lifajiandu*** 立法监督), the offense reporting system (***jubaozhidu*** 举报制度), and central-local checks and balances (***zhongyangdifangzhiheng*** 中央-地方制衡), and so on (Ni, 1996).[7] While Mo's discoveries may be fresh to some in the West, the horizontal checks and balances within the Confucian polity have been well explored by Chinese scholars and to some extent even taken for granted by them. Conceivably, the vast literature devoted to the statecraft of ancient China within Western academia may have unearthed similar discoveries as well, though they have not sought to connect them to the discourse of constitutionalism. It is perhaps in this sense that Mo's article finds its greatest significance.

However, despite the general support received from the peer literature in China, there are three main problems with the claimed relationship between the Censorate and constitutionalism as presented in Mo's work. First of all, it is perhaps a little far-fetched to attribute the Censorate accountability feature to Confucianism alone. As Hucker (1959) points out, while the censorial system does represent "an organized and systematic effort by the government to police itself," it has two main sources, namely Confucianism and Legalism (p. 207). In fact, Hucker attributes the surveillance function of the Censorate largely to Legalism and the remonstration function of the Censorate to Confucianism (p. 193). According to some scholars, the remonstration function played a very limited role in constraining the throne throughout the course of Chinese history (Wang, 2004, pp. 234–235). The second problem concerns the degree to which the horizontal dimension relies on the vertical dimension for its effectiveness. While Mo mentions that the weakest link of the Confucian accountability system is "the absence of vertical accountability [in the democratic sense]" (p. 62), he does not seek to evaluate the significance of this difference on the overall effectiveness of the Confucian Censorate system. In fact, most Chinese scholars who write on these themes tend to highlight this weakness by contrasting the performances of the Censorate at the beginning and the end of a dynasty, where at the beginning it tends to work well and

6 A search of "ancient Chinese power checks and balances" (***zhongguogudaiquanlizhiheng*** 中国古代权力制衡) in the Chinese Journal Database renders 53 articles on that theme, and 377 entries for the theme of "ancient Chinese Censorate" (***zhongguogudaijiancha*** 中国古代监察). There are also quite a few academic monolographs written on these themes, such as Sun and Feng's *The Power Checking Mechanism in Ancient Chinese Bureaucracy Politics* (《中国传统官僚政治中的权力制约机制》) (2010), Yongming Qiu's *The History of Ancient Chinese Censorate System* (《中国古代监察制度史》) (2006), and so on

7 I am just enlisting the institutional aspects here; other aspects covered by the Chinese literature include ethical constraint, cosmic constraints, and so on. For a detailed exploration of these latter aspects, see Sun Jiping and Feng Yong's (2010) book *The Power Checking Mechanism in Ancient Chinese Bureaucratic Politics* (《中国传统官僚政治中的权力制约机制》).

near the end it often performs virtually no function at all. A furthermore fatal problem is with his reductive usage of the concept of "vertical accountability." He quotes from O'Donnell explicating the distinction of vertical accountability over horizontal accountability as "depending on the hierarchical relationship between accounting and accountable agents" (as cited in Mo, p. 57). This definition certainly goes beyond the concept in a democratic sense, but Mo seems to reduce the former to the latter and concludes that the Confucian polity does not have vertical accountability. This is a major problem shared by many Chinese scholars writing on these themes, as they tend to attribute the poor performances of the censorate near the end of a dynasty to the lack of democratic accountability. Nevertheless, conceivably the censorate system may not work at all had there been no vertical accountability, and as we will see, there is such a mechanism of vertical checks and balances in the Confucian polity as well, despite the lack of democratic control in the modern sense.[8]

The vertical dimension largely pertains to the power relationships along the vertical line of the Confucian hierarchy. Correcting the stereotype of absolutism running throughout Chinese history, some scholars contended that there is a certain degree of "checks and balances" even between the king and his subordinates. One good representative work on this is Jaeyoon Song's (2009) article on the complementary yet countervailing relationships between the Sovereign and his Ministers. In his article, Song analyzes Southern Song commentaries on the *Zhou Li* and argues that their elaborations of good government in fact have developed into "a systematic theory of constrained government, an indigenous articulation of 'constitutionalism' in the Chinese tradition" (p. 424).[9] Since this is a systematic and sophisticated analysis of the vertical "checks and balances" within Confucian polity, it is worth presenting a detailed review of the arguments here.

For Song (2009), the relationship between the King and the Grand Steward is not stated very clearly in the "constitution" – *Zhou Li*,[10] which leaves room for Southern Song commentators to articulate their theories. Two such commentators, Zheng Boqian (郑伯谦) and Ye Shi (叶时), give very different interpretations of the sovereign-minister relationship from that of Wang Anshi's harmonious view, an orthodox interpretation in the preceding era. Regarding the reason the Grand Steward is given so much authority among the six

8 In fact, there are many interesting similarities between the Confucian vertical accountability and the modern democratic vertical accountability: in the Confucian case, the government is accountable to the Monarch, who ideally should represent the genuine interests/General Will of the people whose existence has a teleological moral purpose; in modern democracies, the government is also accountable to the elected politicians, who ideally should represent the genuine interests/General Will of the people as well. The vital difference between the two is perhaps the different missions entrusted as well as the differing mechanisms through which the Monarch and elected politicians are held accountable. I intentionally use Rousseau's notion of "General Will" here to denote the inseparable and unerring nature of the term as in contrast to "the will of the people," which is more a sum of the private wills. To see the nuanced distinction, see Rousseau (1987, pp. 155–156). In this sense, it is debatable whether the Monarch or elected politicians (usually "partisan" in nature today) could better represent the General Will.

9 Song does not give a lengthy explication of the concepts "constitution" and "constitutionalism," but just briefly defines them as "the body of doctrines and practices that form the fundamental organizing principles of political state" and "the idea that the coercive power of the state should be constrained" respectively (pp. 424–425).

10 Regarding the constitutionality of the *Zhou Li*, see David Schaberg (2010).

ministries,[11] thereby creating the potential for tyranny, Zheng points out that the guiding principle is

> occupational duties were specified at the bottom; yet the heart of power was unified at the top [like the draw rope of a fishing net]. Every office is united therein. . . . Although things were not done by one or two people, one or two people could possibly lead them.
> (Song, 2009, p. 431)

Zheng further points out that the authority of the Grand Steward over the rest of the bureaucracy is emphasized because there are natural "centrifugal tendencies among lower offices to push for autonomy as they become specialized and routinized," and the measure is a proactive necessity to prevent that from happening (Song, p. 431).

A key constitutional issue is then how to constrain the powers of the Grand Steward to avoid the danger of ministerial tyranny. Targeting this issue, Southern Song commentators resort to the power of the King, especially his use of the Eight Levers (*babing* 八柄) and the Eight Commands (*batong* 八统), as well as the countervailing power of the Royal Secretary (*Neishi* 内史) (Song, 2009). While in the "constitution" the King's role is defined relatively vaguely with more symbolic than actual power for specific state affairs in contrast to that of the Grand Steward, Ye Shi argues that the presence of the King actually serves as an effective constraint on the powers of the Grand Steward, particularly through the division of powers as well as the aid of the Royal Secretary (Song, p. 431). Among the authorized powers of the Grand Steward in the Ten Articles, Ye observes that there are two that the Grand Steward must report to the King, namely those that concern the Eight Levers for the control of the bureaucrats (*yuqunchen* 驭群臣) and the Eight Commands (八统) for the control of the people (*yuwanmin* 驭万民) (Song, p. 431). According to Zheng, these two Articles "concern matters of supreme importance, which should require judicious decision-making beyond the boundaries of the given statutes" (Song, p. 434). Song points out that here it is important to notice that both Ye and Zheng distinguish the expediency (*quan* 权) from the constant (*chang* 常) and established laws (*jing* 经) (p. 434).[12] Concerning the other eight Articles, which the Grand Steward does not need to report to the King, they largely deal with established laws or the management of the constant (p. 434). In other words, "the Grand Steward is in charge of the rule of law while the King is entitled to the rule of man" (Song, p. 434).

Besides this separation of power as an effective constraint on the power of the Grand Steward, Ye points out that the presence of the Royal Secretary also places some constraints on the Grand Steward. According to the "Ministry of Rites of Spring" (*chunguanzongbai* 春官宗伯), the Royal Secretariat is composed of 87 officials, who should report to the King on the matters of the Eight Rafts (*bafang* 八枋) (Song, 2009, p. 432). For Song, what is of vital importance here is that the Eight Rafts is exactly the same as the Eight Levers, namely acts concerning official titles, salaries, prizes, imprisonment, nourishment, confiscation, banishment, and reprimand of the bureaucrats (p. 432). Furthermore, according to Ye, the role of the Royal Secretary is to "closely examine the Grand Steward and to report

11 It is worth noticing that officially the Grand Steward is just the head of the Ministry of Heaven, one of the six ministries, with the rest being the Ministry of Earth, Ministry of Spring, Ministry of Summer, Ministry of Autumn, and Ministry of Winter respectively.

12 Song seems to misinterpret the *jing* (经) here, which usually refers to unchanging truths or principles.

and advise the King on these matters" (Song, pp. 432–433). In this way, the overlapping jurisdictions regarding the Eight Levers between the Grand Steward and the Royal Secretary serve as a double issuance for the prevention of the potential monopoly and abuse of that important power (Song, p. 433).

Song points out that a kind of mutual checks and balances between the King and the Grand Steward is thus unearthed in the Confucian polity (2009). On one hand, the supreme power of the Grand Steward over the bureaucracy is constrained by the King with the aid of the Royal Secretary; on the other hand, the emphasis of the authority of the Grand Steward, especially within its autonomous realms, also serves as an effective means for restraining the power of the King (Song, p. 434). Even within the realms where the King could legitimately intervene in the state affairs of the Grand Steward, the presence of the Royal Secretary reduces the chances of the King making arbitrary decisions (Song, p. 434). In fact, this tension and balance between the Grand Steward and the King might provide great resources even for our contemporary politics, for on the one hand,

> the Grand Steward represents the ideals of meritocracy, bureaucratic standardization, the rule of law, and limits to monarchical autocracy. In contrast, the king represents the ideals of responsive rulership, circumstantial justice, the rule of man, and a check against ministerial tyranny.
>
> (Song, p. 435)

Song's article certainly provides fresh new insights about checks and balances in the Confucian polity along the vertical line. His distinction between rule of man and rule of law along the royal and bureaucratic lines is also quite heuristic and promising. However, there are also two problems. The first concerns the representativeness of Southern Song commentators' political theory within Chinese intellectual history as well as its effectiveness in practice. As we all know, throughout Chinese history, the king and the minister are not always in a "checks and balances," and sometimes such a relationship even does not exist. For example, during the Ming Dynasty, because of the revolt of an early Grand Steward, the position was abolished throughout most of the dynasty, so there was not the kind of king-minister mutual checks. The endeavor of Song is thus similar to those previous attempts seeking to discover liberal tradition in the Chinese history, but the significance of this approach needs our careful scrutiny. This then leads to the second problem, which is about the lack of critical awareness toward the conceptual framework of Western constitutionalism. Basically, Song, just like most other constitutional scholars, regards only hard restraints of power as the defining feature of constitutionalism. That is actually why he is particularly interested in Southern Song commentaries of the *Zhou Li*, which centers on the tension and checks between the King and the Grand Steward. As a result, his account has missed other very important and defining features of Confucian constitutionalism, which are what we will review next.

Ritualistic approach

If the first approach, the institutional approach, largely focuses on the specific institutions of the Confucian polity, the second approach goes a step further by locating the core of Confucian constitutionalism in the *Li* (礼), a unique Confucian concept usually translated as "ritual," "propriety," "rites," "manners," "ceremony," "etiquette," "courtesy" and "rules of proper conducts," and so on.[13] This approach does not focus so much on the internal "checks and balances," but more on the power-restraining or constitutional characteristics of the Confucian *Li* (礼), which has attracted much attention in the academic community. For some, such as Chen Ming (2008), constitutionalism does not have to utilize the separation of power mechanisms to limit political authority because the aim can be achieved through the *Li* (礼), which, as we will see, has several other distinctive advantages as well.

This approach is perhaps the most fully explored among the three approaches covered in this chapter, and here we will mainly review the arguments defending the Confucian *Li*'s constitutional nature as well as its advantages. Regarding the constitutional nature of the Confucian *Li*, Zhang Qianfan (张千帆), a well-known Chinese scholar of constitutional studies at Beijing University, provides a good theoretical defense with some good direct quotes from the classics. For Zhang (2001), the Confucian *Li* is a system of fundamental rules and norms established to maintain social order, cultivate virtuous characters, guide people to constrain their desires, and attune people's social life with the "Heavenly Way" (*tiandao* 天道) (p. 120). Zhang elaborates on three features of the *Li* that qualify it as a constitution. First of all, the *Li* is elevated by the Confucians to the highest norms of a state. It is thought to be created by the ancient sages and taken from the Heavenly Way. Indeed, there are many passages in the *Li Ji* (《礼记》) emphasizing the paramount importance, the source, the scope as well as the functions of the *Li*. Xunzi also regards *Li* as the acme of all laws and ethical rules (*fazhidafen qunleizhigangji* 法之大分，群类之纲纪) ("Advise on Learning" of *Xunzi* 《荀子-劝学》). At the same time, because it is established and maintained by human beings, it is lower than the natural law,[14] but higher than positive laws and social customs. Second, while the all-encompassing *Li* system contains all kinds of trivial and corpulent rules, it has certain core founding principles, such as the Five Relationships (*wulun* 五伦), which establishes and maintains a rational hierarchical structure. The third feature of the *Li* is the stability and durability of its core elements. For example, while certain parts of the *Li* are replaceable, just as the passage that "the Three Kings' world are different and they do not adopt the same rituals" (*sanwangyishi buxiangyanli* 三王易世,不相沿礼) indicates, its core principles, such as "to love those who are kindredly close, respect those who are respectable, obey appropriately the elder siblings, and treat men and women with distinction, and so on" (亲亲也，尊尊也，长长也，男女有别，此其不可得与民变革者也), are not changeable. For Zhang, the *Li*'s highest normative status in the state, the durability and stability of its core, plus its entrenchment of a hierarchical structure thus render it a constitution of the Confucian polity.[15]

Echoing Zhang's defense of the Confucian *Li*'s constitutional nature, Hahm Chaihark (2009) explores in depth the regime-legitimating and -restraining functions of

13 To avoid misunderstandings or mis-associations, I prefer to simply transliterate rather than translate *Li* (礼) here; however, because most scholars have translated *Li* as "ritual," I will keep their usage intact as well, so in the book the two will be used interchangeably, though I am not denying or ignoring the semantic gaps.

14 The author does not clarify the concept of Natural Law here; it seems to be some higher laws that originate from human nature and the universe; hence, these are unchanging in contrast to the positive laws human beings make.

15 In the article, Zhang further discusses and refutes three possible objections, namely: first, the rule of *Li* (礼) is a kind of "rule of man" rather than "rule of law"; second, the *Li* stipulates people's responsibilities and obligations toward the family and state only, but not rights; third, the inherent stability of the *Li* leads to stasis, hence hindering the advancement of society. For a detailed review of his arguments, see pp. 123–126.

the Confucian *Li* and the similarities between the ritual controversies occurred in the *Chosŏn* Korea and modern constitutional crises. For Chaihark, contrary to the modern "secularized" mindset, the Confucian *Li* not only acts as a form of social control and a factor in legitimating power, but also plays the constitutional function of restraining and disciplining political power (2009, p. 199). He further defends this argument by showing, through a case study of the *Chosŏn* Korea, that its ritual controversies have very similar operating mechanisms as modern constitutional crises, for it also involves prolonged political strife, a breakdown of dialogues between different interpretive voices, and a collapse of epistemic foundations underlying the conceptions of the constitution (2009, p. 135).

Besides defending the constitutional nature of the Confucian *Li*, these scholars have also uncovered the unique advantages of a ritualistic constitutionalism. For example, both Hahm Chaihark and Kim Jin-Ha point to the education function of the *Li* as a defining unique feature of the Confucian Ritualistic Constitutionalism. In another article of his, Chaihark (2003) discusses the relationship between constitutionalism and civic virtue and analyzes the latter's importance for the effective operation of the former. For Chaihark, the Confucian *Li* serves such a role of promoting "Confucian civic virtue" because it "lies at the intersection of politics and education" and is "a marvelous combination of education, self-cultivation, training, discipline, restraint, authority, and legitimacy" (p. 43).[16] Chaihark also draws upon Foucault's insights about discipline to support his arguments. This is in fact further affirmed and elaborated in Hahm Chaibong's (2001) article "Confucian Rituals and the Technology of the Self: A Foucaultian Interpretation." In this article, Chaibong argues that, "by mistaking all technologies of the self – such as Confucian rituals – as states of domination that leave no room for freedom and individual initiative, modern theorists have left no room for the possibility of moral education in modern society," and it is particularly in this regard that Confucianism is not only suitable for democracy, but "also fills an important lacuna in modern democratic theory" (pp. 315, 322).

Similarly emphasizing the educational function of the *Li*, Kim Jin-Ha (2007) introduces the other key Confucian dimension of "Music" (乐) into Confucian Ritualistic Constitutionalism (Confucian Religious Constitutionalism) and provides perhaps the most charitable account of the advantages of the Confucian Religious Constitutionalism so far. In his conference paper entitled "Tuning – Constitutional Emplotment under the Confucian Rule of Ritual," Kim applies the Confucian eco-musical principle of "tuning" to the actual working of Confucian Religious Constitutionalism. For Kim, a constitution could be regarded as "the supreme covenant that sets forth the highest normative standards for construction and governance of a political community as premises for the legal order and civic virtue" and "constitutionalism is the foundation of politico-ethical commitment on which a commonwealth should be constructed, affirmed, and changed" (p. 2). He takes the mobilization, distribution, and application

16 According to Chaihark (2003), the process of "ritualization" is also the process of "humanization" and authority-gaining (pp. 44, 49). This may remind us Xunzi's high-threshold for granting ethical maturity, just as Xunxi put it, "to be able to stick to the morals, one could then stand [on his own]; to be able to stand [on his own] one could then respond [in society]; to be able to stand and respond is called to become a human or reach adulthood" (德操然后能定，能定然后能应，能定能应，夫是之谓成人) ("On learning" of *Xunzi* 《荀子·劝学》).

of power as the most salient theme of constitutionalism and operationalizes the exercise of power as a performance, which

> calls for a constitutional framework to check and balance the possible misappropriation of power, that is, an ecological reconstruction of the participatory theater where the actors' role-playing can be inter-subjectively evaluated from the ritually represented ideal-typical performance of the model-homunculi.
>
> (pp. 2–3)

For him, the *Chosŏn* Korea offers an example of this process:

> Envisioning the ideal politico-moral community as a 'Grand Unity' [*da tong* 大同 (Korean: *tae-dong*)] where spontaneous order and harmonious self-governance [: *wu wei er zhi* 无为而治 (Korean: *mu-ui-i-ch'i*)] should prevail, the *Chosŏn* constitutional visionaries mobilized a variety of cultural technologies . . . to ritually embody normative models of moral action and standard procedures of empowerment into the socio-political life world," [with the intention of constructing] "an Autopoietic ritual cosmos where actions actualize potential effects only when enacted in a way congruent to the ritually reconstructed constitutional order.
>
> (pp. 3–4)

Empowerment thus requires attunement and Kim concludes that "the connatural resonance within/without the self as an acting participant in this ritual community reaches eventual politico-musical self-orchestration," which is "the ultimate state of tuning at the zenith of embodied constitutionalism" (p. 4).

From Kim's analyses, there seem to be three prime advantages of Confucian Religious Constitutionalism. The first is the advantage of ritual-personalism over formal-legalism for ethical cultivation or moral development. This may have been well explored and affirmed by comparative moral philosophers. The second is that, although the Confucian polity has a very sophisticated inner balancing and checking mechanism as reviewed earlier, it has the nagging threat of resurgent familialism,[17] which the ritualistic constitutionalism does not have and could help to resolve. Finally, through participating in such an institutional cosmos, which contains the Confucian ethico-ritual positing of meaning and value, the people could participate and ultimately attune with the consummate cosmic order and, hence, become the third pillar of the universe juxtaposing the Heaven and the Earth (*yutiandisan* 与天地参).

So far we have reviewed the main arguments defending the constitutional nature of the Confucian *Li* as well as its advantages. This is indeed an excellent approach towards the study of Confucian constitutionalism. It also has great potential to bridge the insights of the critical legal theorists' critique of the legal-institutional order that dominates much of the contemporary world. However, there are also two problems with the current literature. The first is that the scholars writing with this approach are still more or less influenced by the Western liberal constitutional paradigm. This is particularly shown in Chaihark's keen concern about the restraining and disciplining dimension of

17 Kim does not explain the term in the article, but it seems to be a kind of collusion tendency after becoming familiar with each other and growingly resembling a family.

the *Li*.[18] Chaihark (2003) is in fact aware of Stephen Holmes' thesis that "constitutionalism is as much about enabling and constituting power as it is about disabling power," but he still chooses to employ the concept "as it is commonly understood in Western political and legal discourse" (p. 33). This limitation perhaps partially leads to the second problem of the current literature, which is the negligence of the Confucian *Li*'s other very important function as the entrenchment of natural justice taken from the Heavenly Way.[19] Understanding this function of the Confucian *Li*, we then could have a deeper grasp of the source, scope, and importance of Confucian Religious Constitutionalism, as well as the universal implications it entails. The teleology of entrenching the natural justice behind the Confucian *Li* in fact bridges the Confucian Religious Constitutionalism to the religious approach towards the study of Traditional Confucian Constitutionalism as well, which we will review next.

Religious approach[20]

It is interesting to observe that Korean scholars are leading research in the ritualistic approach; turning to the third approach, it is some of the so-called "mainland new Confucians" who are the pioneers. While Jiang Qing may well be the "flag" of the "mainland New Confucians" or "the Fourth Generation of New Confucians" (labels used to distinguish them from the third generation – the overseas New Confucians), it is worth pointing out that the school is not unanimous on the issue of Confucian Constitutionalism. Some other key "mainland New Confucians," such as Kang Xiaoguang (康晓光), Sheng Hong (盛洪), and Chen Ming (陈明), and so on have been thinking about Confucian constitutionalism as well, but they differ slightly from Jiang Qing's specific proposal, primarily depending on their stance along the spectrum between Confucian fundamentalism and liberal democracy. Another thing worth pointing out is that this religious approach has a strong ideological orientation with a strong sense of religious sentiment, so they are engaging earnestly in the search of a path for contemporary China and also not very rigorous in their arguments. Lastly, because Jiang Qing's proposal is the most systematic and influential, I will just describe and analyze his Confucian Religious Constitutionalism here in some depth.

Following his well-known work on political Confucianism, Jiang Qing recently has been exploring and contemplating constitutionalism with Chinese native characteristics. According to Jiang Qing (2009), this move is mainly a response to the "Fukuyama thesis," which contends that there are no alternatives to liberal democracy as the legitimate political form in the future of human history. He observes that Chinese intellectuals in the past century

18 Kim Jin-Ha is very critical of the liberal constitutional paradigm, but when he made these arguments he was just a graduate student and his view was only expressed in a conference paper, which hence has very little influence in the academia.

19 For a nice discussion of the relationships between the *Dao* (道), the *Ren* (仁), *Li* (礼), and righteousness (义), see Tang (2003).

20 It is worth pointing out that the "religious approach" here does not equate to a more conservative "theocratic" approach. As we can see, Jiang Qing's proposal is religious in some important respects, but it is more complex than a pure theocracy, such as that practiced in some Muslim countries, as he has been cautious in guaranteeing freedom of religion and making explicit room for diverse religious voices in his legislative house. Nevertheless, one might reasonably question the credibility of this promise as well as the sustainability of this solution, as soon as we think about the prospect of reconciling the fundamental differences among the different religions in the world.

have a "Constitutionalism complex" (*xianzhengqingjie* 宪政情结) but criticizes all their specific proposals, including those advocated by Confucians, for lacking native features. For example, for Jiang one common feature of these various proposals is the establishment of a "National People's Congress" (*guomindahui* 国民大会), which denotes the fundamental principle of "Sovereignty with the People" (*zhuquanzaimin* 主权在民). Jiang argues that this is a fundamental Western norm or "transcendental value" that is antithetical to the Confucian fundamental principle of "Sovereignty with the Heaven" (*zhuquanzaitian* 主权在天). So instead, Jiang calls for contemporary Confucians to bravely take on this responsibility of designing a constitutionalism with Chinese/Confucian characteristics.[21] "Confucian Religious Constitutionalism" (Confucian Religious Constitutionalism) (*rujiao xianzheng* 儒教宪政) is his response to it. It is first systematically advanced by Jiang Qing in his keynote address to a conference about Confucianism and China's future held in Confucius' hometown in the summer of 2009 and augmented by the conference devoted to Confucian Religious Constitutionalism at City University of Hong Kong in May 2010. In the following passages, I will seek to offer a brief review of his proposal and discuss some of its problems.

The two fundamental founding principles of Confucian Religious Constitutionalism are its religious nature and its "three-dimensional legitimacy" foundation developed in Jiang Qing's theory of political Confucianism. The first feature is made explicit in the title of the proposal, which Jiang Qing intentionally chooses because he regards Confucianism as a great religion embedded in Chinese civilization that is comparable to Buddhism, Islam, and Christianity. For Jiang, the Confucian religion has been the state religion for most of Chinese history and has performed well several functions, such as its provision of political legitimacy for the government, its provision of ethical norms for the regulation of social conduct, and its provision of religious faith for the people, and so on. Consequently, it has defined the nature of Chinese civilization, molded the cultural identity of Chinese nation, and shaped the axiological consensus and spiritual convictions of the Chinese people. As a result, Jiang is calling for the restoration of the state religion of Confucianism to cope with the all-round challenges from the West.

The second reason for the religious nature of the proposal is Jiang Qing's (2009) contention that the ultimate sovereignty of the regime lies with Heaven, which determines the transcendental, sacred, and religious nature of the Confucian Religious Constitutionalism (p. 4). For Jiang (2009), Heaven is the original source of the polity's legitimacy, as well as its "higher law" or "transcendental value" (p. 5). This, however, is on the metaphysical level; on the mundane level, Heaven is diversified (*fenshu* 分殊) into Heaven, Earth, and People (*tiandiren* 天地人). Accordingly sovereignty is manifested through the "kingly way of politics" (*wang dao zheng zhi* 王道政治), which bridges the three diverse expressions noted earlier (*wangdaotongsan* 王道通三). There are also both a personal manifestation and an institutional manifestation of the "kingly way of politics." On the personal perspective, Heaven assigns the sovereign deputy role to the Sage-kings (*shengwang* 圣王) during the ancient Three Dynasties, and to the Confucian literati (*rushituanti* 儒士团体) thereafter due to lack of subsequent Sage-kings. Institutionally, sovereignty is manifested through the "tri-cameral legislature," which embodies the three levels of legitimacy (*sanchonghefaxing* 三重合法性). This then relates to the second main feature of the Confucian Religious Constitutionalism, which we will review next.

21 Jiang Qing sometimes uses the terms Chinese and Confucian interchangeably.

The three-dimensional legitimacy of political power is a core argument of Jiang Qing's political Confucianism. According to Jiang, the legitimacy of the "kingly way of politics" has three dimensions. The first is the dimension of legitimacy from Heaven, which refers to the legitimacy that derives from sacred sources. More specifically, political power must be sanctioned by the holy, transcendental Heaven that passes the *Dao* to the Confucian Classics with the orthodox Confucians as the exclusive interpreters. The second is the dimension of legitimacy from Earth, which refers to the legitimacy that derives from historical continuity. In other words, political power must not deviate from the mainstream cultural and historical heritage of the nation. The third is the dimension of legitimacy from people, which refers to the legitimacy that derives from people's endorsement or consent. For Jiang, this last dimension would sound most familiar to Western ears, for it is the same as the legitimacy adopted in democratic regimes (Jiang, 2009). However, Jiang Qing vehemently criticizes democratic regimes for the dominance of the last dimension of legitimacy, which consequently has led to many problems. For Jiang, while no dimension of legitimacy should be dominant, he has slightly adjusted his stance and contended that there should be priorities rather than mere balances among the three dimensions. To be more specific, he thinks that each dimension has its autonomous realm, but they are also hierarchical under the idea of "vertical diversification" (*dengchaxingfenshu* 等差性分殊). Jiang has expressed this idea in great detail through his "diagrammatic illustration of 'the kingly way of politics' (*wangdao tushuo* 王道图说)," which we will not get into detail here.

After a brief recounting of the foundational principles of Jiang Qing's Confucian Religious Constitutionalism at the philosophical level, next, we will have a look at its institutional manifestations. As shown in the materials Jiang prepared for the Confucian Religious Constitutionalism conference held in HK, he has been contemplating different institutional forms of Confucian Religious Constitutionalism, such as its parliamentary (*yihui* 议会) form, its supervisory (*jiandu* 监督) form, its national polity (*guoti* 国体) form, its government (*zhengfu* 政府) form, its judiciary (*sifa* 司法) form, and so on, with the last two still in the stage of initial reflection and unwritten. So here we will have a brief review of the first three forms.[22]

For the parliamentary form, based on the three-dimensional legitimacy principle, Jiang proposes a tri-cameral legislature, with each house representing one dimension of legitimacy each, namely the House of the Profound Confucians (*tong ru yuan* 通儒院) representing the legitimacy of the sacred sources, the House of the National Polity (*guo ti yuan* 国体院) representing the legitimacy of historical legacy, and the House of the Common People (*shu min yuan* 庶民院) representing the legitimacy of the people's endorsement (pp. 5–18). Jiang also shares his preliminary reflections on the ways of choosing the members of the different houses. For the House of the Profound Confucians (*tong ru yuan* 通儒院), the members are chosen by nomination and appointment through both civil Confucian organizations and official Confucian institutions. For the House of the National Polity (*guo ti yuan* 国体院), the members should be representatives of various religions as well as descendants of great sages and historical figures. For the House of the Common People (*shu min yuan* 庶民院), the members are chosen through elections just as practiced in contemporary democracies.

22 Because the material on the third form of national polity is quite long and also hard to understand, I only include a review of the first two forms here.

Besides this tri-cameral parliamentary form, Jiang has also provided some clear thoughts about the supervisory form of "the kingly way of politics," namely the "Supervision of the Imperial College system" (*taixuejianguozhi* 太学监国制). For Jiang, because China's political tradition is a "scholar-governed tradition" (*xuezhichuantong* 学治传统), the Imperial College enjoyed many supreme powers of the state in history, including the highest legislative power, executive power, judiciary power, supervisory power, and military power (p. 11).[23] However, because the constitution of the state is very different now, Jiang argues that the power of the new "Imperial College" should be altered accordingly. As a result, it should keep six types of exclusive state power: the highest supervision power (*jianguoquan* 监国权), the highest literati-cultivation and examination power (*yangshikaoshiquan* 养士考试权), the highest ritual and sacrificial power (*liyijisiquan* 礼仪祭祀权), the highest personnel appointment power (renmingquan 任命权), the highest arbitration power (*zhongcaiquan* 仲裁权), and the highest custom-mores maintenance power (*weichifengjiaoquan* 维持风教权). In a way, Jiang Qing is advocating an "Imperial College" that is similar to the status of the ruling communist party in China today.

While this brief review of Jiang Qing's Confucian Religious Constitutionalism certainly has broadened our mental scope and provided some interesting ideas for the constitutional path of China in the future, there are a number of problems with his proposal. In the following, I will present a brief discussion of these. Some might argue that practicability is the most outstanding problem of Confucian Religious Constitutionalism but, as Jiang Qing acknowledges, that his Confucian Religious Constitutionalism is not prescribed for the present but is to be adopted in the future when Confucianism and traditional culture is fully revived, I will not focus on this shortcoming here but instead raise some questions at the theoretical level.

First of all, I think Jiang is not always subtle and cautious enough about the terminology he is using, even though he himself is emphasizing the importance of "rectification of names" (*zhengming* 正名). This shortcoming already has been pointed out by scholars such as Daniel Bell. For example, Bell (2008) questions why the future political reform of China should come from Confucian tradition alone and not include contributions from other traditions (p. 177). As we all know, from a very early stage on, Chinese politics has been deeply influenced by different schools, and it is difficult as well as unnecessary to credit certain features of Chinese political thought or practice to Confucianism alone. Furthermore, some would argue that the boundaries among the various schools in ancient China are not well drawn due to their shared terminology, and consequently contemporary approaches towards them have become a little dogmatic. The title and content of Confucian Religious Constitutionalism are thus doing unnecessary injustice to other schools or traditions in China. One solution here is to treat "Confucian" interchangeably with "Chinese" just as Jiang Qing occasionally does, but based on the importance of "rectification of names," it is perhaps still better to revise the title and content of the view accordingly.

Second, Jiang Qing's Confucian Religious Constitutionalism also needs to add some important additional conceptual clarifications. For example, what is the standard for judging Confucianism a religion? While Jiang Qing (2009) is playing with words when he claims

23 I am not very sure about the validity of the claim about the supreme powers of the Imperial College, nor whether it is precise to call the Confucian political tradition a "scholar-governed tradition" (*xuezhichuantong* 学治传统); "virtue-governed tradition" (*dezhichuantong* 德治传统) may be more accurate, since even though there are some correlations between the two there are also some nuanced differences.

that Confucianism is surely not equal to Confucian religion, just as Christian Theology is not the same as Christian Religion (p. 3), he does not offer clear criteria nor convincing arguments for labeling the Confucian tradition as a religious tradition. The Confucian tradition certainly has many religious features, but it also contains many vital distinctions from other main religions in the world. Even if Jiang had a relatively low threshold for defining a religion, the title may be misleading for many people, so it is better if it is changed as well.

Another conceptual problem is Jiang's failure to distinguish between the Chinese and Western styles of democracy. While the current Chinese political regime does embrace certain liberal democratic values, there are also fundamental differences. In fact, that is why the current Chinese regime is vehemently criticized by liberals, while applauded by some developing countries as an appealing alternative. Unless Jiang engages and successfully challenges the validity as well as the plausibility of the Sinicized Marxist alternative, he should not present his proposal as if that is the only alternative to the Fukuyama thesis.

Finally, there are also some problems with Jiang's interpretations of the Confucian tradition. The plausibility of his idiosyncratic interpretation is further undermined by the lack of rigorous references to the classics.[24] One could easily propose some equally plausible or even superior interpretations. For example, when Jiang is advocating the idea of "sovereignty with Heaven," rather than "sovereignty with the People," he ignores those passages in the classics pointing to the mirroring relationship between the Heaven and the People, such as "the Heaven sees and hears just as the People sees and hears" (天视自我民视，天听自我民听), "the Heaven is clairvoyant, just as the people are clairvoyant; the Heaven punishes and rewards, just as the people punishes and rewards" (天聪明，自民聪明。天明畏，自我民明畏), and "what the people desires, the Heaven will allow it" (民之所欲，天必从之), and so on (*Shangshu* 《尚书》). My call for more exploration here does not assume an unbridgeable gap between Heaven and the people, but we must investigate their subtle relationships as well as to make clear the distinction between the People's Will, in the Rousseauian sense, and volatile public opinion, which is apt to be tricked and misdirected in practice.

Another major problem is with Jiang's idea of three-dimensional legitimacy, more specifically about the second earthly dimension of legitimacy. The proposal has attracted much attention in the academic community and has broadened our vision on a very important issue. While not disagreeing with the overall idea of the three-dimensional legitimacy of Confucianism, I think a more thorough and convincing case needs to be made for the second dimension of legitimacy. As mentioned earlier, the earthly dimension of legitimacy refers to the legitimacy that comes from historical continuity, but it is very hard to know specifically what historical continuity means. If we take seriously the metaphor of history as a current, then all the present could be judged legitimate, because there is necessarily a continuity from the past to the present, hence rendering the earthly dimension of legitimacy unnecessary and relatively meaningless.[25] In that sense, if a "foreign tradition" has been successfully transplanted onto the native soil, it would then have already attained a certain degree of legitimacy. This would undermine Jiang's contention that both liberal democracy and Marxism lack earthly legitimacy in China. Instead, I think an alternative interpretation

24 Daniel Bell (2008) also observes that Jiang's proposal has more to do with his political imagination than rigorous references to the classical texts.

25 This perspective perhaps echoes Hegel's famous statement that "all existence has its *raison d'etre*" (*cunzaijiheli* 存在即合理), or Zhuangzi's similar statement that all things have their pros (*wanwujieyousuoke* 万物皆有所可).

for the earthly dimension of legitimacy is that political power should provide basic material well-being to the people, for that is actually the function and contribution of the earth to human welfare. The obligation of those in political power to provide basic subsistence to the people has been well explored and argued by contemporary Confucian scholars, such as Daniel Bell and Joseph Chan. There are also plenty of references in the classics associating the earth to the mother, whose role is to feed the children, and associating Heaven to the father, whose role is more about moral education.[26]

To sum up, in this section we have reviewed different approaches toward the issue of Confucian constitutionalism. From institutional to the ritualistic approach, and finally to Jiang Qing's religious approach, it seems that the visions are becoming broader but at the same time the arguments are becoming vaguer, especially in the final approach. While the first institutional approach is not as critical as the ritualistic and religious approaches about the conceptual framework of liberal constitutionalism, their rigorous analyses have unearthed excellent resources within the Confucian polity that are compatible and also understandable from the liberal constitutionalism perspective. It seems that the latter two approaches are more defining for Traditional Confucian Constitutionalism, since they are quite distinctive from Western Liberal Constitutionalism perspective. The ritualistic approach is indeed insightful and heuristic and may well shed light on our understandings of Traditional Confucian Constitutionalism, but as we have seen, it also has problems, such as its detachment from the religious layer, which I think is the core of Traditional Confucian Constitutionalism. The religious approach as constructed by Jiang Qing, and so on, is quite thought-provoking but also quite vague and porous. It seems that the discoveries of the three approaches are vertically complementary and may well be combined to establish a full picture of Traditional Confucian Constitutionalism, which will be the task of the next section.

A full picture of Traditional Confucian Constitutionalism

A full picture of Traditional Confucian Constitutionalism will consist of the three layers reviewed earlier and may well have been envisioned by the ancient Chinese sages.[27] A simple diagram of it is shown in Figure 4.1.

In this three-layered Traditional Confucian Constitutionalism, the *Dao* occupies the position of the root/core and is shown at the top. This represents the religious dimension of

26 This may remind us the role of fatherly authority in both Mill and Freud's theories.

27 The plausibility of the ancient Chinese sages' envisioning of the three-layered Traditional Confucian Constitutionalism is conceivable if we subscribe to an understanding of constitution as Rousseau (1987) puts it:

> It is not engraved on marble or bronze, but in the hearts of citizens. It is the true constitution of the state. Everyday it takes on new forces. When other laws grow old and die away, it revives and replaces them, preserves a people in the spirit of its institution and imperceptibly substitutes the force of habit for that of authority. I am speaking of mores, customs, and especially of opinion, a part of the law unknown to our political theorists but one on which depends the success of all the others; a part with which the great legislator secretly occupies himself, though he seems to confine himself to the particular regulations that are merely the arching of the vault, whereas mores, slower to arise, form in the end its immovable keystone."
>
> (p. 172)

This understanding will also echo the belief that Confucius is the legislator of all ages in Chinese history (*weiwanshilifa* 为万世立法).

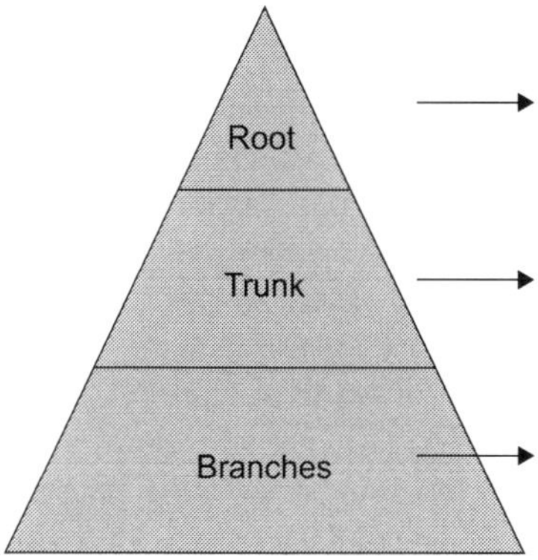

Religious layer	Dao (道) (mainly Daoist & Huang.Lao school)	Sage (圣) King (王)	(spirit) 神
Ritualistic layer	Li-yue (礼乐) (Confucianism)	Gentlemen (君子) Ministers (臣僚)	(blood) 血
Institutional layer[1]	Xing-zheng (刑政) (Legalism)	Petty men (小人) Mass (庶民)	(*qi*) 气.

Figure 4.1 The three layers of Traditional Chinese Constitutionalism

Traditional Confucian Constitutionalism. The second layer is that of *Li* and *Yue* (*liyue* 礼乐) and locates in the middle, and this is where the Confucian ritualistic constitutionalism we reviewed earlier mostly fit in. The bottom layer is about Xing and Zheng (*xingzheng* 刑政), which manifests as power checks and balances at the institutional level. I take constitutionalism as the idea and practice of entrenching certain core political ideologies and arrangement with some normative justifications so that later people could not easily overthrow or change them. It is in this sense that I argue that the Chinese tradition not only has constitutionalist thinking from a very early stage, but also has the longest, stablest, and grandest constitutionalism the world has ever have. Because my interpretation of the religious layer is significantly different from Jiang's religious approach reviewed earlier, next, I will first seek to give a full account of this layer, then discuss about the main features of Traditional Confucian Constitutionalism as well as its implications.

Before delving into it, a few clarifications are needed. First of all, as we have seen from earlier discussions, the Western vision towards the ancient Chinese constitutionalism is significantly limited by its parochial imaginative horizons, so I will seek to return to the perspective of the ancient Chinese sages.[28] One move towards this is to rely as much as possible on the ancient Chinese classics and may occasionally use contemporary literature to affirm certain interpretations. Consequently, the methodology should be directly in accord with the wisdom of the ancient Chinese epistemology as I have suggested in the first chapter. The direct implication here is the adoption of the *Tongbian* (通变) thought rather than Western causal thought, which also entails the utilization of the holistic approach and the genealogical approach, with the key as the attaining and seeing through the Way. For the *Tongbian* thought, Tian Chenshan (2005) has given a wonderful elaboration in his book *Chinese Dialectics: From Yijing to Marxism*, in which he argues that the Tongbian thought

28 In fact, this seems to be foreseen by Zhuangzi explicitly, as he says "the knowledge is dispersed to all under heaven but the core is established in the Middle Kingdom" (其数散于天下而设于中国) and "the scholars of later ages unfortunately would not see the undivided purity of heaven and earth, and the Great Way of the ancients" (后世之学者, 不幸不见天地之纯，古人之大体，道术将为天下裂) ("The All Under Heaven" chapter of *Zhuangzi* 《庄子-天下篇》).

is the primary mode of thought inherited from the *Yijing* that has deeply influenced the thought of Chinese people even in contemporary China. For Tian, "bian" suggests becoming in light of difference, while "tong" expresses the kind of becoming in light of continuity, so "tongbian" is "continuity through change between any correlative pairing" (pp. 22–23). The *Tongbian* thought also entails the holistic approach and genealogical approach, which are crucial for tracing the phenomena of ontogenesis and interanimation back to its origin in order to have a full grasp of the nature and reality. As the Way is regarded as the original source of all creations in ancient China, the core here is then to attain and see through the Way.[29] A furthermore substantive implication of my current approach is that I do not focus on Confucianism alone, but seek to take the full Chinese traditions into account, particularly their origin. Here I completely agree with Sima Tan's (司马谈) reading of the complementariness among the different pre-Qin schools as well as their respective natures, as shown in his "On the Cores of the Six Schools" in the Sima Qian's preface to his *Shiji* (《史记-太史公自序》). Following this reading, we can regard Confucianism as the "trunk" of the Chinese cultural tradition while Daoism (including the Huang-Lao school) and Legalism as the "root"/"core" and "branches" respectively.[30] Consequently, we can largely see the three layers in the traditional Chinese constitutionalism framework, which we will discuss next.

As we can see from the diagram, at the top is the religious layer.[31] This has some similarities with the articulations of the "mainland New Confucians" but also many crucial differences. For example, I agree with Jiang Qing about the supreme status of the Heaven but I do not share his institutional constructions inspired from it. As a result, I will spend some length here to develop a new account by clarifying what the religious layer is, its distinctive features, as well as its constitutional roles.

First of all, I think religious thought not only exists in ancient China, but actually occupies the center of the ancient thought system, if we do not subscribe to a very narrow definition of religion.[32] According to one encyclopedia, religion in the narrow sense refers to the belief in and worship of a god or gods, but in a broad sense refers to a set of beliefs explaining the existence of and giving meaning to the universe, usually involving devotional and ritual observances. There are certainly many similarities and also distinctions between the ancient Chinese belief system and other counterparts in the world. If we derive the criteria of defining a religion from the "overlapping" part between those belief systems, we could then have no problems in the naming. I think the definition of religion in the broad sense falls within this "overlapping" part, and historians of ancient world may well have affirmed this. As for

29 For textual evidences to support this point, see chapter 4, 14 of *Daodejing*, the "Daofa" chapter of *Huangdi Sijing* (《黄帝四经-道法》), and the "Tiandi" chapter of *Zhuangzi* (《庄子-天地篇》).

30 This is not contradictory to Chen Guying's reading of the "trunk" status of the Daoism, because he is stating that in the realm of philosophy, and he also agrees that Confucianism could be regarded as the trunk in the cultural realm.

31 I regard religion as the core of philosophy, which is the core of a culture. This is so, because religion deals with the crucial question of the meaning of existence, human nature, etc., while philosophy is a conscious effort to formulate views and values as expressions of the fundamental beliefs of a people (Cheng, 2000, p. 493). Culture, on the other hand, has a broader meaning, as it includes all kinds of behaviors, norms, customs, and so on.

32 In the article, I will use "Chinese religion" and the "religious dimension of ancient Chinese thought" interchangeably. By "Chinese religion," I mean something similar to Legge's (1880) understanding as shown in his notion of "the religion of China." For a good defense of the religious character of the Confucian tradition, see Taylor (1998).

the narrow sense, if we do not subscribe a narrow definition to the idea of "god" or "gods," we could still acknowledge that the Chinese belief system has a religious dimension as well. The distinction, just as Tian Chenshan points out, is only that the Western counterparts subscribe a seriously assigned name "God" to the unfathomably wonderful "thing" which at the very beginning created the ten thousand things and brought them into "ordered" actions, but the Chinese ancestors only describe its manifestations with words such as *shen* (神), *dao* (道), and "Heaven," and so on (p. 40).

From a hindsight post-modern perspective, however, the religious dimension of ancient Chinese thought seems to be more rational-oriented than the Western counterparts, which makes it standing out among the world religions. This orientation could be seen in two main aspects. The first is about the conceptual evolution from *Shangdi* (上帝) to *Heaven*. As Cheng (2000) points out, because of the tradition of reverence to the ancestral spirits, the common source of the family is regarded as the supreme divinity *Shangdi* during the Xia and Yin periods, which, however, is replaced by the notion of *Tian* during the Zhou Dynasty, perhaps as a search for the common source for all lives in the natural world, including the human beings (p. 498). With the expansion of the semantic range, the core meanings of the concepts have also evolved from the notion of "creator" to "fecundator," which is even more manifested in the later elaborations of the roles of the Heaven and Earth.

This conceptual manifestation of the rational-orientation of the religious belief in ancient China also echoes Cheng Chung-ying's insight about the core of *sheng* (生) as well as the changing and becoming aspect it entails in ancient Chinese thought. As Cheng (2000) points out, while the ancient Chinese do show a reverence and trust to the natural spirits, "they responded to the natural processes of nature by accepting the natural world without excessive mythological personification" (p. 498). What preoccupies their attention most is instead the life in the totality of nature. The organically changing or transforming dimension of nature is thus a very important part of ancient Chinese thought. It is in this regard that Tian Chenshan subscribes a materialist account of religion to the ancient Chinese world. Tian Chenshan (2005) focuses on the concept of *Shen* (神) as shown in *Yijing* and argues that, "when a human being attains a thorough comprehension of change, he accesses to shen, for 'changing' always presents itself as something spirit-like or mysterious" (p. 28).[33] This seems to provide an excellent bridge to modern explanations about religion. For example, according to Spinoza, the main characteristic of the multitude is uncertainty, resulted from ignorance of true causes and the lack of adequate ideas (Yovel, 2002, p. 437). This uncertainty renders the multitude prey to the alteration of fear and hope, and consequently breeds superstition, which is also the essence of historical religions for Spinoza (p. 438).[34] No wonder for some, the rationalization of life originates in our irresistible desire for emancipation from fear and was first initiated in religious spheres, as Weber describes (Kim, 2007, pp. 4–5).

The rational-orientation of the Chinese religion also renders it a striking parallel with the ideal theological-political arrangements prescribed by Spinoza in his *Theological-Political Treatise (TPT)*. As Spinoza's TPT is quite relevant for our understanding of the religious

33 The relevant passages here are: "the onto-genesis is called the *Yi*-'change'" (生生之谓易) and "the one who know the way of change must have known the actions of the *shen* or God" (知变化之道者，其知神之所为乎) (*Jici of Yijing* 《易经-系辞》).

34 This may remind us Marx's critique of religion as the "opium" of the mind. For a detailed elaboration, see *Marx's Selected Writings* (1994, pp. 28–34).

layer of Traditional Confucian Constitutionalism, I will take a detour to have a review of Spinoza's key arguments here. First of all, for Spinoza, there are three mental states corresponding to the people in a society, namely *imaginatio*, *ratio*, and *scientia intuitiva*, something very similar to the mental state of the petty men, the gentleman, and the sages in the Chinese thought. The individuals have the potential to rise above the *imaginatio* and attain *ratio*, even *scientia inuitivia*, but it is a reality for Spinoza that the great majority is incapable of doing this at a given time and place (Yovel, 2002, p. 435). Meanwhile, Spinoza thinks that the psychology of the *imaginatio* tends to breed discord, violence, and war, as well as fanaticism and the various forms of intolerance, and is the source of social instability and insecurity in life, so the whole project of his *Theological-Political Treatise* aims to reshape and re-channel the effects that *imaginatio* has on the multitude (Yovel, p. 435). The result is a project of "mental and institutional mechanisms that would transform the imagination into an external imitation of reason, using state power and the purified popular religion as vehicles of a semi-rational civilizing process" (Yovel, p. 435).

Spinoza's prescription includes two steps. The first step is to have the historical religion undermined and replaced by the universal popular religion. The historical religions to Spinoza are all *vana religio*, spurious religions of the imagination, which perpetuate repression and alienation within the multitude's mental world (Yovel, 2002, p. 438). The universal popular religion, on the other hand, is "a popular version of the religion of reason which remains rooted in passion and the imagination and is rational only externally or by imitation" (Yovel, p. 439). Tailored for the multitude, the universal aspect of it "lies in its stressing the same patterns of conduct which reason, too, will recommend; but it does not presuppose any true knowledge, only obedience" (Yovel, p. 439). This is indeed where the semi-rational nature of this religion lies, for it is being "a mere imitation of reason within the realm of imagination" (Yovel, p. 439). Another manifestation of the semi-rational nature is the reduction of "the content of the word of God and the true meaning of the prophets to a nuclear set of general (and rather secular) principles such as justice, solidarity, and mutual help," but at the same time relying partly on the authority of Revelation to provide the motivational source for the multitude's conduct (Yovel, pp. 439–440).

If this is the first step to solving the theological part of Spinoza's grand scheme, the second step is then the political part of the grand scheme that spells out the Word of God by the secular state. This is so because for Spinoza the general principles reduced from the word of God are too general and vague as guiding basis for actions, so they need to be articulated out in legislations and adapted to the specific social context (Yovel, 2002, p. 440). Furthermore, it is hard to conceive a better "candidate" than the state "as the most potent mechanism" to accomplish Spinoza's goals. As a result, the state

> becomes in Spinoza not a mechanism of power only but equally a civilizing agent, an instrument of education. In both ways it uses the typical psychology of the multitude to create an institutionalized form of semi-rationality, imposed by obedience and enhanced by habit, repetition, and the memory of its advantageous results.
>
> (Yovel, p. 442)

For Spinoza, the other very important aspect central to his project is the use of rhetoric. Just as Yovel points out, "Using metaphor, allusion, equivocation, and other rhetorical devices is essential to Spinoza's program no less than strict philosophical discourse and as an indispensable complement to it" (p. 442). This is so because Spinoza's TPT is not merely a theoretical work but "a form of philosophic engagee" that seeks to "trigger and enhance the execution of its own recommendations in the very act of putting them forth" (Yovel, p. 442). The practical and performative side of the work thus requires "the TPT must use several levels of discourse simultaneously, address different audiences in the same text, exploit the connotations of old words to serve radically new meanings" (Yovel, p. 442).

After this brief review of Spinoza's grand blueprint, one may have already attained a sense of the striking parallel between Spinoza's prescriptions and the endeavors as well as practices of the ancient Chinese sages. The conceptual evolution from the Shangdi to Tian as we mentioned earlier clearly could be regarded as the ancient Chinese sages' endeavor to undermine historical religions as Spinoza advocates. In fact, as Mircea Eliade put it well:

> This passage from "creator" to "fecundator" [in Eliade's another term, solarization of supreme beings], this slipping of the omnipotence, transcendence, and impassiveness of the sky into the dynamism, intensity of new atmospheric, fertilizing, vegetation figures, is not without significance. It makes quite clear that one of the main factors in the lowering of people's conceptions of God, most obvious in agricultural societies, is the more and more all-embracing importance of vital values and of "Life" in the outlook of economic man.
>
> (as cited in Kim, 2007, p. 47)

The humanistic turn in ancient China as widely noticed in the academia certainly could affirm this reading.[35] Confucius also explicitly calls for the gentlemen to "preoccupy with what is proper for the human beings, and respect the spiritual beings but keep a distance from them" (*wuminzhiyi jingguisheneryuanzhi* 务民之义，敬鬼神而远之) ("Yongye" chapter of *the Analects* 《论语-雍也》). Confucius himself serves as an exemplar of what he preaches, as he "does not talk about extraordinary things, feats of strength, disorder, and spiritual beings" (*zibuyuguaililuanshen* 子不语怪、力、乱、神) ("Shuer" chapter of *the Analects* 《论语-述而》). In fact, just as Spinoza prescribes, Confucius not only resorts to reason to defend his political and ethical visions, but also appeals to the authority of Tian for the justifications (Ivanhoe, 2007). Perhaps as part of what is proper for the human beings, Confucius also established a religion that is similar to the semi-rational universal religion Spinoza advocates. That is actually what Confucius may intend by his preaching that "the people could be led but not know" (*minkeshiyouzhibukeshizhizhi* 民可使由之不可使知之).[36] Confucius also reduces the unfathomable concepts of *Dao*, *De*, and so on to the principles of benevolence (*ren* 仁), justice (*yi* 义), *Li* (礼), *Yue* (乐), filial piety (*xiao* 孝), and so on and has painstakingly appealed to the state to carry out the grand plan.[37]

35 The understandings of the term "humanistic turn" in the academia may not be unanimous, and I do not intend to get into these debates here.

36 I do not think what it means here is to keep the people in perpetual ignorance. What is intended here is actually quite consistent with Spinoza's understandings; in Mengzi's words, "people move towards goodness each day yet without knowing" (民日迁善而不知为之) ("Jinxing I" of *Mengzi* 《孟子-尽心上》). One could argue that this is actually paving the way for their later enlightenment, which echoes Aristotle's insight in his *Nicomachean Ethics* regarding the tension between habit-forming and knowledge-attaining.

37 There is perhaps little question about the unison of politics and religion (*zhengjiaoheyi* 政教合一) in Confucianism. For a wonderful elaboration, see Yang Yang's (杨阳) (2007) book *The Cultural Order and the Political Order: A Political-cultural interpretation of the Confucian China* (《文化秩序与政治秩序 – 儒教中国的政治文化解读》).

The other very important dimension where Confucianism meets Spinoza's prescription is about the use of language or rhetoric. For careful and thoughtful students of the Chinese philosophy, one must wonder whether there are deep reasons behind Confucius' emphasis on the unity of knowledge and practice, as well as his careful choices of the terminologies, such as *Junzi* (君子), *Tian* (天), *Ren* (仁), *Li* (礼), and so on, Spinoza's account seems to offer a good explanation about it. In fact, a careful study of the wide semantic ranges of the terms used in ancient Chinese philosophy may well demonstrate the ancient Chinese sages' intention to "address different audiences in the same text" as Spinoza advocates (Yovel, 2002, p. 442). This may well be what the passage "the teaching of the gentlemen is hermeneutically open: he guides and does not drag; he strengthens and does not discourage; he opens the way but does not conduct to the end" (故君子之教喻也，道而弗牵，强而弗抑，开而弗达) intends ("On learning" chapter of *Li Ji* 《礼记-学记》). The character *yu* (喻) here literally means to "tell" but with a metaphorical connotation, so I regard it has a hermeneutical dimension, which seems to be quite consistent with the meaning of the sentence as well.

After a review and discussion of the existence and importance of religious thought in ancient China, its defining distinctive feature of rational-orientation, as well as its match with the ideal theological-political framework Spinoza prescribes, the constitutional role of the religious layer is perhaps already clear to some. To understand this from a modern perspective, one needs to see the connection between a political constitution of a state and the normative universe the people in the state inhabit. This connection has been acknowledged by various scholars. For example, supported by Cover, Frederick Schauer, and Clifford Geertz, Hahm Chaihark (2003) points out that the normative power of a constitution relies on its being embedded in a nomos, "the normative cultural vocabulary of a people through which they understand and evaluate political action" (p. 39). Laurence Tribe's (2008) latest book *The Invisible Constitution* may well affirm this point as well. Another legal scholar, Lawrence W. Beer, also connects the constitution to the particular "religion" of a people, by which he means "the most important, most binding ideas at the heart of that culture" (as cited in Chaihark, 2003, p. 40). In fact, the controlling function of the religious layer in the political realm may well be affirmed by discoveries in modern phenomenology, and semiology, and so on[38] The latest discovery of the information-controlling mechanism as the core of the *Zhouli*, a political constitution inspired and emulated from the Natural Order of the Heavenly Way (Schaberg, 2010) may well render support to this prospect.

The relevance of religious thought for modern constitutionalism is thus clear, but how does the religious layer we reviewed earlier actually contribute to Traditional Confucian Constitutionalism? I think the actual operation mechanism has two aspects. The first has to do with its prescription of norms signified from the natural order of the Heavenly Way, which is phenomenologically projected onto the human mental world to serve as the guidance for

38 While the contention by scholars of semiology that their subject is the common denominator of all humanities and social sciences may not be well received by outsiders, it seems their more moderate claim that semiology is the key to the study of culture has certain validity (Zhao, 2009, p. 169). The controlling function of culture seems to have been well acknowledged by the academia now, so semiology certainly has a great potential to shed light in that regard. In fact, Geertz (1977) has made the point when he states that "human thought is basically both social and public" as it is not just "happenings in the head" but of a traffic of "significant symbols," which include "words for the most part but also gestures, drawings, musical sounds, mechanical devices like clocks, or natural objects like jewels – anything, in fact, that is disengaged from its mere actuality and used to impose meaning upon experience" (p. 45).

human affairs.[39] The elaborations about the heaven and the earth, the four seasons, the yin and yang (*yinyang* 阴阳), and the five elements (*wuxing* 五行), and so on are all constitutive to the natural order the ancient Chinese sages have envisioned.[40] Against this natural order of the Heavenly Way, the concept of *Zheng* (正), widely used in the ancient world to denote legitimacy, also finds its meaning.

Besides this phenomenological project of entrenching the norms to the human world, the other aspect is the ancient Chinese sages' holding fast to the roots by a thorough understanding and accurate articulation of the natural order, human nature as well as their necessary evolutions. For them, while the myriad things all have their luxuriant growth, they nevertheless without exception would return to their roots (夫夫物芸芸，各复归其根) (chapter 16 of *Daodejing*), so they hold fast to the *Dao*, the root of all creations, and consequently nothing would not follow them just as following their own natures. This is captured very well in the following metaphors: "just as the relationship between the root and the branches: drag them from the root, then none of the myriad branches and leaves would not follow" (譬犹本与末也，从本引之，千枝万叶，莫不随也) ("On spirit" of *Huainanzi* 《淮南子-精神训》):

> hold the *Dao* as the fishing rod, *De* as the fishing line, *Li* and *Yue* as the fishhook, *Ren* and *Yi* as the bait, throw it into the river and let it flow in the ocean, then which among the myriad things would not be within your grasp?
>
> (夫道有经纪条贯，得一之道，连千枝万叶. . .是故以道为竿，以德为纶，礼乐为钩，仁义为饵，投之于江，浮之于海，万物纷纷孰非其有) ("On innocence" of *Huainanzi* 《淮南子-俶真训》)[41]

Behind their confidence is certainly their deep grasp of the root, but I include an accurate articulation dimension here, so it could induce "resonance" among those exposed to it. I do not interpret their ideal of *wuwei* (无为) as "no action at all." In fact, even for their ideal *wuwei* metaphors such as the relation between the seasons spring and autumn to the grasses and the fruits, the presence of the seasons may seem to be a kind of "articulation" that are necessary to induce the "growth" or "fruition" within their nature.[42] This is perhaps more manifested in Zhuangzi's parable of playing the *se* (瑟), an ancient Chinese musical instrument with 25 strings, in which a single play on the "lordly string" could induce all 25 strings to vibrate ("Xuwugui" of *Zhuangzi* 《庄子-徐无鬼》).

The constitutional role of the religious layer is thus clear; as for the second and third layers shown in the diagram, because the literature reviewed earlier have given excellent analyses, I will not seek to elaborate again here. What I want to do is just to point out certain important features of the three-layered Traditional Confucian Constitutionalism as shown

39 For a good discussion of this, see Wu (2006).

40 For textual evidences of this point, see "Jici" of *Yi Jing* (《易经-系辞》), the "Heavenly Way" chapter of *Zhuangzi* (《庄子-天道篇》), and so on.

41 This may be a perfect example of the utilization of the Archimedean Point as it was originally meant: given a place to stand, one solid point, and a long enough lever, one could lift the earth.

42 The passage I have in mind here is: "When the airs of spring come forth, all plants grow; and, when the autumn arrives, all fruits mature. Don't spring and autumn have these effects without taking any actions?" (夫春气发而百草生，正得秋而万宝成。夫春与秋，岂无得而然哉？) ("Gengsangchu" of *Zhuangzi* 《庄子-庚桑楚》).

in Figure 4.1. The first is that there is a hierarchical order among the three layers, which are also complementary. The hierarchical order is manifested in the sense that the lower layers should not contradict the spirit of the higher layers. The three layers are also largely complementary, just as the relations among their respective dominant schools.[43] Surely, there are also some disharmonious contentions among the schools, just as most people tend to hold themselves right while others wrong (*shijierfeiren* 是己而非人). But from the perspective of the necessary evolution trajectory of the natural order, namely from the *Dao*, to the *De*, to the *Ren*, to the *Yi*, and to the *Li*, they all have their respective stages of play and contribution (故失道而后德，失德而后仁，失仁而后义，失义而后礼。夫礼者，忠信之薄，而乱之首) (《道德经》). While the law is not included in this evolutionary picture, it is obvious that the prescriptions of the legal school are needed when disorder emerges after the *Li* has lost. Confucius' goal is indeed to return to the Grand *Dao* but, at the same time, keep the *Li*, *Yue*, *Xing*, and *Zheng* all playing their respective functions without blocking each other's paths (礼乐刑政四达而不悖, 则王道备矣) ("Record of Music" of *Li Ji* 《礼记-乐记》).

The second feature is that the three layers correspond to different schools, with different foci. As shown in the table beside the diagram in Figure 4.1, the first layer largely corresponds to the Daoist and Huang-Lao schools, with the second and the third layers correspond to the Confucian and Legal schools respectively. Their targeting groups are also different. From the targets' mental state perspective, the first layer is preoccupied with the sages, with the latter two layers preoccupied with gentlemen and petty men respectively. This trichotomy is quite parallel to that of Spinoza's ***imaginatio***, ***ratio***, and ***scientia intuitiva*** as mentioned earlier as well. In the political realm, these three mental states correspond to the King, the ministers/officials, and the common people respectively. In the ideal of Traditional Confucian Constitutionalism, "the King should be *wuwei* but hold fast to the ultimate righteous order [perceived from the Nature]" (王中心无为也，以守至正) ("Liyun" of Li Ji 《礼记-礼运》), leaving the human affairs to the ministers and officials. The divisions between Heaven's Way (*tiandao* 天道) and Human's Way (*rendao* 人道), King's affairs (*jundao* 君道), and Ministers' affairs (*chendao* 臣道) are thus clear in Traditional Confucian Constitutionalism. This reading is affirmed by Sima Tan's summary of the various schools' respective natures as well ("Sima Qian's Preface" of *The Records of Historians* 《史记-太史公自序》). The last column in the table is the bodily correspondence to the three layers. It may not be very rigorous, especially with the middle layer, but nevertheless, there are some passages in the Chinese medicine to lend support to this reading. For example, the ancient Chinese sages, including Mengzi, have elaborated on the relationship between the heart/mind, the spirit (*shen* 神), and the aspiration of the heart (*zhi* 志) as well as the *qi* (气). Under the paradigm of Chinese medicine, the blood also provide nutrients to the *qi*, which is the driving force of vitality, much like the role of the people as the driving force of history. Liu Chang's (2009) latest book titled *The Isomorphism of the Heart and the King: A Prototypal Study of the History of Ancient Chinese Political Thought* (《心君同

43 I do not subscribe to a conflictive reading of the various schools, because just as Sima Tan (司马谈) says well,

> [A]ll under the heaven reach the same goal with various considerations, and reach the same destiny with different paths. The schools of Yin-Yang, Confucianism, Mohism, Naming, Legalism, and Daoism, all aim at the grand governance, but differ in the paths they take as well as their respective emphases.
>
> (天下一致而百虑，同归而殊涂。夫阴阳、儒、墨、名、法、道德，此务为治者也，直所从言之异路，有省不省耳). (《史记-太史公自序》).

构 – 中国古代政治思想史的一种原型范畴分析》) may well shed light on this dimension. Indeed, the literature on body politic may well lender support in this regard and it is worth further research as well.

Summary and conclusion

So far we have reviewed current explorations regarding Traditional Confucian Constitutionalism and sought to establish a full picture of Traditional Confucian Constitutionalism. It is a plausible account, as there are plenty of passages supporting this interpretation. If the validity of my portrait of Traditional Confucian Constitutionalism is granted, it would have several important implications. First of all, it may pose a challenge to the current paradigm of liberal constitutionalism prevalent in the academia throughout the world. As Chaihark (2003) points out, there is actually a contradictory element to the notion of "constitutional democracy" since "democracy" refers to "a form of politics in which the people are the source of power and legitimacy" while "constitutionalism" refers to "the notion of regulating and restraining the political process and government power according to some higher norm that cannot be changed even if the majority wants to change it" (p. 31). By the definition of constitutionalism itself, it is clear then that Traditional Confucian Constitutionalism could be regarded as an exemplary that successfully entrenches the ancient norms. The persistence and stability of Traditional Confucian Constitutionalism as confirmed by Jin Guantao's (金观涛) famous thesis about the "super stable structure" (*chaowendingjiegou* 超稳定解构) running through most of Chinese history may well render it the longest and stablest constitutionalism the world has ever have. Conceivably without the intervention of Western imperial powers, Traditional Confucian Constitutionalism may well have continued to exist in China.[44] We certainly should not deny the status of constitutionalism to other constitutional systems as long as they do not conform to certain substantive contents of our own, such as individual rights. Another related point is about the inclusion of religious dimension into the constitutional framework. Given the crucial differences between the Chinese religion and Western counterparts, the religious dimension certainly should be taken into consideration when we study constitutional systems that are different from those of the West.

Second, it may lead some people to rethink the criteria we use to judge regimes. Future scholars may well find that the ancient Chinese and Greeks share a same vision of the ideal regime, but simply differ in their aspirations as well as practices. For some, the structure of the ideal regime described in Plato's *Republic*, which corresponds metaphorically to the three hierarchical parts of the soul, is very much similar to the Traditional Confucian Constitutionalism we have portrayed.[45] The difference is perhaps that the ancient Chinese sages

44 On this, the ancient Chinese sages may not have a negative view at all, since it is quite consistent with their principle of "acting only when being pressed hard" (*poerhoudong* 迫而后动) of the *wuwei* ideal. This is also a necessary step towards greater enlightenment just as the mutual interaction of the yin and yang in the character *Ming* "enlightenment" (明) entails (日往则月来，月往则日来，日月相推而明生焉) ("Jici" of *Yijing* 《易经-系辞》).

45 In fact, one could argue that the ideal political orders envisioned by Spinoza and Hobbes were implemented in ancient China as well. For the Spinoza case, we have discussed it earlier. For Hobbes, his discourse may have been tailored to his specific context of civil wars, but his ideal was to establish an absolute sovereign whose legitimacy though should be based on following the natural laws he prescribes. Recalling his first two fundamental laws centering on the pursuit of peace and the ancient Chinese sages' preoccupation with disorder-aversion, the match between them is thus clear if we can be rid of our biased pre-conceptions.

are aspiring to carry it out despite the seemingly insurmountable challenges,[46] while Plato and Aristotle are just apathetically describing the "the utopia in speech" as well as the necessary evolution of the regimes after failing to reach the utopia.[47] Consequently, the ancient Chinese sages engages paternalistically with the prescription of the *Li* and *Yue* system, while the ancient Greek philosophers may well be preoccupied with some pure theoretical contemplation off the ground and let the world be on fire just as Aristophanes and Nietzsche vividly depicted. Indeed, future scholars may well be awed by the grandeur as well as the subtlety of the ancient Chinese sages' prescriptions, such as the "noble lie" to entrench the hierarchical order, the carefully designed mobility mechanism among different classes within society, and the meticulous measures to harmonize ideal with reality, and so on.[48]

Finally, after unearthing Traditional Confucian Constitutionalism, further research is needed to investigate its impacts as well as manifestations in contemporary China. Given that the rationalist trend of modern society made well known by Weber is largely inevitable, a simple re-invocation of Traditional Confucian Constitutionalism in its traditional form certainly would not succeed in current China. This is indeed the main problem of the mainland New Confucians, such as Jiang Qing's constitutional proposals. A more plausible and fruitful endeavor may well be to explore the continuities and changes between Traditional Confucian Constitutionalism and the Sinicized Marxist constitutional arrangement currently being practiced in China today, which will be our investigating topic in the next chapter.

46 This kind of idealist aspiration is expressed in the following dialogue very well:

> Gong Sun Chou said, "Lofty are your principles and admirable, but to learn them may well be likened to ascending the heavens – something which cannot be reached. Why not adapt your teaching so as to cause learners to consider them attainable, and so daily exert themselves!" Mencius said, "A great artificer does not, for the sake of a stupid workman, alter or do away with the marking-line. Yi did not, for the sake of a stupid archer, charge his rule for drawing the bow. The superior man draws the bow, but does not discharge the arrow, having seemed to leap with it to the mark; and he there stands exactly in the middle of the path. Those who are able, follow him."
>
> (公孙丑曰："道则高矣，美矣，宜若登天然，似不可及也；何不使彼为可几及而日孳孳也？"孟子曰："大匠不为拙工改废绳墨，羿不为拙射变其彀率。君子引而不发，跃如也。中道而立，能者从之。") ("Gongsunchou" of *Mengzi* 《孟子-公孙丑》)

47 In the case of Plato, he describes how the regime would necessarily evolve from an aristocracy to democracy, and then to tyranny, the latter part of which is unfortunately largely ignored nowadays, while in the Aristotle's case, he largely shows how the regime would evolve into a mixture of democracy and oligarchy.

48 For the last point, Kenneth Holloway's (2009) new discovery about the harmonization of aristocracy and meritocracy in ancient Chinese philosophy based on the newly excavated Guodian Chu Slips text would provide a good example.

5 Sinicized Marxist Constitutionalism

Its emergence, contents, and implications

Introduction

As we all know, the liberal perspective historically views the constitution of a Marxist-Leninist state as a "sham" that serves as "an artifice of propaganda designed to impress and mislead foreigners" (Cohen, as cited in Wong, 2006, p. 1), or a "useless" document to rein in the government (Possony, as cited in Wong, 2006, p. 1). Consequently, scholars influenced by this paradigm look contemptuously at the current Chinese constitution, which for them needs to be abolished, significantly revised, or judicialized (Jiang, 2009, p. 12). However, in recent years, in light of the significant progress of the constitutional framework of China, including its values and practices regarding the rule of law, this dominant liberal perspective has been challenged. Stephanie Balme and Michael Dowdle (2009), for example, have devoted their latest book *Building Constitutionalism in China* to exploring the empirical impacts of the emerging constitutionalism on many aspects of Chinese society, including its juridical, political, and social realms. A US constitutional scholar, Larry C. Backer, has also sought to establish a party-state model to grant legitimacy to China's current constitutional development in the international community. This effort has been echoed by the separate articulations of Jiang Shigong, Lin Feng, Chu Jianguo, and Randall Peerenboom, and so on as well. Mainstream legal scholars in China have made similar efforts and recently convened a conference on "Socialist Constitutionalism with Chinese Characteristics" in May 2010 in Changsha City of Hunan Province.

In light of these developments, we can see that a new paradigm of Sinicized Marxist Constitutionalism[1] is emerging. Why is Sinicized Marxist Constitutionalism emerging? What are its contents and its implications? These are the questions this chapter seeks to explore. The chapter is divided into four sections. The first introduces the emerging context of Sinicized Marxist Constitutionalism. The second reviews the main approaches towards Sinicized Marxist Constitutionalism as well as their contents. The third elaborates the philosophical foundation of Sinicized Marxist Constitutionalism that is rarely heard or well understood by other two schools. The final section summarizes the chapter and draws some implications concerning the emergence of Sinicized Marxist Constitutionalism. As we will see, the emergence of Sinicized Marxist Constitutionalism has deep historical roots; the paradigm is rich in content and carries some profound implications.

1 The reason I prefer the title of "Sinicized Marxist Constitutionalism" over other titles such as "Party-State Constitutionalism" or "Socialist Constitutionalism with Chinese Characteristics" has to do with its semantic range as well as preciseness, which will be clearer later.

Emerging context of Sinicized Marxist Constitutionalism

There are three main sources motivating the emergence of Sinicized Marxist Constitutionalism. First, there is the significant progress of the values and practices regarding the rule of law in China over the past four decades. From a virtual legal vacuum at the end of the Cultural Revolution, China has established a comprehensive and well-codified legal system, which has been put into effective practice as well. The fact of legal progress has been widely noticed and acknowledged by scholars both in and outside China. In China, these achievements are well summarized and reflected in the government white paper *The Building Up of China's Rule of Law* (《中国的法制建设》) (Chinese Government, 2008), as well as in various survey books published in the past 2 years, such as *Thirty Years of China's Rule of Law* (《中国法治 30 年, 1978–2008》) (Legal Studies Institute of Chinese Academy of Social Sciences, 2008) and *China's Thirty Year March toward Rule of Law* (《中国走向法治 30 年, 1978–2008》) (Legal Studies Institute of Chinese Academy of Social Sciences, 2008),[2] to name just a few. In Western academia, China's legal progress is well acknowledged and discussed in books such as Randall Peerenboom's (2002) monograph *China's Long March toward Rule of Law*, Donald C. Clarke's (2008) edited book *China's Legal System: New Developments, New Challenges*, and so on.

Because the rule of law is widely taken as the core and defining element of constitutionalism, achievements in the legal realm provide a foundation for surging interest in constitutional development in China as well as the emergence of Sinicized Marxist Constitutionalism. In fact, the constitutional framework of China has also undergone profound changes. During the reform and opening-up period, Deng Xiaoping repeatedly emphasized the importance of the institutionalization and legalization of democracy in China. Near the end of the 20th century, the Communist Party of China also called for the the rule of law and building up a socialist rule of law state during the 15th Congress of the Communist Party of China in 1997 and later entrenched this goal into the Chinese Constitution during the 9th National Congress in 1999. Recently, a "human rights" clause has also been written into the Constitution, widely regarded as a landmark in China's constitutional development.

Nevertheless, despite the remarkable progress of legal reform in China, most scholarly attention seems to have been preoccupied with the gap between Chinese constitutional reality and the ideal liberal constitutionalism developed in the course of Western constitutional experience.[3] This is largely due to the dominance of the liberal constitutional paradigm in Western academia as well as its deep penetration into the Chinese intellectual realm. For example, some foreign-based China scholars distinguish the "rule by law" from the "rule of law" and attribute the former to current Chinese reality while emphasizing the significant barriers for China to attain authentic rule of law as practiced in the West. For them, "the concept of rule of law belongs to the West and connotes a pluralistic law reflecting a delicate balance of social forces, acting as a shield to protect various socioeconomic classes and strata against the arbitrary tutelage of government," while "the rule by law in China means statist instrumentalism and invokes both the doctrines of traditional Chinese legalism and the bureaucratic ethos of Soviet socialist legality" (Baum, as cited in Zheng, 2004, p. 50). Accordingly, "rule by law has become a major goal of Chinese political development" because the government realizes that law is not only an institutional necessity to promote

2 The latter is also recently translated and published in English, see Cai and Wang (2010).

3 It is worth pointing out that the liberal constitutionalism advocated in China is still quite ideological and parochial as reviewed in chapter 2, which is why I call it an "ideal."

socioeconomic development, but also "an effective means of coping with social, economic, and political problems resulting from rapid social and economic changes," as well as an important instrument to reduce arbitrariness on the part of officials while strengthening the state's legitimacy (Zheng, pp. 63, 69).[4] Zheng further summarizes three main types of barriers for China to attain rule of law, namely cultural, organizational, and structural barriers (p. 63). Culturally, both the large tradition of Confucianism and Legalism and the small tradition of communism are quite remote from the ideal of the rule of law; organizationally, the entrenchment of the supremacy of the Communist Party of China as well as its unwillingness to concede its leading power still poses a significant obstacle to China's march towards the rule of law; structurally, China is still a developing country, so the Chinese state is not merely a coordinator of different interests, but also a provider of political order and a facilitator of socioeconomic development (Zheng, pp. 63–66). Similarly, Jean-Pierre Cabestan (2005) analyzes in detail the political and practical obstacles, such as the lack of financial and human resources, rampant corruption, and local protectionism, and so on that prevent China from reforming its judiciary and establishing a rule of law state.

The deep influence of the Western liberal constitutional paradigm is also well manifested in the constitutional scholarship in China. With the steady progress of legal reform in China, especially the official advocacy of "rule of law" by the Communist Party of China leadership in 1997 and the entrenchment of this ideal into the constitution in 1999, constitutional consciousness in China has increased dramatically; at the same time, scholarship on constitutional law and constitutionalism in China has proliferated. Although constitutionalism is largely a Western idea, it has nevertheless transcended its parochial origins to become a universal norm of the world (Jiang, 2009, p. 11); its influence on Chinese constitutional thinking is also remarkable. As shown in his article "Western Constitutional Ideas and Constitutional Discourse in China, 1978–2005," the impact of Western constitutional ideals and discourses in China is so significant that Yu Xingzhong (2009) acknowledges that "it is no exaggeration to say that Chinese constitutional discourse has been significantly 'Westernized'" (p. 114). It is in this regard that Pan Wei, a well-known coiner and advocate of the notion of "Chinese Model" (*zhongguo moshi* 中国模式), regards the realm of legal study as the "hardest hit area" of Chinese academia by what he regards as Western ideological imperialism (personal communication, June 10, 2010). The impact is also manifested in the sensibilities as well as sense of what problems are most important (*wenti yishi* 问题意识) of the majority of Chinese constitutional scholars. While not daring to openly call the Chinese constitution a "sham" or "useless" document as some Western critics have, they nevertheless take the divergence between the constitutional expression and practice as a tacit truism (Jiang, 2009, p. 11). The problems they are most concerned about and preoccupied with are consequently how to revise the current Chinese constitution to meet Western standards and particularly how to implement the constitution in juridical practice in order to avoid its irrelevance in daily life (Jiang, 2009, p. 12).[5]

4 The latter reading of the political controlling function of law is supported by He Xin's (2009) in-depth study of administrative litigation in China. This idea is also vividly captured by the title of Stanley Lubman's (2000) book *Bird in a Cage: Legal Reform in China after Mao*.

5 It is worth noting that after the People's Supreme Court's first invocation of constitutional provisions in its judicial interpretation to the "Qi Yuling case" in 2001, the problem of "the judicialization of the constitution" (*xianfa sifahua* 宪法司法化) has been hotly debated and discussed; nevertheless, in response to the significant impact it generated, the Supreme Court annulled the interpretation together with a number of other interpretations in 2008.

Meanwhile, the deep penetration and influence of the Western liberal constitutional paradigm in China has induced two remarkable reactions. The first is the "constitutionalism abolition thesis" (*xianzheng quxiaolun* 宪政取消论), and the second is the advocating of constitutional proposals based on and loyal to China's indigenous traditions by some cultural conservatives in mainland China. The first reaction is mainly shown among scholars of political studies. If the realm of legal studies is indeed the "hardest hit area" of Chinese academia by Western ideological imperialism, the situation in the realm of political studies is relatively better, perhaps due to greater caution of the part of supervising political authority in China as well as the distinctive natures of the two subjects. The difference is reflected in their distinct stances towards the issue of constitutionalism. Constitutionalism is by no means a hot topic among political scholars in China; in fact, some prominent figures among this group have openly criticized the concept as well as the ideology behind it.[6] Their views seem to have been accepted by political authorities, which is perhaps why some books written on constitutionalism face some implicit barriers for publication (anonymous, personal communication, May 22, 2010). The appeal of the "constitutionalism abolition thesis" to current political leaders is not hard to understand as soon as one questions where the Four Cardinal Principles (*sixiang jibenyuanze* 四项基本原则)[7] that serve as the foundation for China's reform and development are placed in the new constitutional discourse, which usually centers on the three core elements of "democracy, rule of law, and human rights." This is actually one of the primary motivations for the conference on "Socialist Constitutionalism with Chinese Characteristics" in Changsha in May 2010 by legal scholars in China; most of the participants had the hidden agenda of using the title of this meeting to rectify the name and restore the leading status of constitutionalism in directing China's political reform in future. This may well be shown in the speech of the convener Li Buyun, who confesses his strategic concerns for holding the conference. While the conference was attended by many important figures within the field of legal studies, including several presidents of the University of Politics and Law (*zhengfa daxue* 政法大学), and some major media representatives in China, such as the *People's Daily*, and so on as well as an important former state leader, Luo Haocai (罗豪才), the conference received little media coverage and consequently had little impact on the public. The struggle over the issue of rectifying the name of constitutionalism has thus not undergone significant changes.

Another reaction to the penetration of the Western liberal constitutional paradigm in China is the emergence of Confucian constitutionalism discourse advocated by some so-called "mainland New Confucians," represented by Jiang Qing (*Jiangqing* 蒋庆), Kang Xiaoguang (*Kangxiaoguang* 康晓光), Sheng Hong (*Shenghong* 盛洪), and Chen Ming (*Chenming* 陈明), and so on (Fang, 2006, p. 6). While having not reached a consensus among themselves for a specific constitutional blueprint, this school is united in bemoaning the fact that the liberal constitutional proposals of the past century, including amendments of the current Chinese constitution, all lack native features. In other words, contemporary Chinese politics is still diverging from its native tradition and getting more "Westernized."

6 For example, see Chen Hongtai (2004), Wang and Chen (2004), and Xie Yi (2004).

7 The "Four Cardinal Principles" includes the "leadership of the Communist Party, guidance of Marxism-Leninism and Mao Zedong Thought, people's democratic dictatorship, and adherence to socialism." It was advocated by Deng Xiaoping in 1979 as the foundational or baseline principles for China's reform and opening-up policy. It was explicitly written into the Charter of the Communist Party of China and implicitly included in the Preamble of the Constitution. For the latter, see Lin Feng (2000), chapter 2.

As a result, they have been seeking to develop constitutional blueprints that are based on and also loyal to China's cultural tradition. One notable proposal is Jiang Qing's "Confucian Religious Constitutionalism" (*rujiao xianzheng* 儒教宪政), which is supported by his theory of "political Confucianism" and consists of a series of concrete proposals for realizing the blueprint. An international conference entitled "Confucian Religious Constitutionalism and China's Future" has been convened in May 2010 in Hong Kong as well.

If the constitutional achievements of China in the past four decades provide the foundation, while the deep penetration of the Western Liberal Constitutional paradigm in China serves as a kind of catalyst for the emergence of Sinicized Marxist Constitutionalism, the surging interest in exploring and theorizing the so-called "Chinese Model" (*zhongguo moshi* 中国模式) within current Chinese academia and the prevailing trend of shaking off the yoke of dominant paradigms in the Western academia may have provided a supporting environment for its emergence. Tacitly endorsed by Chinese government, whose intellectuals have sought to bridge the notion of "Chinese Model" with the official line of "The Path and Theoretical System of Socialism with Chinese Characteristics" (*zhongguotese shehuizhuyidaolu he liluntixi* 中国特色社会主义道路和理论体系), the exploration and theorization of the "Chinese Model" based on China's successful modernization path has proliferated in Chinese academia in the past few years, especially in the past 2 years since the unfolding of the financial crisis in the West. This is well reflected in the change of the number of core social science journal articles published on the theme, as shown in Table 5.1.

In the period of 2009–2010, there were 91 articles containing the phrase "Chinese Model" in their titles and 167 articles with "Chinese Model" as the keyword; this is nearly three times the number published during the period of 2001–2008, which had 29 and 57 instances respectively. There have also been various conferences, research projects, and books devoted to the theme in China recently.[8] While it is hard to give a specific definition to the term "Chinese Model," some key characteristics could be identified, such as its objection to the prevailing doctrinaire adoption of Western institutions and values, as well as its emphasis on the theorization of indigenous experiences of the past 60 years.

The current popularity of the "Chinese Model" does not seem to have spread far from the Chinese border, but nevertheless, in Western academia, there is a trend to rethink the dominant paradigms as well as re-engage alternative discourses that were previously ignored or suppressed. This trend is particularly well manifested in the area of China studies, since the bare facts of China's rapid economic growth as well as the regime's continuing resilience have betrayed the limitation of the existing frameworks and have led some to explore new categories and perspectives to better capture China's realities. This seems to be well shown

Table 5.1 Number of core social science journal articles on the "Chinese Model"

	1980–2000	*2001–2008*	*2009–2018*
"Chinese Model" in title	18	70	1321
"Chinese Model" as keyword	4	49	904

Source: China Academic Journals Full-text Database of the CNKI on June 8, 2018.

8 Taking the books for example, in recent years there are already books such as *The Chinese Model: Experience and Dilemma* (Zheng, 2010b), *Dialogue: The Chinese Model, On the Chinese Model* (Qi, 2010), *Chinese model – understand the 60 years of PRC* (Pan, 2009), and so on.

in Backer's, Perenboom's, Balme and Dowdle's endeavors. The easier access of information from China as well as increased interactions with Chinese realties due to technological advances and the rising tide of globalization certainly have contributed to this change.

To sum up, we have reviewed three factors in the background that have contributed to the emergence of Sinicized Marxist Constitutionalism. As we have seen, the progress of the rule of law and constitutional framework in China surely play a foundational role, as without these transformations, the Chinese variant of constitutionalism may not have attracted much attention at all. However, the prevailing acceptance of the liberal constitutional paradigm in China has induced some reactions from various quarters and consequently has served as a catalyst for the emergence of Sinicized Marxist Constitutionalism. Finally, interest in exploring the "Chinese Model" within current Chinese academia and dissatisfaction with the dominant paradigms in the West have provided an amiable environment for a Sinicized Marxist Constitutionalism to emerge. Surely behind all of the three major factors mentioned earlier is the common denominator of China's continuing rapid economic growth. This may echo Marx's thesis about the dialectical relationship between economic base structure and ideational superstructures. Next, let's have a look at the contents of Sinicized Marxist Constitutionalism.

The contents of Sinicized Marxist Constitutionalism

As shown in Figure 5.1, we could identify five main approaches toward constitutionalism in China.[9] The first approach is surely the prevailing Western Liberal Constitutionalism approach mentioned earlier, which focuses on the gap between China's current constitutional reality and certain Western ideals. Due to the scope and purpose of this chapter, I will not elaborate it further here. The second approach is a little more moderate as it acknowledges and focuses on the legal and constitutional progress seen in China over recent decades, which I call an "empirical transitional approach." This is represented by the work of Balme and Dowdle's edited book *Building Constitutionalism in China* (2009), which

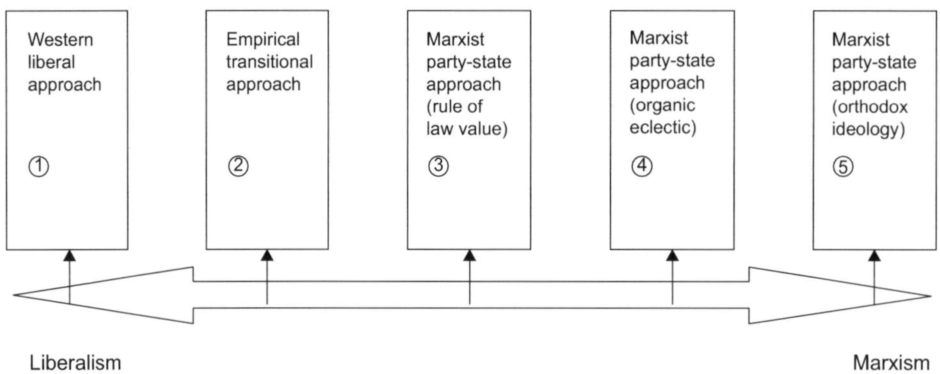

Figure 5.1 An ideological spectrum of approaches towards Chinese constitutionalism

9 The boundaries among the five approaches may not be clearly delineated, nor are the categorization of the scholars to the approaches absolute; the preliminary categorizations are for general organizational as well as illustrative purposes.

is largely empirical in nature; it mainly explores different conceptual frameworks towards Chinese constitutionalism and the impacts of this emerging constitutionalism in a variety of areas, including not only the juridical realm such as legal practice, judicial decision-making, and legal scholarship and education, and so on, but also the political and social realms, such as political consciousness, social resistance, mobilization, and citizen empowerment, and so on. While marking an advance over the first approach, the "transitional constitutionalism" approach is still operating within the paradigm of Western Liberal Constitutionalism, and so does not yet fully realize the Chinese characteristics of the constitutionalism emerging in China. As a result, I will not go over it in detail here. Most relevant to the theme of this chapter are the third to the fifth approaches because they all capture some core elements of Chinese constitutionalism, namely the party-state constitutional order, as well as the importance of ideology in the constitutional framework. Nevertheless, they differ in terms of center of gravity among ideological values, with the third approach pivoted on the rule of law value, the fifth approach on the orthodox ideology of regime, and the fourth approach on an organic eclectic of the third and fifth approaches. Next, I will provide a review and analysis of each approach to Sinicized Marxist Constitutionalism.

Marxist party-state approach pillared on the rule of law

The third approach is well represented by Larry C. Backer's party-state model of Chinese constitutionalism. According to Backer (2009b), to understand this model with Chinese characteristics, one needs to first understand that "the Chinese constitution exists as a combination of polity and governing ideology, on the one hand, and the state apparatus, on the other hand" (p. 110). A key component in this constitutional arrangement is the Communist Party, not as a political party or private actor in the Western sense, but as the institutionalization of the polity and the source of its substantive values. In other words, the Communist Party as an autonomous community serves as the gatekeeper of political citizenship and the provider of the value framework for the state. As a result, Backer (2009b) concludes four major features of the party-state model of the Chinese constitutionalism: 1) the division of citizenship between social and economic citizenship held by all, and political citizenship exercised through the Communist Party of China[10]; 2) the subordination of state power and institutions to political authority; 3) institutionalization of political authority within a collective space (the Communist Party of China) beyond the control of any individuals, that serves as the source and conduit of constitutional values to be implemented by the state apparatus[11]; and 4) reliance on state and party self-discipline for the elaboration of rule of law values (p. 102).

While this approach is quite distinctive from previous approaches in that it brings the Communist Party of China as well as its ideologies into the constitutional structure, it is located near the center of the spectrum because it still emphasizes rule of law as the defining feature of constitutionalism. As a result, Backer (2009b) argues that the Communist Party

10 On this issue, as we shall see, Jiang Shigong differs slightly, as he includes other political parties as holding some political citizenship as well.

11 For Backer, Jiang Zeming's "Three Represents" and Hu Jintao's policy of "scientific development and harmonious society," which incorporate sustainable development, social welfare, a people-centered society, and increased democracy, and so on, are such value frameworks derived from the vanguard party. For a good discussion of "Three Represents" as the foundation of Sinicized Marxist Constitutionalism, see Zhang and Jiang (2002).

of China "retains its constitutionalist character to the extent that in its internal operations it observes the same rule of law framework as that imposed externally on the state apparatus" (p. 111).[12] It is Backer's (2009b) emphasis on rule of law as the defining feature of constitutionalism that leads him to regard pre-Deng Chinese state governance architecture as anti-constitutionalist, a kind of truism shared with previous approaches (p. 126). While Backer (2009b) is right in claiming that "the basic premise of constitutionalism is to distinguish it from despotism or tyranny" (p. 107), it seems that further support is needed to argue that the absence of the rule of law necessarily leads to despotism and tyranny.[13]

This approach, represented by Backer's model, is also shared by some famous scholars, such as Jiang Shigong and Chu Jianguo in China and Randall Peerenboom at UCLA. Responding to the prevailing sensibilities and problem awareness of the majority of legal scholars in China, especially their exclusive focus on the written constitution, Jiang Shigong (2009) advocates an "unwritten constitution" perspective to study China's constitutionalism. With some compelling arguments, the author contends that the actual operation of constitutionalism in all countries relies on an unwritten constitution, and he demonstrates that China's constitutional order actually has four sources, namely the party constitution, constitutional conventions, constitutional doctrines, and constitutional statutes. The most remarkable characteristics of the Chinese constitutional order, according to Jiang, is the compound interactional structure between the political and the legal, represented by the party and the state respectively.[14] Historically, the PRC was founded politically under the leadership of the Communist Party of China with alliances of other political parties. This is well shown in *The Common Program of the Chinese People's Political Consultative Conference* proclaimed in 1949, the first constitutional document of the PRC. According to Jiang, the diverse background of the first political consultative conference attendees as well as their representativeness could well provide the legitimacy needed to politically establish the PRC; however, as a "political" foundation lacks certain formal elements, it needs a legal foundation to entrench and stabilize the polity, which is the reason for the proclamation of the formal Constitution in 1954.[15] Consequently, Jiang (2009) argues that the sovereignty of China is represented in two ways: the first is through the Communist Party-led multiparty cooperation system, which consists of representatives based on their political ideas, historical missions, and class interests; the second is the People's Congress, which consists in representatives elected through certain legal and formal electoral procedures from the

12 To be fair, it is worth pointing out that Backer does regard the ideology of the Communist Party of China, such as the "Three Represents," as a distinctive feature of Sinicized Marxist Constitutionalism, but I think he still emphasizes the rule of law values.

13 The assumed dichotomy of the rule of law versus despotism seems to have been taken for granted by the liberal paradigm; nevertheless, we should be aware that this pre-conception has excluded some plausible alternatives. For example, as I have shown and elaborated earlier in Chapter 4, the core of Confucian constitutionalism is to design a subtle cultural mechanism to contain the potential abuses of government power without excessive reliance on legal means; for some, the socialist legal system as practiced in China during Mao's period is founded on a "radicalized version of Confucianism," also representing a socialist alternative to the liberal paradigm (Hipkin, 1984, p. 125).

14 For a more detailed discussion of the compound feature of China's political reform as well as the overall reform and opening-up movements of the late 1970s, see Tong Dezhi (2010, pp. 8–23), which argues that the compound feature is manifested not only in the overall strategy, institution system, and end goals of China's reform, but also shown in the relationships between state and civil society, intra-party democracy and people's democracy, democracy and rule of law, democracy and economics, and democracy and culture, and so on.

15 For a good discussion of Stalin's influence on this, see Hua-yu Li (2001).

citizenry (p. 22). This echoes Backer's insights about the two main divisions of citizenship as well. While emphasizing the unique Chinese constitutional party-state structure, Jiang seems to share the power-constraining dimension of Backer's view. For Jiang (2009), while state sovereignty, represented by the People's Congress, is indeed a kind of "rubber stamp" in a neutral sense, since political wills of Communist Party of China and NPC are themselves supposed to be identical, legitimization of the party will through the NPC assumes the additional function of "taming the emperor" (p. 23). Jiang does not elaborate the reasons but points out the differences through a comparison with that of the Cultural Revolution period where the Communist Party of China ruled directly without any resort to legal legitimatization. Conceivably, the need to go through the NPC in order for Communist Party of China's will to be elevated to state level may serve to slow the deliberative process hence making the proposals more cautious as well as representative (remember that the approval rate by the votes in the NPC still indicates something). In fact, this is supported by Robert Benewick's (1998) observation of the dualistic feature of Chinese constitution as "the Communist Party contending and proposing and the state amending and disposing" (p. 447). To Jiang (2009), this is similar to the difference between "absolute monarchy" and "constitutional monarchy" as manifested and aspired to in recent Chinese history (p. 23).[16] Another scholar Chu Jianguo (2006) shares this view and further elaborates the advantages as well as necessity of what he calls "One Party Constitutionalism" (*yidang lixian* 一党立宪) in a web-based article. Nevertheless, it is hard to know whether Chu truly endorses the leadership of the party or is just expressing a realistic compromise, since he thinks that the purpose of the "One Party Constitutionalism" is to bring all political power, including the Communist Party of China, under effective constraints while not alternating the leadership role of the current ruling party (p. 10).

Marxist party-state approach pillared on orthodox ideology

If these approaches are largely preoccupied with constraining governmental power through the rule of law mainly due to the deep influence of the liberal constitutional paradigm, the fifth approach then, as an alternative, concentrates its attention on the constitutional order of Chinese politics as it is and takes its ideological dimension as the distinctive feature of Chinese constitutionalism.[17] First of all, this approach sees a consistent constitutional developmental trajectory in China and has been well explored in books such as Han Damei's (2005) *A Study of the Constitutionalism of New Democracy* (《新民主主义宪政研究》), Qing Qianhong and Ye Haibo's (2008) book *A Study of Socialist Constitutionalism* (《社会主义宪政研究》), and Han Dayuan's (2008) *The 1954 Constitution and Chinese Constitutionalism* (《1954 年宪法与中国宪政》), and so on.[18] Here I will review Ren Xirong's synoptic account as a representative. In her presentation at the "Socialist Constitutionalism with Chinese Characteristics" conference, Ren Xirong (2010) from Jilin University reviews the developmental trajectory of socialist constitutionalism from

16 For a good discussion of the similarities and differences between the Communist Party of China and the Emperor in the Chinese history, see Zheng Yongnian (2010), *The Chinese Communist Party as Organizational Emperor: Culture, Reproduction, and Transformation.*

17 For pioneering research on constitutionalism in authoritarian settings, see Suisheng Zhao (1996), *Power by Design: Constitution-Making in Nationalist China.*

18 This is a major reason for my preference for using the title "Sinicized Marxist Constitutionalism," because only it precisely and comprehensively covers the whole period; other titles, such as "Party-state

Mao's time to later leaders. According to her, Mao Zedong and his contemporary Marxist theorists are the founders of the Chinese Socialist Constitutionalism theory and system. This is so not only because the core of Mao Zedong's constitutional thought, namely "constitutionalism is the politics of democracy," has deeply influenced the way Chinese people today understand constitutionalism,[19] but also because, during Maoist times, the fundamental categorical system of the Chinese socialist constitutionalism, including constituents such as the Constitution, the National Polity (*guoti* 国体), the state/government (*zhengti* 政体), the people, citizenship, democratic centralism, people's congress system, the fundamental rights and obligations, legislative power, judicial power, administrative power, chief of state, autonomous governance, and so on, and the actual working mechanisms of the constitutional order were formed. Constitutional structure and thought was further developed by Deng and Jiang. During his time, Deng not only established the "Four Cardinal Principles" for China's reform and opening-up and set up the goal of institutionalizing and legalizing the peoples' democracy, but also developed the ideology of "Socialist Theory with Chinese Characteristics" (*zhongguotese shehuizhuyililun* 中国特色社会主义理论).[20] This constitutional trajectory is further developed by later leaders, as shown in the incorporation of "the rule of law," "human rights," and "Three Represents" clauses into the Constitution.

Second, this fifth approach is distinct for its emphasis on the orthodox ideology. For example, tracing the constitutional development of China from the Common Program of 1949 to the current 1982 Constitution, Kam Wong (2006) points out that the Chinese

> constitutions were not there to limit the government's power but to promote the ideology of the state and advance the cause of the Communist Party, that is to contribute to building a Communist State under Mao (the 1954 PRC Constitution) or to facilitate the social and economic reforms under Deng (the 1982 PRC Constitution).
>
> (p. 37)

In other words, Wong (2006) further explains, "Traditional 'constitutionalism' in the West is built upon an individualistic foundation, adversarial processes and a zero-sum gain calculus," but Chinese "constitutionalism" is "premised more upon a collective mentality, centered more on a cooperative spirit and on a mutually beneficial understanding [that] Power need not be held in check but must be guided and directed to achieve collective goods" (p. 37). It is also in this sense that Ren (2010) regards the "Four Cardinal Principles" as the

---

Constitutionalism" and "Socialist Constitutionalism with Chinese Characteristics" tend to be either not indicative of its philosophical foundation, as the former, or not comprehensive enough, as the latter, which tends to be associated with Deng's reform period in the Chinese context. For a more detailed elaboration on the evolution and continuity of Marxism in China, see Ni Degang's (2009) book *A Study of the Sinicization of Marxism*.

19 This core, according to Ren (2010), is not a sign of Mao's pragmatic attitude towards constitutionalism, as some liberal scholars criticize, but actually denotes a Marxist attitude and perspective on constitutionalism: first, constitutional movement should have different tasks at different period of time; second, there is close connections between democracy and constitutionalism; and third, it is a more comprehensive understanding of the intensions of constitutionalism over the liberal perspective (p. 1).

20 According to Chinese scholars, this theory system was developed during Deng's time but theorized afterwards.

cornerstone of Chinese constitutionalism and the fundamental feature distinguishing it from its Western counterparts (p. 2). While in his article Wong (2006) points out that the 1982 Constitution of the PRC marks a breakthrough from previous ones by incorporating the ideas of "rule of law, individual rights, limitation of state powers" for the first time (p. 3), he does not elaborate much on them, nor regard them as essential for Chinese constitutionalism. In fact, Wong acknowledges that the Chinese authorities drafting the 1982 Constitution did not subscribe to a liberal understanding of these core values and has called for further research on the impacts of the reform and opening-up period on the Party's thinking as well as the people's understanding of constitutionalism in the past four decades.[21]

Given this approach's reliance on the orthodox ideology of the Communist Party of China as well as its canopy of the Cultural Revolution period, a third feature not hard to conceive is the legacy of Marxist and socialist legal philosophy. Just as the third "rule of law" approach does not exclude the ideological dimension of Sinicized Marxist Constitutionalism, this fourth ideological approach does not exclude the "rule of law" either, though it presents it in terms of a very different Marxist or socialist understanding. In Western academia, there is very little written on Marxist or socialist legality, let alone their philosophy. This is understandable, since classical Marxism is well-known for dismissing law as a class instrument and capitalist institution, which will "wither away" with the state after the revolution (Wong, 2006, pp. 4–5). Nevertheless, Marxist legal theory, advocated and endorsed by the authority, has been hotly explored and discussed in Chinese academia, especially its adaption to the current context. I will leave a review of this aspect until later; what I want to suggest here is a plausible defense of the fifth approach's inclusion of the Cultural Revolution period, which is widely perceived as a lawless era. This reading is taken from Brian Hipkin, who suggests that a key difference between the legal realms of Mao's period and Deng's period is not whether the period has laws or not, but whether the rules of justice are codified or informal. For Hipkin (1984), during the Mao period, "rules were created and maintained at the level of interpersonal relationships and it was possible for them to both generate a sense of solidarity and to give the masses a chance to control their situations"; after the transformation, however, "codification, the intervention of formal state legal organizations, control by higher courts and notions of precedent" emerged, and these measures led to rules that "stand outside of the interpersonal recognition of solidarity and socialist equality" (p. 126). Consequently, it has led to the alienation of the ordinary people, particularly rural peasants and the urban proletariat from legal practices, and partly resulted in future inequality (Hipkin, 1984, p. 126). Hipkin (1984) attributes much of this "massline" style of socialist legality to China's immense cultural heritage, which had contributed to the longevity and efficiency of China's informal justice system as shown in the history of managing such a big country with little more than 5,000 lawyers (p. 125).

It is beyond the scope of my current project to go into details about the change (*bian* 变) and continuity (*tong* 通) between traditional Chinese jurisprudence and Sinicized Marxist jurisprudence, but to help the reader better understand this perspective, I will mention two key theses.[22] The first is the discovery by Yu Ronggen (俞荣根) (1998, 2006), a widely recognized authoritative scholar on Confucian legal thought, that the distinctive core as well

21 In this regard, the title of Wong's article "Human Rights and Limitation of State Power: the Discovery of Constitutionalism in the People's Republic of China" is more a kind of stunt than an informative window to the content.

22 For a good discussion of the value of the former to the latter, see Zhang (2010).

as spirit of Chinese jurisprudence is the trinity of natural law or Universal Principles (*tianli* 天理), state laws (*guofa* 国法), and commonsensical sentiments or the actual condition of the people (*renqing* 人情). In this framework, the common people are not alienated from the legal realm mainly because they occupy one pole of the trinity, and they can utilize common sense as a weapon against doctrinaire or deviant interpretations of state laws, which is supposed to be consistent with natural law that in turn is also based on the sentiments and actual condition of the people (Yu, 1998, p. 14). This is in fact supported by a second thesis advocated by Jin Guantao (金观涛) and Liu Qingfen (刘青峰), two well-known scholars of Chinese intellectual history. Drawing on discoveries from a large quantitative database for the study of modern Chinese intellectual history that they developed, Jin and Liu (2010) argue that the Chinese concept of *Li* (理) as the criteria for judgments of propriety and legitimacy is radically different from its counterpart in the West, rationality. For Jin and Liu (2010), one could read the Chinese concept of *Li* as "common sense rationality" (*changshilixing* 常识理性), which is meticulously entrenched in "common sense (常识)" and "natural sentiments or facts (*renzhichangqing* 人之常情)" (p. 26).

Hipkin's reading of socialist legality clearly renders support to the fifth approach towards Sinicized Marxist Constitutionalism.[23] Bearing the two theses in mind, we could then also better understand Mao Zedong's statement that

> The peasants are clear sighted. Who is bad and who is not quite vicious, who deserves severe punishment and who deserves to be let off lightly – the peasants keep clear accounts and very seldom has the punishment exceeded the crime.
>
> (as cited in Wong, 2006, p. 7)

Further, we could also better understand Mao's later shying away from codified laws for governing the people. This perhaps could also help us understand the current Chinese judiciary's strategic turn towards populism, its re-emphasis on mediation of disputes (Peerenboom, 2010, p. 21),[24] as well as the hot debate in China over the advantages of substantive justice (*shitizhengyi* 实体正义) over procedural justice (*chengxuzhengyi* 程序正义) and established legal scholars' surging interest in "soft law" (*ruanfa* 软法), and so on.[25]

Marxist party-state approach pillared by a new organic eclectic ideology

The fourth approach towards Sinicized Marxist Constitutionalism marks the latest turn in constitutional thought among the leadership as well as some leading established intellectuals in China. First of all, it is worth pointing out that, given the dense liberal flavor of the notion of "constitutionalism" in the Chinese context, which has induced the

23 For a similar but more moderate account, see the critical legal theorist James P. Brady's (1982) *Justice and Politics in People's China: Legal Order or Continuing Revolution*. Conceivably, as critical legal theory is more akin to Marxism than its liberal alternative, it could perhaps render much support to the fifth approach reviewed here.

24 For an in-depth and sophisticated analysis of the actual working mechanisms of legal realm at the grassroots level, see Zhu Suli (2000) *Sending Law to the Countryside: Research on China's Basic-level Judicial System*.

25 This is well shown in the growing number of articles containing "soft law" in the title: before 2005, there are only 5 articles, and now the number has increased to 29 in total (statistics from China Academic Journals Full-text Database); for a good elaboration of the importance of "soft law," see Luo and Song (2009).

"constitutionalism abolition thesis" mentioned earlier, the terminology is rarely used by party leaders and established intellectuals, with the exception of some legal scholars mainly in the legal community. Party leaders have used the notion of the "rule of Constitution" (*yixianzhiguo* 依宪治国), but the most common counterparts of "constitutionalism" in the Chinese discourse have been "socialist democratic politics" (*shehuizhuyiminzhuzheng-zhi* 社会主义民主政治), "Chinese style democracy" (*zhongguoshiminzhu* 中国式民主), and "socialist political civilization" (*shehuizhuyizhengzhiwenming* 社会主义政治文明), and so on. Since the political authority's public pronouncement and advocacy of these notions with Chinese characteristics, the literature devoted to these themes has proliferated. Though these different notions emerged in different contexts and differ to some extent in terms of their respective intensions and extensions, they all share an essential core in the Chinese case, which is the organic unity of "the leadership of the Party, the position of the people as masters of the country, and the rule of law" (党的领导，人民当家做主，依法治国). This constitutional trinity was included in the reports of both the 16th and the 17th Communist Party of China National Congresses. Since then, an enormous literature has been devoted to this constitutional trinity as well. Next, I will just take Wang Jinyuan's explication of the organic relationships among the trinity as a representative.[26]

The three parts are held to be organically united since the leadership of the party is the guarantee of the latter two, while the concept of people as masters is the essential requirement of socialist democratic politics and rule of law is the fundamental strategy of the Communist Party of China to lead the people to govern state affairs (Wang, 2003, p. 30). According to these authors, the leadership of the Communist Party of China has been proven by both history and reality to be indispensable for the setting up of the socialist system and the continuing march towards socialist democracy in China.[27] In fact, from the very moment of the birth of the Communist Party of China, it has embraced the realization and development of people's democracy as its main task, so there is no divergence between the leadership of the Communist Party of China and the people as masters. Accordingly, all Chinese leaders have repeatedly emphasized the crucial leading role of the Communist Party of China for the socialist causes and endeavors China is aiming at (Wang, 2003, pp. 30–31). As for the people as masters, that is surely a necessary requirement of socialist democracy, which itself is the inherent nature and requirement of socialism (Wang, 2003, p. 32). The concept of people as masters means that all endeavors should serve the interests of the people, who have the inherent rights to participate in governing state affairs and supervise the operation of state apparatuses. At the same time, rule of law as an important mark of modern civilization has been accepted as the necessary requirement of socialist democratic politics and also the guarantor of the realization of the latter and, consequently, the goal of people as the master. Rule of law is also the bridge as well as nexus between the Communist Party of China and the people as masters.

From this brief introduction, we can see that the fourth approach combines certain core ideas from both liberal constitutionalism and Marxist ideological constitutionalism as reviewed earlier. In this regard, it is similar to the effort of the third approach, but it transcends the third approach by developing an organic outlook on the three core elements

26 I only provide a brief account of the organic relationship here; for a discussion of what each pole entails, see Zhang and Jiang (2002), Xi (2007), and Gao and Tong (2010).

27 The victory of China in overcoming the so-called "Three Mountains," namely imperialism, feudalism, and bureaucratic capitalism, as well as the deviation of the Soviet Union from socialism caused by its abandonment of the Communist Party's leadership all shows the indispensability of the leading role of the Communist Party of China in China (Wang, 2003, pp. 30–31).

rather than tilting towards the rule of law value. As we can see from the spectrum of Figure 5.1, this latest development of constitutional thought also could be regarded as the result of the interactions and dialogues between liberal constitutionalism and Marxist ideological constitutionalism. Marxist constitutionalism, as shown in the fourth approach, takes the orthodox ideology as the defining element of constitutionalism and, to some extent, adopts a kind of consequentialist philosophy that enables the government to use ends to justify means as practiced during the pre-Deng eras. However, due to increasing Western influences as well as China's own development, the importance of the rule of law and individual rights has been widely accepted by both the authority and the public and consequently integrated into this latest constitutionalism discourse. This eclectic reading is also supported by He Baogang (2010), who argues for a constitutionalism that is able to transcend both the left and the right ideologies and maintain a dynamic coordinating balance among them with a comprehensive outlook.

The eclectic nature of the fourth approach is also well illustrated in the new discursive terminologies of the current ideology. Shying away from the slogans of the Maoist period yet without embracing Western values in a wholesale manner, party leaders and established intellectuals have sought to develop a "theoretical system of Socialism with Chinese Characteristics" (*zhongguoteseshehuizhuyililuntixi* 中国特色社会主义理论体系) that incorporates those newly coined ideas such as the "Three Represents," "Scientific Outlook on Development," "People-centeredness," "Harmonious Society," "Socialist Political Civilization," and "Socialist Legal Ideas," and so on. This discursive turn of Chinese ideology has been well captured by China scholars in Western academia as well. For example, through the application of discourse theory to an analysis of the newly emerging ideology of "Socialism with Chinese Characteristics" and "Scientific Outlook on Development," Xing Guoxin (2009) argues that the Chinese party leaders and established intellectuals have "boiled socialism down to abstract values, independent of and autonomous from the economic base, marking a retreat from class and class struggle" (p. 213). Nicholas Dynon's (2008) article "'Four Civilizations' and the Evolution of Post-Mao Chinese Socialist Ideology" also offers an in-depth analysis of the emergence of "civilization discourse" in China's current ideology. What is remarkable about this collection of terminology is that both the left and the right could interpret and utilize them in ways consistent with their respective core tenets, while the "Party rhetoric defines the opportunity structures for debate" (Gilley & Holbig, 2009, p. 342). For example, employing a similar attempt to take "people centeredness" as the foundational norm of Chinese constitutionalism, liberals try to associate it with the protection of human rights and dignity (Liu & Yang, 2004; Li & Zhu, 2005; Yuan, 2010), while Marxists tend to emphasize the superiority of the Marxist understanding on the issue over that of Western liberal alternatives (Xu & Xie, 2005; Chen & Jin, 2009).

A related issue worth pointing out is the emergence of corresponding legal theory in the name of "Socialist Legal Ideas" (*shehuizhuyifazhilinian* 社会主义法治理念) for Sinicized Marxist Constitutionalism. It is a summation and theorization of China's legal reforms both in its practical and theoretical dimensions over the past four decades and an inherent part of the grand theory of "Socialism with Chinese Characteristics" dealing with the juridical aspect; it is also a direct result of the adaptation and innovation of Marxist jurisprudence in the contemporary Chinese context. As mentioned earlier, while Marxist jurisprudence is not so popular in mainstream Western academia, it is nevertheless a hot topic in Chinese legal studies. This is well shown in the number of articles written on this theme, especially its Sinicization. For example, the core social science journal articles that have "Marxist jurisprudence" (*makesizhuyifaxue* 马克思主义法学) in their title have increased from 5 in

2000 to 31 today.[28] The focus of this literature has also shifted from mainly an introduction to the original legal theory of Marxism to an exploration of its Sinicization for application in contemporary China; the recent high-level conference devoted to this theme this past summer at Renmin University is a good illustration of the ascendance of this topic.[29] A more telling statistics perhaps is the number of articles written on "Socialist Legal Ideas" (*shehuizhuyifazhilinian* 社会主义法治理念), explicitly claiming to be a result of the process of the Sinicization of Marxist jurisprudence in China. Since the term was first coined in 2006, there have been a total of 43 articles in the core journals containing this idea in their title.[30] State authorities have tried to advocate it in society with promotional campaigns, such as knowledge and speech contests, and so on. The Politics and Law Committee of the Communist Party of China has also published a *Socialist Legal Ideas Educational Reader* in 2008 and have included "Socialist Legal Ideas" in China's Judicial Test (*sifakaoshi* 司法考试) as a separate section heavily weighted for scoring starting in 2009. There is no need to go into further details about the contents as well as justifications for these ideas; it suffices to point out that the core essence of "Socialist Legal Ideas" is the constitutional trinity explicated earlier. Consequently, "Socialist Legal Ideas" has eclectically combined values such as "managing state affairs in accordance with law" (*yifazhiguo* 依法治国), "implementing law for the people" (*zhifaweimin* 执法为民), "equity and justice" (*gongpingzhengyi* 公平正义), "serving the overall interests" (*fuwudaju* 服务大局), and "leadership of the Communist Party of China" (*dangdelingdao* 党的领导), "respect and protection of human rights" (*zunzhonghebaozhangrenquan* 尊重和保障人权), "maintenance of the authority of law" (*weihufalvquanwei* 维护法律权威), "supervision and checks" (*jianduzhiyue* 监督制约), and "liberty and equality" (*ziyoupingdeng* 自由平等) (Xie, 2006; The Politics and Law Committee of Communist Party of China Central, 2009).

The philosophical foundation of Sinicized Marxist Constitutionalism

As we can see from our review, the three approaches all take the party-state structure into consideration but differ in where they see the center of gravity among ideological values, with Backer's version relying primarily on the rule of law value, the Marxist one on the orthodox ideology of the regime, and the contemporary Chinese official one on an organic eclecticism combing various aspects of the two. Even though the current eclectic approach does mark a combination of certain values of Backer's "rule of law" approach and the Marxist ideological approach, it is clear that the orthodox ideology of the regime represented and guaranteed by the Communist Party of China leadership still occupies a position prior to the rule of law.[31] It is in this sense that I regard the orthodox ideology as the

28 Statistics from China Academic Journals Full-text Database.

29 The conference is attended by over 120 leading legal scholars and practitioners in China, with some important political figures present in the opening ceremony, such as the Vice-president of the Central Party School, the former Director of the Central Military Committee Office, and so on.

30 Statistics from China Academic Journals Full-text Database.

31 This is not hard to understand as soon as we take seriously the order of the three pillars of the current constitutional thought in China, namely the leadership of the Communist Party of China first, the people as master second, and the rule of law last. In fact, the orthodox ideology epitomized in the "Four Cardinal Principles" is well entrenched in the Preamble of the Constitution, and the government may well evoke it within the current constitutional framework, yet the government has not sought to do so and has taken a non-contention (*buzhenglun* 不争论) attitude and approach instead.

defining element of Sinicized Marxist Constitutionalism. As there are quite some prejudices towards the orthodox ideology of the Marxist regime, which to some extent denotes an insurmountable barrier for engaging dialogues with Sinicized Marxist Constitutionalism, I seek to remove this barrier by providing an account of the philosophical foundations of the Marxist orthodox ideology in this section. Even though Marxist political philosophy has been hotly explored and developed in Chinese academia in recent years,[32] the justification of Sinicized Marxist Constitutionalism at a philosophical level has not been fully developed. As a result, I will draw on various resources and seek to establish such a foundation for Sinicized Marxist Constitutionalism in the following pages.

To fully understand the foundation of Sinicized Marxist Constitutionalism, there are three points that are particularly worth pointing out. First of all, the Marxist teleological view of humanity may well be the "Archimedean point" of Sinicized Marxist Constitutionalism. In a nutshell, I summarize the *telos* of humanity in Marxism as to "free its animalistic nature and become a free creator humanizing the nature harmoniously."[33] As scholars of Marxism have well observed, the central theme in all of Marx's work is liberation/emancipation, not only from natural forces arising and imposing themselves from outside, but also from social forces people themselves create, as well as their bodily nature, which imposes constraints upon them from within (Han, 2007, p. 2). To understand this, a grasp of Marx's concept of "species-being" as "a radical reconceptualization of the philosophical tradition's use of the idea of a human essence" as well elaborated by Wartenberg is crucial. According to Wartenberg, while Marx's statement that "Man is a species-being . . . and free conscious activity constitutes the species-character of man" was dropped from his later writings,[34] it nevertheless functions as the centerpiece of Marx's view of human beings and their society, as well as the ground for his critique of capitalist society and the various "ahistorical" theories of human nature prevalent in the mainstream Western philosophical tradition (p. 77).[35] As Wartenberg points out, translated from *Gattungswesen*, the concept "species-being" has two meanings: first, it refers to a type of things in the sense that it can only exist in a social or communal situation with others of its type, which Marx uses to criticize the atomistic view of bourgeois political theory, echoing Aristotle's notion of *zoon politikon*; second, it refers to the species-essence, with "being" denoting a metaphysical sense of specific difference, and accordingly the human "species-being" is the species-essence or species-character of human beings, possession of which qualifies them as the distinctive creatures that they are (p. 79). Previously, the concept of human essence has played a crucial role in Western philosophy, as well articulated by Aristotle, who takes rationality or reason as the "species-essence" of

32 For example, in 2006, the Marxist scholars in China convened an important conference titled "Marxist Political Philosophy: Elaboration and Innovation" at Nankai University in Tianjing, with some of the papers published in a book with the same title. Since then, many articles have been written on Marxist political philosophy, and several monographs have appeared, such as *Initial Exploration of the Categories of Marxist Political Philosophy* (2007), *Introduction to Marx's Political Philosophy: A Contemporary Interpretation from the Perspective of Human Studies* (2009), and so on.

33 This teleological understanding may remind us that of the ancient Chinese sages, who call for the humanity to become the third pillar juxtaposing the Heaven and the Earth (*yutiandican* 与天地 叁) and facilitating the growth of nature (*yifuwanwuzhiziran* 以 辅万物之自 然). They share a kind of anthropocentrism but nevertheless do not ignore the harmonization aspect given the objective and unchanging rules of nature (Han, 2007, p. 125).

34 For a fuller discussion of the reason for this, see Wartenberg, (1982, pp. 82–84).

35 I would contend that Marx's statement is the key to understand all his other core concepts, such as alienation, exploitation, emancipation, religion, state, class, revolution, communism, and so on as well.

human beings and accordingly regards the "contemplative life" as the ideal life a human being should aspire to (Wartenberg, 1982, p. 78). What is most innovative about Marx's reconceptualization, according to Wartenberg (1982), is his generalization of "rationality" as articulated in the intellectualist tradition of Western philosophy to "free conscious activity" as well as his use of that theory to criticize bourgeois society (p. 79). It is perhaps beyond my ability here to provide a convincing account of the teleological view of humanity as well as the role of Marxism in achieving this *teleos*. Nevertheless, without taking this "Archimedean point" seriously, we could not then understand the second point of the constitutional structure of Sinicized Marxist Constitutionalism as follows.

If the Marxist teleological view of humanity is granted, we could then see why the party-state structure, including its democratic centralism principle,[36] is so crucial to Sinicized Marxist Constitutionalism, as the structure is not only more efficient but also necessary for guiding society towards its teleological end.[37] In another way of expression, the party-state constitutional order is most efficient and necessary for promoting "virtue cultivation,"[38] and consequently "happiness" in the Aristotelian sense as "activity in accordance with virtue." To understand this, we need to be aware that Marxism is not at all a body of dogmas, but rather a system of thought that allows us to learn about "unfolding historical processes." In this regard, Marxist-Leninism is an adaptation of Marxism to a particular time and place, namely Russia in the early 20th century, and Sinicized Marxism is a further adaptation of Marxist-Leninism to the Chinese context. The linkage between Marxism's teleological view of humanity as well as the political structure it entails is perhaps more complex and requires a separate work to elaborate it. Given the moral and entrepreneurial nature of the Marxist vision of the state, inherited from Hegel's philosophy, there are perhaps good reasons to support such a constitutional structure as manifested in the Chinese regime, and contemporary discoveries in business administration or public administration may well lend support to this reading.[39] For Marxists in contemporary China who "truly study, truly understand, truly believe, and truly apply" the Marxist stand, viewpoints, and methodologies, this is obvious and taken for granted. For example, Chinese leaders such as Deng Xiaoping have repeatedly emphasized the vital importance and indispensability of a leading vanguard party that consists of highly enlightened, self-disciplined, and full of self-sacrificial spirit members, for uniting the thoughts and minds of the billions of people to march towards socialism (Wang, 2003, p. 30).

Accordingly we could also understand the prominence of political authority over judicial authority in Sinicized Marxist Constitutionalism. Challenging the liberal obsession with judicial independence, some point out that "the term 'judicial independence' begs

36 For a relatively more moderate and unbiased reading of the democratic centralism, see Steven Angle's (2005) article "Decent Democratic Centralism."

37 For a pioneering discussion of this idea, see Xu and Xie (2005).

38 By "virtue" here, it does not refer to some specific kinds of substantive moral goods but rather its original Aristotelian use in the Greek *arête* sense, which refers to the goodness, excellence, or right operation of a person or thing.

39 One could argue that the party-state constitutional structure in Sinicized Marxist Constitutionalism resembles to some extent the ideal state as described in Plato's *Republic*, with the Communist Party of China, the Peoples' Liberation Army, and the National People's Congress corresponding to the three parts of the ideal regime respectively. While it is true that Plato's plan has never been put into practice anywhere anytime, it is not clear why the ideal political form should not be aspired in all time across all societies, especially through more moderate means with more acceptable cost.

an unspoken propositional object – that is, independent *from what*" (Balme & Dowdle, 2009, p. 11) in the Chinese context. As the questioners further point out, the court or the judiciary surely should not be independent from laws and the constitutional order, or the *grundnorm* of the state order (Balme & Dowdle, 2009, p. 11). Even for judicial independence from political parties in the US constitutional order it is largely due to historical reasons; there is no clear reason, however, for this rule to apply to the case of China. As Zheng Yongnian (2010a), a well-known foreign-based scholar of Chinese politics, points out,

> [W]hilst the concept of political party in China was imported, the Communist Party of China is a Chinese cultural product: it is an entirely different breed of political party from those in the West – an organizational emperor, wielding its power in a similar way to Chinese emperors of the past.
>
> (back cover)

In fact, the Communist Party of China has clearly stated that its leadership will be political, ideological, and organizational. In this sense, the notion of "organizational emperor" used by Zheng does not cover the whole semantic range. If the Communist Party of China truly meets what it preaches to be, namely the "Three Represents" (*sangedaibiao* 三个代表) of advanced social productive forces, advanced culture, and the interests of the overwhelming majority, there are then good reasons to not only bring the party in, but also regards it as the embodiment of the polity as Backer and others have advocated. The emphasis on political authority over judicial authority may well echo Aristotle's thesis that human beings are by nature political animals and the political authority is the highest among all associated relationships in the *polis* (1252a3–6, 1253a15–19). A genealogical investigation of the reasons why the judicial emerges in Western history to assume its current prominent power may well render further insight into the issue here. In fact, the recent book *Judicial Independence in China: Lessons for Global Rule of Law Promotion* (2009), containing the latest discoveries on the issue of judicial independence by the leading scholars in the field, provides an excellent defense of the plausibility as well as legitimacy of China's unique judicial-political arrangement. Understanding these, we could also better comprehend why the Communist Party of China encourages the development of the judicial in China yet confines it within a clearly demarked "cage" as vividly captured in the title and cover page of Lubman's (2000) book.[40] This is also one of the main reasons why conservative political scholars are not willing to grant constitutionalism its normal status, since it is "not merely an academic problem, but an ideological question" of which subject assumes the leading role in the discourse of China's future political development (Chen, personal interview, June 10, 2010).

The key criterion of evaluating the legitimacy of Sinicized Marxist Constitutionalism then lies with the vanguard nature of the Communist Party of China as well as the degree of it living up to its aspirations, which is then the third point for our understanding of the philosophical foundation of Sinicized Marxist Constitutionalism. To do so, we then need to know both the goals of the Communist Party of China at different stages of its history

40 For example, Li Peng (李鹏), the fourth Premier of the PRC and the then Chairman of the Standing Committee of the National People's Congress (NPC), explicitly points out that all comrades working in the NPC should never be obscure about the leading role of the Communist Party of China for the work of the NPC, as entrenched in the Preamble of the Constitution (as cited in Jiang, 2009, p. 23).

and the results of its practices. It is beyond the scope here to review its historical record, but it is worth pointing out that the Communist Party of China has indeed undertaken many measures to attain its goals in contemporary China, which include:

> unfolding activities to educate the Communist Party of China members in retaining their advanced character, pushing ahead the building or development of the study-type political party, going in for the inner-party democratic construction, developing inner-party democracy, improving the Communist Party of China members' conduct and building a clear government, still bettering the Party's leading and governing methods, and further improving the inner-Party supervision.
>
> (as cited in Backer, 2009b, p. 136)

How successful these measures have been is hard to know. Just as Backer (2009b) acknowledges,

> The trick will be to see if the Party's bureaucracy is as adept in developing its praxis as the intellectual organs of the party are in recognizing problems and shaping theoretical approaches to its solution. . . . If the party cannot practice what it preaches, it will lose its mandate.
>
> (p. 136)

The result will certainly be finally judged by history, but if we take a crude indicator of whether the Communist Party of China could remain in power, there are mixed messages as David Shambaugh's (2008) latest book *China's Communist Party: Atrophy and Adaptation* and Zheng Yongnian's (2010a) book *The Chinese Communist Party as Organizational Emperor: Culture, Reproduction, and Transformation* have compellingly demonstrated. The biggest barrier for engaging dialogues with Sinicized Marxist Constitutionalism is thus to dismiss its legitimate aspirations and judging its legitimacy from our own norms. Indeed, if we are confident that the Communist Party of China would not be able to live up to its promises and would ultimately lose its mandate, there is perhaps good reason to just wait for history to exert its forces for the fall of Communist Party of China then. The impatience as well as the unbearable calling of conscience to condemn or intervene in the affairs of other "kingdoms" may actually necessitate greater caution as well as introspections about our possible limitations due to our partial understandings as well as fallibilities.

Conclusion and implications

To sum up, in this chapter, we first described the emerging context of the newly developed Sinicized Marxist Constitutionalism. The progress of the rule of law in both its theoretical and practical dimensions over the past 30 years in China surely plays the foundational role for the surging interests among scholars on the issue of constitutionalism in China. Meanwhile, the deep penetration and domination of Western Liberal Constitutionalism have induced two reactions from scholars outside of the legal realm, namely the articulation of the "constitutionalism abolition thesis" as well as some cultural conservatives' proposal of developing a constitutionalism that is based on and also loyal to China's indigenous tradition. Within the legal realm, it has pushed some to rethink the pre-conceptions of the Western liberal constitutional paradigm both in and outside China and has catalyzed their articulation of Sinicized Marxist Constitutional paradigm. The fad of advocating the

"Chinese Model" within Chinese academia and the popular trend of shaking off the yoke of currently dominant paradigms in the West, especially since the Western financial crisis, may have offered an amiable and supporting environment for the emergence of Sinicized Marxist Constitutionalism as well.

We then reviewed the three main approaches towards Chinese constitutionalism that are under the canopy of Sinicized Marxist Constitutionalism. The first one is represented by Larry Backer's model, which takes into consideration the Communist Party of China as well as its ideologies but still emphasizes rule of law in Western Liberal Constitutionalism sense as the defining feature of constitutionalism. The second also takes the party-state structure into the constitutionalism but emphasizes more the orthodox ideology. Its understanding of rule of law is also significantly different from that of the liberal paradigm and is more akin to jurisprudences such as Critical Legal Theory, and so on that are largely marginalized in the contemporary Western legal studies. The third is the one currently developed and promoted by the political authority as well as the pro-government scholars in China. It combines certain core ideas from the previous two approaches and emphasizes on the organic trinity of party leadership, people as the master, and rule of law. This approach has also developed corresponding legal theories such as the "Socialist Legal Ideas" to match it.

Because the orthodox ideology still plays a defining role in the constitutional thinking of the current Communist Party of China leadership, I have sought to elaborate its philosophical foundation to help the audience understand this feature. The defining orthodox ideology is well shown in the intact cornerstone of the "Four Cardinal Principles," which has allowed not even just a plot of strike. Nevertheless, as the prejudice towards the orthodox ideology of Sinicized Marxist Constitutionalism is prevalent and deeply rooted, which is also the prime barrier for Western Liberal Constitutionalism and Traditional Confucian Constitutionalism to engage dialogues with Sinicized Marxist Constitutionalism, I have sketched some points to help to understand the rationale of Sinicized Marxist Constitutionalism. This rationale includes the teleological understanding of humanity in Marxism, the self-perceived role of Marxism in the endeavor, as well as the indispensable constitutional structure of party-state for realizing these goals. For these reasons, I suggest that we should not judge the legitimacy of Sinicized Marxist Constitutionalism by some norms of other constitutional paradigms and may fare better to let history exert its forces rather than commit some irreversible mistakes that could be caused by our fallibility.

Because of these findings, the implications of Sinicized Marxist Constitutionalism would also be profound. First of all, the emergence of a lively heterogeneous constitutionalism discourse certainly poses a challenge to the dominant Western Liberal Constitutionalism and consequently contributes to the pluralistic orientation of current constitutional discourses both in China and around the world.[41] It will perhaps force some liberal scholars to rethink their pre-conceptions of constitutionalism and generate more dialogues between different constitutional communities. Second, it may remind us of the relevance of Marxism in contemporary China as well as within the global society. After a 30-year embrace of a market economy and the penetration of external forces, is Marxism-Leninism still relevant in China as the official line proclaims? Are the top Communist Party of China leaders who call for cadres at all levels to "truly study, truly understand, truly believe and truly apply" (*zhenxuezhendongzhenxinzhenyong* 真学真懂真信真用) "the stand, viewpoint, and methodologies

41 For a good capture and analysis of the competition of different constitutionalisms at the global level, see Backer (2009a).

of Marxism," or are what they call the "living soul of Marxism" merely hypocrites or are they doing something imprudent or deluded? We did not tackle this problem directly in this chapter, but the answer may be quite obvious. The constitutional structure of China has remained largely the same throughout the past six decades and the current ideology of the regime is eclectic and vague enough to retain flexibility for both left and right turns. To a clairvoyant observer, the current Chinese ideology is very much taking Marxist values as the Ti (体) and liberal values as the *Yong* (用), though with both adapted and contextualized to the current reality and time.[42] In fact, there is sufficient evidence to support such a reading, such as the current leadership's heavy investment in the Marxism Theory Research and Construction Project (*makesililunyanjiuhejianshegongcheng* 马克思理论研究和建设工程), which aspires to lead the whole humanities and social sciences in the Chinese academia, and its firm stance towards reforms in the area of civil and political rights that lie at the core of the liberal paradigm. Indeed, Yan Jirong (2011), the director of the Department of Political Science at Beijing University, has contended that "totalism" is still the most accurate word to describe China's current politics. The third implication is then the impacts of such a "communist" China on the world order. While the ideology has successfully shied away from traditional class politics and incorporated a market economy as well as private property, it still subscribes to the "stand, viewpoint, and methodology" of Marxism; hence, it is perhaps unacceptable to hard-core liberals. This certainly necessitates more careful research and reflection for anyone who is concerned about the development of China as well as the future of the world order. In the following chapter, I will provide an account of the current strategic configurations in the ideological realm of China and shed light on the prospect of the three "kingdoms" to become the unifier.

42 The prominent Marxist Confucian scholar Fang Keli (2010) recently has advocated the thesis of "Marxism as the soul, Nationalist studies as the Ti (体), and Western studies as the Yong (用)," which seems to be shared by a number of pro-government scholars.

6 The romance of "three constitutional kingdoms"

Who will unify the world?

The opening lines of the Chinese classical novel the *Romance of the Three Kingdoms* (*Sanguo yanyi* 《三国演义》) say, "What is long divided must be united, what is long united must be divided" (*fenjiubihe, hejiubifen* 分久必合，合久必分). This describes the ideological realm within Chinese society as well as the constitutionalism realm within Chinese academia well. The ideological realm of China was united under the banner of Sinicized Marxism after the Communist Party of China took control of the state in 1949, but with the reform and opening-up of Chinese society, it has become significantly jumbled; one finds a similar situation in the constitutional realm of Chinese academia, where the hegemony of Western Liberal Constitutionalism has started to move towards a more divided and competitive state much like in the *Romance of the Three Kingdoms.* In previous chapters, I sought to provide an account of the state of play of the three "kingdoms," and now, it is time to analyze their respective strengths and weaknesses and discuss the possible outcomes of this grand "constitutional game."[1] Accordingly, this chapter consists of three main sections. The first section presents a brief recapitulation of the respective states of the three "kingdoms" as reviewed earlier. The second section offers a preliminary comparison of the three players and discusses their respective virtues and vices. The final section analyzes the current strategic configurations as well as their developmental trends and provides some predictions about the possible results of this new "romance of three kingdoms," which is likely to have profound implications for both China and the world in the 21st-century China.

A recap of the developing state of the three kingdoms

Because Western Liberal Constitutionalism has been well explored in academic circles, I have mainly reviewed its history in China, its core claims, and the major challenges it faces today in China. As we have seen, the history of Western Liberal Constitutionalism in China consists of two main periods, the first during the late Qing and early Republican period and the second being the post-Deng reform period of the past four decades. For the half century following the forced opening up of China by the British Opium War in 1840, the spread of Western Liberal Constitutionalism in China was quite slow, but it gained significant momentum with the defeat of the imperial Qing court at the hands of the relatively small yet "constitutionally" organized Japanese state during the Sino-Japanese

1 It is should be pointed out that although the metaphors of "three kingdoms" may appear to refer to the three constitutionalism discourses per se, it is used in the chapter in a broader sense to cover the liberal, Confucian, and Marxist approaches.

War of 1894–1895. Shortly after that, the spread of Western Liberal Constitutionalism ideas was transformed into a movement for setting up and implementing Western Liberal Constitutionalism institutions. This was shown not only in the "Hundred Days' Reform" (*bairiweixin* 百日维新) launched by reformists such as Kang Youwei (康有为) in 1898, and the first proto-constitution of China, called "the General Principles of the Constitutional Government by the Imperial Order" (*Qinding Xianfa Dagang* 钦定宪法大纲) in 1908, but also in the actual practices of drafting and implementing various constitutions throughout the republican period. However, Western Liberal Constitutionalism started to decline in China when the revolutionary wave of New Democracy (*xin minzhuzhuyi geming langchao* 新民主主义革命浪潮) emerged in the 1920s.[2] The success of the proletarian revolution in Russia as well as the spread of Marxist-Leninism in China since then has greatly impacted the development of China. Even the Nationalist Party was influenced by the Soviet Komintern and transformed into a revolutionary "tutelage" party in 1923. Nevertheless, as the Nationalist Party did not "exorcise the specter" of Western Liberal Constitutionalism as completely as the Communist party, Western Liberal Constitutionalism ideas have persisted in the former and even taken control of it as shown in Taiwan today. In mainland China, the "specter" of Western Liberal Constitutionalism was not a problem in the first three decades of the founding of the PRC, because the Communist Party of China had been cautious about it with the strategy of "taking class conflicts as the first priority" (*yi jieji douzheng wei gang* 以阶级斗争为纲); nevertheless, the "specter" has gradually resurfaced as this priority was replaced by economic development beginning with the reform and opening-up period launched by Deng Xiaoping in the late 1970s. This change, which initiated and undergirded China's rapid economic rise, has unleashed a second wave of Western Liberal Constitutionalism in China. As the spread of Western Liberal Constitutionalism in China during this period has been all encompassing, I have limited my review to the constitutional realm within academia. As we have seen, the constitutional realm has been significantly "Westernized" and could be well regarded as the "headquarters" of the new Western Liberal Constitutionalism kingdom in China. Its impact on officials could also be shown in the ideological changes of the government as well as four constitutional amendments in the past four decades, which have gradually moved China closer to Western Liberal Constitutionalism prescriptions.

These achievements, however, have not satisfied the hard-core advocates of Western Liberal Constitutionalism, who consequently have advocated *Charter 08* and called for greater political reforms, and I have reviewed their core claims and theoretical justifications, as well as the main criticisms Western Liberal Constitutionalism faces in China today. I have taken *Charter 08* as a representative manifesto of Western Liberal Constitutionalism claims in China today and reviewed its theoretical justifications as shown in the works of Li Buyun, the most authoritative figure in this area. As we have seen, Western Liberal Constitutionalism claims not only include some declarative values such as freedom, human rights, equality, and so on, but also some specific proposals for political reforms. Constitutional scholars in China also have established a four-pillar explication of this Western Liberal

2 According to the Chinese official line, the "newness" refers to its transcendence as well as superiority over the Xinhai Revolution (*xinhaigeming* 辛亥革命) led by Sun Yat-sen in 1911, which was part of the worldwide, old bourgeois democratic revolutionary wave of the time.

Constitutionalism edifice, namely the democracy pillar, the rule of law pillar, the human rights pillar, and the supremacy of the constitution pillar. The claims and theoretical justifications are very comprehensive and to some extent summarize all the major features of Western Liberal Constitutionalism as practiced in Western countries, especially the US. The topics covered are also diverse as they range from judicial independence, checks and balances of power, fair and free elections, to fiscal reform, environmental protection, and so on. Behind these normative claims and justifications, however, is the common agenda of getting rid of the current foundations of the contemporary Chinese regime, namely the "Four Cardinal Principles" (*sixiang jiben yuanze* 四项基本原则). This is indeed one of the major problems Western Liberal Constitutionalism faces in China. Besides its compatibility with the persistent yet resilient party-state regime, I have also reviewed other challenges Western Liberal Constitutionalism faces in China such as its acclimatization in the Chinese cultural soil deeply influenced by the Confucian tradition, the exposure of the parochial and sectarian nature of Western Liberal Constitutionalism proposals in the eyes of some intellectuals in China, as well as greater awareness by some Chinese of the gradual erosion of Western Liberal Constitutionalism's theoretical pillars back in its matrix in the West.

After a brief review of the state of Western Liberal Constitutionalism in China, I then turned to Traditional Confucian Constitutionalism, where I mainly introduced the institutional, ritualistic, and religious approaches towards it; analyzed their respective strengths and weaknesses; and offered a full three-layered picture at the end. For the institutional approach, I mainly reviewed the works of Jongryn Mo and Jaeyoon Song. Mo uncovers the accountability system of the Confucian polity along the horizontal line through a case study of the Censorate of the *Chosŏn* Dynasty, and Song mainly shows the existence of a mechanism for "checks and balances" along the vertical line between the King and the Grand Steward through a careful elaboration of Southern Song commentary on the counterbalancing sovereign-minister relationship in the *Zhou Li*. The defining approaches towards Traditional Confucian Constitutionalism, however, are the ritualistic and the religious approaches. For the ritualistic approach, I mainly reviewed Zhang Qianfan's, Hahm Chaihark's, and Kim Jin-ha's works, which have not only compellingly demonstrated the constitutional nature of Confucian *Li* or rituals, but also elaborated the unique advantages of such a ritualistic constitutionalism. The religious approach is mainly advocated by some cultural conservatives in China such as Jiang Qing, who have articulated a "Confucian Religious Constitutionalism" and working out its specific forms. There are two main foundational principles in Jiang's proposal, namely its religious nature and three-dimensional legitimacy. The religious nature is shown not only in how Jiang regards Confucianism as a great religion, but also in his view of "sovereignty with the Heaven" as the cornerstone of Confucian Religious Constitutionalism. This three-dimensional legitimacy is derived from Jiang's political Confucianism and consists of the legitimacy of Heaven, Earth, and People, which corresponds to the legitimacy derived from sacred sources, from historical continuity, and from the consent of the people respectively. Jiang's well-known tri-cameral legislature is also directly based on this idea of three-dimensional legitimacy.

After describing the three approaches, I discussed their respective strengths and weaknesses and offered my vision of a three-layered Traditional Confucian Constitutionalism. The arguments of the institutional approach have unearthed excellent resources within the Confucian polity for modern constitutionalism, but this approach is also the least critical towards the conceptual framework inherited from the liberal paradigm. The ritualistic approach is generally very insightful and heuristic, but it also misses the important dimension of rituals as the embodiment of natural justice taken from the Heavenly Way, which is well captured by the religious approach. Nevertheless, the arguments of the religious approach are quite vague and porous even though they are quite thought-provoking. To some extent, the three approaches all uncover very important dimensions of Traditional Confucian Constitutionalism, and I have sought to combine them to render a full picture of a form of constitutionalism that is consistent and also loyal to the visions of the ancient Chinese sages. In constructing the three-layered Traditional Confucian Constitutionalism, I also offered a different reading of the religious core of Traditional Confucian Constitutionalism from that of Jiang Qing's.

Regarding Sinicized Marxist Constitutionalism, I mainly reviewed its emerging context, analyzed the three main versions held by different scholars under this general and overarching canopy, and suggested a philosophical foundation for it. For the emerging context, I identified three factors that have made particularly important contributions to the emergence of Sinicized Marxist Constitutionalism, namely the progress of rule of law in post-reform China as a foundational factor, the deep penetration and wide acceptance of Western Liberal Constitutionalism as a catalyst, and the fad of exploring the "Chinese Model" in contemporary Chinese academia as a supporting factor. Regarding the contents of Sinicized Marxist Constitutionalism, I mainly reviewed the three approaches, all of which take the party-state structure into consideration but differ in where they see the center of gravity among ideological values, with Backer's version relying primarily on the rule of law value, the Marxist version on the orthodox ideology of the regime, and the contemporary Chinese official version on an organic eclecticism combing various aspects of the previous two. Backer's approach marks a path-breaking theorization of Sinicized Marxist Constitutionalism, but because it regards "rule of law" value as the defining feature of constitutionalism, it shares with the Western Liberal Constitutional paradigm the view that the Maoist period is "anti-constitutionalist." This approach thereby excludes the option of a Marxist constitutionalism that is founded on the orthodox ideologies. This latter approach does not see a rupture between the Maoist period and Deng's reform period and relies on a Marxist and socialist legal philosophy that is akin to critical legal philosophy in Western jurisprudence. In fact, even though the current eclectic approach, based on the organic trinity of "the Communist Party of China leadership, people as masters and the rule of law," does mark a combination of certain values of Backer's "rule of law" approach and the Marxist ideological approach, I have suggested that the orthodox ideology still occupies a position prior to the rule of law in the Communist Party of China's constitutional thinking. It is in this sense that the orthodox ideology is still the defining element of Sinicized Marxist Constitutionalism. To help to render this clearer, I have also provided an elaboration of the philosophical foundation of Sinicized Marxist Constitutionalism.

Their respective virtues and vices

After a recap of the current state of play in the three constitutional kingdoms, it is crucial to have a comparison of the three and be aware of their respective strengths and weaknesses in order to make informed predictions concerning the likely outcome of the "constitutional game." A preliminary comparison of the three is shown in Table 6.1.

As we can see, the three constitutional paradigms are very different in regard to their constitution status, regime types, power structures, locations of sovereignty, roles of judiciary, trumping values, main governance methods, primary target, as well as their ontology and epistemologies. To some extent, Sinicized Marxist Constitutionalism is an eclectic approach that combines certain elements of Western Liberal Constitutionalism and Traditional

Table 6.1 A preliminary comparison of the three constitutionalisms

	Western Liberal Constitutionalism	*Traditional Confucian Constitutionalism*	*Sinicized Marxist Constitutionalism*
Constitutional status	Concrete and judicialized	Vague and unjudicialized	Eclectic
Regime type	Liberal democracy	Authoritarian monarchy	Tutelage republic[1]
Power structure	Polyarchy[2]	Hierarchy	Hierarchy with gradual transfer
Sovereignty	People in name but individuals in reality	Heaven in name but Confucians in reality	People in name but the Communist Party of China in reality with gradual transfer
Judiciary	Independent and strong	Subordinate and weak	Subordinate but increasing strength
Trumping value	Freedom and equality[3]	Virtue and harmony	Eclectic
Main governance method	Rule of law	Rule of ritual	Eclectic
Primary target	External constraints of individuals	Internal constraints of individuals	Eclectic
Ontology	Individualistic and disparate world	Holistic and relational world	Eclectic
Epistemology	Rationalism	Intuitionism[4]	Eclectic

Notes:

[1] For a good elaboration on this, see Fang (2011); for the differences between a republic and a democracy in the Chinese context, see Jin, Liu, and Lam (2005).

[2] For a good elaboration on this, see Zhou (2005).

[3] It is not that Western Liberal Constitutionalism does not seek to promote virtue, but that virtue is not their primary concern or they have very different understandings of the notion.

[4] The terminologies for the two distinctive epistemological traditions are taken from Wu Qiong (2006, p. 17), who has translated Spengler's *The Decline of the West* into Chinese. On intuitionism in ancient Chinese thought as well as its adoption in legislation, see Du Daoming (2003) and Chen Guangxiu (2009) respectively.

Confucian Constitutionalism. It is beyond the scope of this work to elaborate in detail each of these differences; nevertheless, as we will see, their respective strengths and weaknesses are largely derived from these differences. It is also worth pointing out that, just as everything exceeding its limit tends to have the opposite effect, so are the respective virtues of the three constitutional paradigms, which could also be transformed into their vices. Next, I will have a look at the primary virtues and vices of each paradigm.

The greatest virtue but also the biggest vice of Western Liberal Constitutionalism has to do with its elevation of the individuals to the status of sovereign. This may sound contradictory, but as I will elaborate in the following, it does not. I regard the *de facto* sovereignty of the individual as the "soul" of Western Liberal Constitutionalism, so accordingly the constitutional status of being concrete and judicialized (*sifahuade* 司法化的), the regime type of liberal democracy, the power structure of polyarchy, the trumping value of freedom and equality, the independent and strong judiciary, the entrenchment of rule of law, the primary target of external fetters, the perception of an individualistic and disparate world, as well as the prevalence of rationalism, and so on of Western Liberal Constitutionalism are all serving this "soul."

The virtue of this paradigm is its perfecting of the external environment for the individual to be free, which also represents the *teleos* of humanity. This teleological view of human history is well articulated by Nietzsche (1998):

> The task of breeding an animal that is permitted to promise includes, as condition and preparation, the more specific task of first *making* man to a certain degree necessary, uniform, like among like, regular, and accordingly predictable. The enormous work of what I have called "morality of custom" (cf. *Daybreak* 9, 14, 16) – the true work of man on himself for the longest part of the duration of the human race, his entire *prehistoric* work, has in this its meaning, its great justification – however much hardness, tyranny, mindlessness, and idiocy may be inherent in it: with the help of the morality of custom and the social straightjacket man was *made* truly calculable. If on the other hand, we place ourselves at the end of the enormous process, where the tree finally produces its fruit, where society and its morality of custom finally brings to light that *to which* it was only the means: then we will find as the ripest fruit on its tree the *sovereign individual*, the individual resembling only himself, free again from the morality of custom, autonomous and supermoral (for "autonomous" and "moral" are mutually exclusive), in short, the human being with his own independent long will, the human being who *is permitted to promise* – and in him a proud consciousness, twitching in all his muscles, of *what* has finally been achieved and become flesh in him, a true consciousness of power and freedom, a feeling of the completion of man himself.
>
> (II: 2)

From this passage, we could see that the aspirations of Western Liberal Constitutionalism match those of the end stage of human history well, which perhaps underlies the natural appeals of Western Liberal Constitutionalism to people everywhere. This also echoes Tocqueville's insight that the effort to stop the liberal democratic trend would be in vain just like resisting almighty God himself. Indeed, one might be awed by the subtlety as well as delicacy of Western Liberal Constitutionalism both in its theoretical and institutional dimensions. The achievements of Western countries certainly have reinforced the appeal of Western Liberal Constitutionalism throughout the world as well.

The vice of Western Liberal Constitutionalism, however, is also related to the elevation of the individual to the "sovereign" status and is well revealed in Nietzsche's passage. As we can see, Nietzsche's vision of the "sovereign individual" as the "the ripest fruit" actually requires enormous work of cultivation through the aid of society and the "morality of custom." As the Chinese idiom says well, it takes 10 years to grow a tree but 100 years to cultivate an individual (*shinianshumu,bainianshuren* 十年树木,百年树人), the lengthy duration as well as enormous work required for fruit-bearing thus should not be ignored. Nevertheless, this aspect seems to be the "shorter slab" (*duanban* 短板) of Western Liberal Constitutionalism "wooden barrel." Various works, such as Sungmoon Kim (2009), Dennehy (2007), Kupperman (2004), and Warren (1989), and so on have all shed light on this. Philip Ivanhoe's (2000) thorough exploration of the Confucian tactics of self-cultivation may well render support to this reading as well. It should be acknowledged that external freedom provided by Western Liberal Constitutionalism is indispensable for the flourishing of humanity, but it is also clear that successful cultivation of the virtuous characters seem to be a vital prerequisite.

The problem with Western Liberal Constitutionalism, to use Marx's words, is then that it exalts the individual man "as *sovereign* and supreme," when he is still a man

> in his uncivilized and unsocial aspect, in his fortuitous existence and just as he is, corrupted by the entire organization of our society, lost and alienated from himself, oppressed by inhuman relations and elements – in a word, man who is not yet an *actual* species-being.
>
> (p. 13)[3]

To put it metaphorically, we could well regard the internal character as the essential root (*ben* 本) and the external free environment just as the trivial branches (*mo* 末). From the perspective of Traditional Confucian Constitutionalism and Sinicized Marxist Constitutionalism, the biggest vice of Western Liberal Constitutionalism is thus its "pursuit of the branches at the cost of the roots" (*she ben zhu mo* 舍本逐末), or "inverting the orders of the branches and the roots" (*ben mo dao zhi* 本末倒置). This fatal vice of Western Liberal Constitutionalism certainly has good historical reasons and is perhaps a necessary trade-off for its achievements in perfecting the "branches," though with profound implications. As we will see, Traditional Confucian Constitutionalism's virtue and vice seem to be just the opposite of Western Liberal Constitutionalism.

For Traditional Confucian Constitutionalism, its greatest virtue may well be its capacity to penetrate into the individual and cultivate their moral character. This "soul" is actually manifested in all the three layers of Traditional Confucian Constitutionalism that we have reviewed. There is perhaps no need to go over the unique advantages of ritualistic constitutionalism and religious constitutionalism for virtue cultivation. Even for the legal dimension of Traditional Confucian Constitutionalism, its distinctive feature, when compared with other forms of jurisprudence, is actually also its educational functions, which is well elaborated in Zhang's (2010) article on Chinese jurisprudence. Bearing this in mind, we could better understand the differences between Traditional Confucian Constitutionalism and Western Liberal Constitutionalism as shown earlier in Table 6.1. For example, the status of the constitution in Traditional Confucian Constitutionalism is vague and unjudicialized because it does not seek to provide the individual the kind of "psychological comfort" rendered by Western Liberal Constitutionalism but endeavors to entrench a hierarchical political structure that enables moral sages to perform their "civilizational" (*wenming huacheng* 文明化成) duties. Seen from this perspective, the constitution of Traditional Confucian Constitutionalism could well be regarded as a meta-constitution, which is well elaborated by Rousseau (1987):

> It is not engraved on marble or bronze, but in the hearts of citizens. It is the true constitution of the state. Everyday it takes on new forces. When other laws grow old and die away, it revives and replaces them, preserves a people in the spirit of its institution and imperceptibly substitutes the force of habit for that of authority. I am speaking of mores, customs, and especially of opinion, a part of the law unknown to our political theorists but one on which depends the success of all the others; a part with which the great legislator secretly occupies himself, though he seems to confine himself to the

3 People influenced by Western Liberal Constitutionalism may rebut Marx's accusation here, largely due to their very different perceptions of the reality as well as diverging conceptions of the criteria.

particular regulations that are merely the arching of the vault, whereas mores, slower to arise, form in the end its immovable keystone.

(p. 172)

The vice of Traditional Confucian Constitutionalism, however, is also quite clear. First of all, it certainly leaves more room for the abusive use of public power given its preoccupation with "soul-craft." Second, if Spinoza is correct that the *cupiditas*, or the desires of the people, are indeed the eternal driving force of history, Traditional Confucian Constitutionalism's endeavor to constrain their desires may well lead to a lack of strength and vitality. This may be particularly manifested in the neo-Confucian eras of the Song and Ming dynasties in Chinese history, when the prevalent norm was to "preserve the heavenly principle and annihilate the humanly desires" (*cun tianli mie renyu* 存天理灭人欲). This feature of Traditional Confucian Constitutionalism would also render it unpopular among the masses, hence lacking popular support in contemporary societies. Third, Traditional Confucian Constitutionalism may become static, hence hindering the development of human history. This is indeed one of the main problems that liberals in the West, such as John Stuart Mill, have with the Chinese tradition. Recalling Nietzsche's teleological description of human history, we certainly should not forget that the "morality of custom and the social straight-jacket" are only the means rather the end. Furthermore, freedom will be genuine freedom only when there are choices to make, so an external free environment is certainly needed.

Finally regarding Sinicized Marxist Constitutionalism, as it is largely a compound of Western Liberal Constitutionalism and Traditional Confucian Constitutionalism, its virtues and vices are also related to its eclectic nature. Its primary virtue lies in its potential to combine the virtues of both Western Liberal Constitutionalism and Traditional Confucian Constitutionalism, and its primary vice may well be its failure to do so and its combination of the vices of the two instead. Its self-perceived virtue could be metaphorically shown in the anecdote Zhuangzi used to illustrate his preaching that "the one good at nourishing life is like a herder of sheep – he watches for stragglers and whips them up" (善养生者，若牧羊然，视其后者而鞭之):

In Lu there was Shan Bao – he lived among the cliffs, drank only water, and didn't go after gain like other people. He went along like that for seventy years and still had the complexion of a little child. Unfortunately, he met a hungry tiger who killed him and ate him up. Then there was Zhang Yi – there wasn't one of the great families and fancy mansions that he didn't rush off to visit. He went along like that for forty years, and then he developed an internal fever, and died. Shan Bao looked after what was on the inside and the tiger ate up from outside. Zhang Yi looked after what was on the outside and the sickness attacked him from inside. Both these men failed to give a lash to the stragglers.

("Dasheng" chapter of *Zhuangzi*)

鲁有单豹者，岩居而水饮，不与民共利，行年七十而犹有婴儿之色，不幸遇饿虎，饿虎杀而食之。有张毅者，高门、悬薄，无不走也，行年四十而有内热之病以死。豹养其内而虎食其外，毅养其外而病攻其内，此二子者，皆不鞭其后者也。

（《庄子-达生》）

From the perspective of Sinicized Marxist Constitutionalism, Traditional Confucian Constitutionalism is like the Shan Bao in the anecdote, who largely lives a solitary life and is concerned more with internal transformation than external strength. As a result, he is vulnerable to external attacks just as manifested in the humiliation of China's recent history. On the other hand, Zhang Yi is like Western Liberal Constitutionalism, which produces all kinds of "party-men" who would ultimately be plagued by some "internal fevers" due to lack of moderation as well as self-cultivations.[4] To some extent, the Maoist period and the reform period correspond to the metaphorical state of Shan Bao and Zhang Yi respectively as well.[5] From the perspectives of Western Liberal Constitutionalism and Traditional Confucian Constitutionalism, however, Sinicized Marxist Constitutionalism has failed to learn and adopt their virtues and has just retained their "drosses" instead.

To sum up, in this section we have briefly discussed the virtues and the vices of the three constitutional discourses. These internal virtues and vices certainly contribute a lot to their strengths and weaknesses in the constitutional game, but as we will see, there are also some other external factors that should be taken into consideration, which we will review next.

The prospect of the new "romance of three kingdoms"

To make plausible forecasts about the future of the constitutional game, three factors need to be examined. First of all, we need to know the respective strengths and weaknesses of each "kingdom" as derived from their internal virtues and vices. Second, we need to have a grasp of the current strategic configurations. Finally, a reliable sense of the development trend of each "kingdom" as well as the overall situations is also crucial. As the virtues and vices of each have been discussed earlier, next, I will mainly review other factors before suggesting a possible result.

The strategic configurations of the constitutional game are shown in Figure 6.1. The innermost circle is the constitutionalism realm within Chinese academia.[6]

In this realm, Western Liberal Constitutionalism is dominant, and Traditional Confucian Constitutionalism and Sinicized Marxist Constitutionalism are just emerging, so the latter two have not challenged the dominant status of Western Liberal Constitutionalism in significant ways. Because the underlying social and economic foundations of Traditional Confucian Constitutionalism, such as China's agrarian economy and closely knitted kindred relationships, have largely ceased to exist in the modern world, and because advocates of Traditional Confucian Constitutionalism have not offered a plausible way for Traditional Confucian Constitutionalism to be transplanted to modern context,[7] the prospect of Traditional Confucian Constitutionalism replacing Western Liberal Constitutionalism in China at the moment is quite low.[8] For Sinicized Marxist Constitutionalism, because the political

4 It is perhaps worth directing one's attention to Thucydides' similar description of the "internal fevers" plaguing the democratic Athens during the Peloponnesian War.

5 The analogy is not unfounded, as Maoist China did remain "puritan" to some extent but was also quite weak and vulnerable during the period, while the reform period indeed witnesses dramatic increase of China's strength and vitality, but its morality seems to have degenerated accordingly as well.

6 It needs to be pointed out that the location of the realm in the center of the diagram does not imply a central status or an endogenous nature but simply indicates that Western Liberal Constitutionalism has successfully carved out a sphere within the ideological realm of China.

7 For a good discussion of the difficulties for re-institutionalizing Confucianism in contemporary China, see Zhang Shibao (2008).

8 Here I have in mind the advocates of Traditional Confucian Constitutionalism such as the cultural conservatives in China, who conceive an unbridgeable gap between Marxism and Confucianism. They are different from those compatibilists subscribing to a "continuity through change" mode of thought (*biantongsiweimoshi* 变通思维模式), such as Tian Chenshan, Feng Tianyu, and so on.

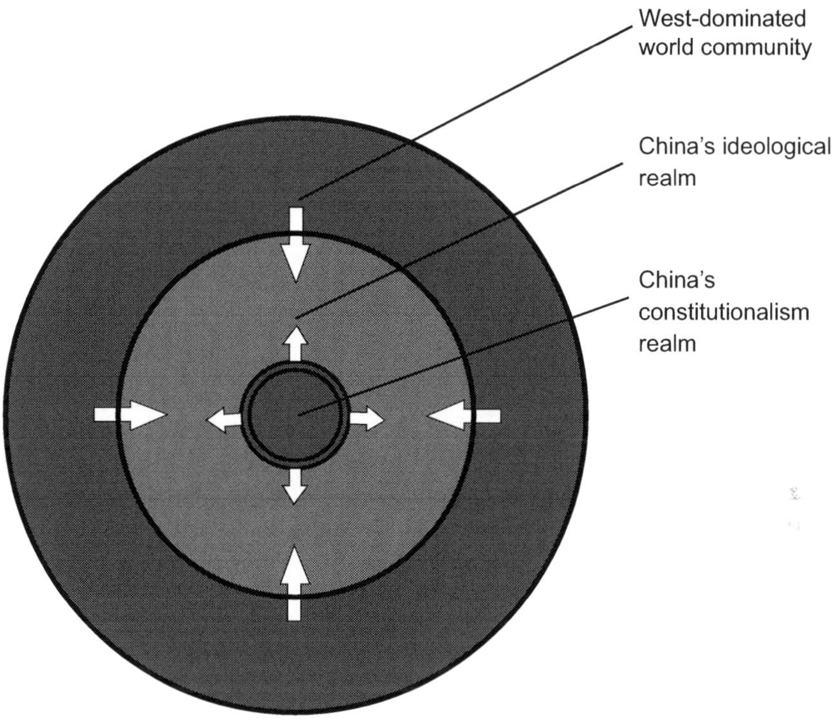

Figure 6.1 Current strategic configurations and developmental trend

authority and the established scholars' strategy has been to evade the notion of "constitutionalism" (*xianzheng* 宪政) and seek to constrain the development of Western Liberal Constitutionalism by force rather than engage in argumentation with it, Sinicized Marxist Constitutionalism may not challenge the dominant status of Western Liberal Constitutionalism in the realm of constitutionalism discourse in the short term as well. This strategic choice on the part of the leadership may have to do with the reality that there is a shortage of politically correct and also competent scholars in the constitutional realm to advocate and defend Sinicized Marxist Constitutionalism at the moment. Furthermore, given that Chinese society is becoming more and more pluralized and that Western Liberal Constitutionalism has been particularly refined for this fact of modern society both theoretically and practically, Western Liberal Constitutionalism may have some advantages in attracting the loyalty of some intellectuals in China.

However, within the second ideological realm of China, Sinicized Marxist Constitutionalism is certainly the dominant player at the moment, and it occupies a very advantageous position from which to shape the development of the game. The main advantages include the endorsement of the political authority and the enormous resources rendered by the latter, such as research funding priority, propaganda advantage, direct repression of any viable challenges, and so on. While the ideological control of the authorities has been weakened by economic reform and opening-up, its controlling tactics has also been advancing with time (*yushijujin* 与时俱进) and the vital aspects of the ideological realm is still within the

Communist Party of China's reign.[9] Despite the penetration of Western Liberal Constitutionalism values from the outer realm of the West-dominated world community, the political authority has painstakingly established certain "walls" to stop or have them filtered. As for the outer realm of the world community, Western Liberal Constitutionalism is certainly in the predominant position, despite also being challenged from various quarters. Nevertheless, the predominant status of Western Liberal Constitutionalism has not been shaken in any fundamental ways perhaps just as the US President Obama's proclamation in his recent speech to the British parliament that the leadership of the West has not been fundamentally challenged. The current strategic configuration is thus clear. What needs to be investigated next is the likely development trend of the current situations.

The development trend of the current strategic configurations is marked by the arrows in the Figure 6.1 earlier. First of all, Western Liberal Constitutionalism-dominated constitutionalism realm marked by the innermost circle and the West-dominated world community marked by the outer ring are likely to continue to expand as this is determined by their natural propensity, which to some extent resembles the preaching nature of Christianity.[10] There is no deliberate plotting or conspiracy involved as this is largely a necessary consequence of globalization as well as their respective natures. A direct result of this development would be to squeeze the strategic space of the orthodox ideology in China denoted by the middle ring and provoke certain reactions from the latter. The collaboration between the inner and the external forces (*liyingwaihe* 里应外合) would render China's orthodox ideologies vulnerable to being "attacked" from both front and rear (*fubeishoudi* 腹背受敌).[11] This situation may have partly induced the elevation of "planning the international and the domestic grand games in one entirety" (*tongchouguoneiguojilainggedaju* 统筹国内国际两个大局) to the national grand strategy since the 17th Congress of the Communist Party of China in 2007.[12] This trend is likely to drive the constituencies of Traditional Confucian Constitutionalism (including some cultural conservatives) and Sinicized Marxist Constitutionalism together in both the constitutionalism realm and the ideological realm as well, as the latter two have more in common than with Western Liberal Constitutionalism.[13] While not deliberately seeking a regime change in China, the strategy of Western Liberal Constitutionalism both in and outside China will nevertheless be to act in accordance with the tide of globalization (*shunshierwei* 顺势而为) and give it a push whenever needed. Advocates of Western Liberal Constitutionalism would not refrain from doing so, because they may well think that it is their calling and obligation. As globalization does not seem to be stoppable and

9 For a good elaboration of this, see Yan (2011).

10 Here I have primarily their resemblance on the surface in mind. For deeper resemblances, one might consult Marx's (1994) critique of the "Christian" nature of modern liberal democracies (p. 10) for insight.

11 The idiom borrowed here is a neutral one mainly serving to depict a realistic picture of the "battle" of the three "kingdoms."

12 For a good elaboration of this grand strategy, see Ling Jihua (令计划) (2007), Hu Jintao's (胡锦涛) close consultant and also the Secretary of the Secretariat of the Central Committee of the Communist Party of China (中央书记处书记).

13 If the "invasion" of the West on China's ideological realm escalated into a more comprehensive confrontation no matter for whatever causes, some constituency of Western Liberal Constitutionalism may shift to Sinicized Marxist Constitutionalism and Traditional Confucian Constitutionalism as well; ultimately some advocates of Western Liberal Constitutionalism in China are nationalist first and liberals second, which is well captured by the Chinese idiom: "internal disunity dissolves at the threat of external invasion" (*xiongdixiyuqiangwaiyuqiwu* 兄弟阋于墙外御其侮).

it is inevitably accompanied by the expansion of Western values and institutions, Western Liberal Constitutionalism seems to be on the offense in the constitutional game.[14] On the other side, Sinicized Marxist Constitutionalism's coping strategy will be to "subdue the active by being inactive" (*yijingzhidong* 以静制动) and "wait at one's ease for the exhausted enemy" (*yiyidailao* 以逸待劳). Because Traditional Confucian Constitutionalism and Sinicized Marxist Constitutionalism believe that Western Liberal Constitutionalism is ultimately not sustainable, the optimal strategy of the Chinese leadership would be to avoid a direct confrontation with them both inside and outside China as long as China's three-layered core interests, as articulated by Dai Bingguo (2010), the highest official in China in charge of foreign affairs, are not threatened.[15] It is worth pointing out that the regime nature as shown in the "Four Cardinal Principles" occupies the most important layer in the minds of the Chinese leadership (Dai, 2010, p. 7).

Looking from this perspective, we might have a rather dark picture of the future of the ideological realm in China. The competition seems to be zero-sum, and the prospect of peace seems to be quite low. For a clairvoyant outsider perspective, the problem seems to have more to do with Western Liberal Constitutionalism rather than Sinicized Marxist Constitutionalism or Traditional Confucian Constitutionalism, as Western Liberal Constitutionalism is on the offensive while Traditional Confucian Constitutionalism and Sinicized Marxist Constitutionalism are on the self-defensive, echoing Newton's (2006) insight about the similar logic of Western Liberal Constitutionalism and imperialism. Perhaps even this "fact" could not be agreed upon, which is why the hope of peace is slim. History is indeed full of tragedies caused by ideological assertions, but humanity in the 21st century does not seem to have learned its lesson. Ultimately, if each side, especially those on the offensive, could forget their rights and wrongs (*shifei* 是非) and take no actions (*wuwei* 无为), just as Zhuangzi has advocated, the world will be better. In other words, if we could satisfy with the status quo; uphold the principle of non-interference, including unintended penetration among the three "constitutional kingdoms"; and come to understand Nietzsche's (1968) insight that "It is our needs that interpret the world; our drives and their For and Against. Every drive is a kind of lust to rule; each one has its perspective that it would like to compel all the other drives to accept as a norm" (481), the casualty to humanity may be lessened. This, however, will seem to remain a dream even in our precious 21st century, because it is against Western Liberal Constitutionalism's nature to stop "shining," or "seducing" to use the opponents' words, in this increasingly borderless world.[16]

Nevertheless, there is also some hope for an alternative harmonious integration among the three traditions in China's future. This prospect will depend on a number of factors such as whether stability in the political, social, and economic realms can be secured. Stability is of crucial importance because the regime is very fragile, and the collapse of the first "card" may well lead to the collapse of the regime like a domino, as has happened repeatedly to

14 For a good insight of the advantages as well as disadvantages of this tactics, one might want to consult Thucydides' *History of the Peloponnesian War*, where the democratic league led by the Athens has adopted the strategy.

15 According to Dai (2010), the core interests of China include three layers: the first and also most important is the nature of the nation and the regime, as well as political stability; the second is the safety of sovereignty and national unity; the last one is the basic protection of sustainable development of China's society and economy (p. 7). The latter layer seems to include the safety of China's importation of natural resources from overseas.

16 Borders of sovereign states as envisioned by Western Liberal Constitutionalism are merely artificial barriers set up by the dictators for accomplishing the liberals' salvation missions.

Marxist regimes. The inevitable collapse of the regime is the vision held by Western Liberal Constitutionalism, which regards itself as the only sustainable path. This vision is consistent with Fukuyama's thesis about the "end of history," which suffered some challenges in the past two decades largely due to the continuing resilience of the Chinese regime. The recent democratic wave in the Middle East and North Africa, however, have rekindled their passions and increased their confidence greatly. This is perhaps well reflected in Hillary Clinton's recent comments on China's recent suppression of dissidents as "a fool's errand" "trying to stop history," adding further that "They cannot do it. But they're going to hold it off as long as possible" (Goldberg, 2011). However, if the stability in all three realms was granted, the final result is unlikely to be that envisioned by the liberals. Instead, we might witness a continuous integration of the three schools both theoretically and practically in the 21st-century China even though with Sinicized Marxist Constitutionalism taking the leadership (*zhudao* 主导) role. There are several reasons for this possibility, which I will briefly discuss next.

First of all, as the established scholars in China have well captured, the competition of the three constitutional discourses ultimately is a competition over the leadership role for directing China's future political path (Chen Hongtai, personal communication, June 10, 2011). As a result, we should not obscure the fact that their focal divergences are not whether some specific elements such as human rights protection, rule of law, and so on should be adopted or not, but rather whose discourse should serve as the leading ideology. In other words, it is the crucial matter of holding what kinds of "flags" for China. The metaphor of "flag-holding" (*juqi* 举旗) has been frequently used by Sinicized Marxist Constitutional constituencies, including the top Chinese leadership, but has not been invoked by Western Liberal Constitutionalism and Traditional Confucian Constitutionalism constituencies, for obvious and understandable reasons. Nevertheless, it is clear that, unless Western Liberal Constitutionalism and Traditional Confucian Constitutionalism could successfully transform or convert the Communist Party of China, their triumph would imply the "lay-off" of the Communist Party of China, which is hard to conceive in contemporary China without certain kinds of revolutions. Since I have assumed the stability of China as our starting point, we could then exclude the scenario of the "lay-off" of the Communist Party of China and just focus on the first possibility. As we will see, it seems that a successful conversion of the Communist Party of China is unlikely in the foreseeable future as well.

The unlikelihood of converting the Communist Party of China ideology into that of Western Liberal Constitutionalism and Traditional Confucian Constitutionalism is the second reason for the forecast of the final result. There are two indicators for this. First of all, the current Chinese leadership has been very clear that they will not change their current flag. This is well shown in reform and opening-upthe reports of both the 18th and 19th Congresses of the ruling party in China. Second, there seems to be little question that the current Chinese leadership is beginning to make a "left" turn at the moment, which may well continue in the future. Perhaps a "left" turn is inaccurate and misleading, since it will not be a return to the "left" of the Maoist period, but a synthesis of the first three decades of "left" experimentation and then three more decades of "right" experimentation in the PRC's near 70-year history. It may appear to be a "left" turn because China has been marching towards the "right" quite far in the past four decades.

The third reason has to do with the social-political foundations of the various constitutional proposals. For any new proposals to be adopted and implemented in current or future China, there are certainly needs for social and political support at both the elite and the popular level. Nevertheless, it is hard to conceive that the Traditional Confucian

Constitutionalism proposal as Jiang Qing has advocated would attract wide supports in contemporary or future China, where a certain degree of pluralism seems to have emerged and may well continue into the future. For the model of Western Liberal Constitutionalism, even though some of its values have clearly taken root in society and even penetrated to some officials, they still lack the political support of the current leadership, and the thesis of Western Liberal Constitutionalism that the emergence of middle-class in the modernization process would ultimately bring democratic transformation is yet to materialize.

Finally, Sinicized Marxist Constitutionalism has the open-mindedness and infrastructure to embrace the valid parts of other traditions and have them play their respective roles for the development of China. Given that the traditions of Western Liberal Constitutionalism and Traditional Confucian Constitutionalism all have their respective merits to contribute, it is unlikely that they will die away in the future. In fact, China's endeavors in the past four decades have manifested such a synthetic feature. For example, the Chinese government has selectively adopted certain Western Liberal Constitutionalism values and institutions such as human rights protection, rule of law, service-oriented government, and so on, as long as they do not pose a threat to the fundamental nature of the regime. Given that Western Liberal Constitutionalism indeed embodies some important values that represent the needs of humanity at the end stage of history as we have discussed earlier, Chinese leadership may have to deal with this reality. Meanwhile, however, to cope with the potential vices brought by the values of Western Liberal Constitutionalism, the government may resort to Traditional Confucian Constitutionalism for insights as well as prescriptions. To some extent, this endeavor of innovative synthesis may well be represented by Sinicized Marxist Constitutionalism literally, with the "S" linked to the tradition of Traditional Confucian Constitutionalism, "M" linked to the Marxist tradition, and the "C" linked to the tradition of Western Liberal Constitutionalism. In the Chinese context, as long as the pressures of Western Liberal Constitutionalism and Traditional Confucian Constitutionalism are kept below the threshold of creating instability and other troubles, they may well manifest their positive sides and play a constructive role for the development of China in the 21st century. This may well be the contribution of Sinicized Marxist Constitutionalism towards the world. It is hard to conceive that Western Liberal Constitutionalism or Traditional Confucian Constitutionalism could adopt certain Marxist elements at the moment. So both theoretically and practically, it seems that the only likely outcome would be a further integration of the three traditions with Sinicized Marxist Constitutionalism taking a leadership role.

To sum up, we first recapitulated the state of play of the three "constitutional kingdoms" as captured in previous chapters, then conducted a preliminary comparison of the three players and discussed their respective virtues and vices, and finally analyzed the prospects of the game based on some perceptions of the current strategic configurations as well as their development trends. At the first glance, the three constitutional kingdoms are indeed engaging in a kind of zero-sum competition, but as I have suggested, in the Chinese context, the dark side of the competition may well be under control, and their positive sides may have full play. If this happens, it would indeed be a significant contribution of Sinicized Marxist Constitutionalism to the world. Whether this will be realized, however, will have to wait for the history to tell.

7 Implications for the world[1]

As previous chapters have shown, China serves as a fascinating case for the study of the consequential effects of globalization on ideology, and this project clearly demonstrates how the emergence of three constitutionalism discourses for the future of China is a direct result of the various interactions under the influence of globalization. We have touched on themes such as the internationalization of Western Liberal Constitutionalism, the attempt to harmonize the Western legal tradition into the Sinicized Marxist political infrastructure by the Chinese government and established scholars, and the reactions of some cultural conservatives within Chinese society towards the spread of Western norms and institutions, as well as the likely evolution of the strategic configurations. Nevertheless, China certainly is not a passive receptor of influence from the outside world only, but also a potential active exporter of ideas and concepts. Indeed, this dimension has attracted much attention and exploration by Chinese policy-makers and scholars alike. They have actually undertaken many initiatives to push China's views and discourses to spread abroad. But most importantly, with China's overall national strength continuing to grow, its influence in the world will be greater even if China does not undertake any intentional campaigns. Thus, conceivably the constitutionalism discourse, once driven from developed Western states to other parts of the world may now also see some positive engagement from places like China. That may have a potentially important effect on the quality and shape of the future of constitutionalism as ideology and legitimating measure of governments worldwide. This chapter will thus discuss the implications of China's rising constitutionalism.

As we all know, the issue of constitutional legitimacy and the ideologies for authentic constitutionalism has acquired a global dimension over the last several decades, so the hot discussion of constitutionalism in China, the most dynamic and also now the second largest economies in the world, certainly would have much to say or contribute. Depending on the viewer's horizon, the implications could be at discursive, theoretical, and practical levels, with each level going one step further than the previous one. On the surface is the discursive level, where one may take the rising Chinese constitutionalism discourse as a sign of constitutionalism's discursive diversification in the world, breaking the yoke of liberal monopoly of the concept of constitutionalism. The three constitutionalism discourses in China may also remind us the similar and parallel constitutionalism discourse at the global

1 Parts of this chapter have been reproduced with kind permission from the article "Why the Ukraine Crisis Is the West's Fault: A Historical and Philosophical Perspective," Peng Chengyi, in *International Critical Thought* © Chinese Academy for Social Sciences, reprinted by permission of Taylor & Francis Ltd, www.tandfonline.com on behalf of Chinese Academy for Social Sciences.

level, namely the Islamic constitutionalism, the Marxist constitutionalism, and the liberal constitutionalism, despite the Islamic constitutionalism and Marxist constitutionalism are seldom mentioned in the mainstream academia of the West. One step further is the theoretical level, where the advantages of Traditional Confucian Constitutionalism and Sinicized Marxist Constitutionalism, as well as the vices of Western Liberal Constitutionalism could provoke reconsiderations of our mainstream political theories, especially regarding notions of freedom, authority, tyranny of majority, etc. With China's constitutionalism growing ripe both in practice and in theory, it may well bring a revolution to the field of normative political science. If the viewer's horizon is bigger with keener insight, he or she may well sense the practical implications of the rising Chinese constitutionalism, especially regarding its efficiency in coping with the rising populism worldwide than the alternatives as well as its prospect for a peaceful world order. Next, we will thus elaborate on the implications at each of the three levels.

Discursive implications

First of all, the emergence of Chinese constitutionalism may contribute to the legitimization of Chinese polity in the West-dominated liberal order. Just as Backer has rightly pointed out, an important function of constitutionalism is its determination of the legitimacy of a constitutional system as conceived or as implemented. Even if the Chinese constitutionalism may not be acknowledged and accepted by the mainstream in the West, it at least raises the awareness that there are different criteria of judging the legitimacy of different regimes. Just as the UK polity was not granted the status of constitutionalism initially when viewers conceived constitutionalism only through the lens of constitutional judicialization, we may not acknowledge Chinese constitutionalism if we only think about constitutionalism through Western criteria. In fact, just as many scholars have well found, there are actually many different versions of constitutionalism across the West amid different stages of history; hence, we certainly should not be "blinded" by our parochial visions even though this self-rectification process is neither pain-free nor easy.

Second, the emergence of Chinese constitutionalism discourse may well push forward discursive diversification of constitutionalism at the global level. In fact, due to the dominance of the West led by the US both materially and culturally, constitutionalism has been largely taken as equivalent to liberal constitutionalism as exemplified in the US case. However, just as Foucaultian discourse analysis reveals, behind the discourse actually lies the power relationships. In this respect, with China's power continuing to grow, it may also break the cultural and ideological monopoly of the West led by the US and induce legitimate ideologies towards more diverse directions. Even if the Chinese government does not embrace the notion of constitutionalism due to some strategic considerations, the discourse is likely to further expand in the academia as well as at the grassroots level. It is thus conceivable to see more diverse constitutionalism discourses at the global level sooner or later.

Third, there is also a striking similarity and parallel between the tri-party competition of constitutionalism discourse in China and at the global level. For the latter, there is actually a competition among theocratic constitutionalism, liberal constitutionalism, and Marxist constitutionalism (Backer, 2009a) that is very similar to the competition among Traditional Confucian Constitutionalism, Western Liberal Constitutionalism, and Sinicized Marxist Constitutionalism in China. As Backer (2009a) points out, a distinctive feature of the constitutionalism discourse at the global level since WWII is the increasing primacy of value frameworks; consequently, the old consensus of constitutionalism prior to WWII, largely grounded in domestic law and the peculiar will of the territorially defined demos, has been replaced by a new consensus grounding constitutional legitimacy on its conformity to a higher norm shared by the community of nations (101). And accordingly, there are largely three such communities of nations, namely the Islamic group, the Marxist group, and the liberal group, corresponding to three constitutionalism discourses based on different norms (Backer 2009a, p. 111).[2] There is no need perhaps to mention liberal constitutionalism since it is the dominant constitutional paradigm in the world today and has been embraced by the majority of countries. It is even taken as the standard of modern political civilization in the world. The other two notions may sound fresh to our readers, since they are mainly used by Backer.[3] According to Backer (2009a), even though theocratic constitutionalism is very young in many aspects, only about one generation old, it has become a powerful system for constructing and legitimating constitutions among countries embracing a religious framework within which the constitution operates (p. 159). The focus of the constitutionalism is a search for a grounding in values beyond the will of individuals, with the rules of institutional organization and behavior derived from the holy texts and the rule systems of organized religions, and consequently, it merges the substantive normative systems with the procedural *Rechtsstaat* protections of traditional constitutions (Backer 2009a, p. 159). It seems that the Traditional Confucian Constitutionalism reviewed in Chapter 4 is very similar to the kind of theocratic constitutionalism as practiced in the Islamic world. Marxist constitutionalism, according to Backer (2009a), seeks to ground constitutions within a Marxist normative infrastructure as explicated by the pioneering Marxist party. This, accordingly, is well represented in certain strands of Sinicized Marxist Constitutionalism as reviewed in Chapter 5 of this book. Other countries such as Vietnam and Cuba would belong to this camp as well.

The discursive significance of the Chinese constitutionalism will thus not only seek to grant legitimacy to the Chinese regime in the international community, but also drive global constitutionalism discourse towards diverse directions and enrich the constitutionalism discourse at the global level, especially the schools of Traditional Confucian Constitutionalism and Sinicized Marxist Constitutionalism. It will also serve as an epitome of the theocratic, liberal, and Marxist constitutionalisms at the global level. Given China's sheer size and increasing influence, its constitutionalism discourse, when fully theorized and elaborated, would have significant impacts on political theory and practice worldwide as well, which will be reviewed next.

Theoretical implications

As we can see, the Chinese discussion has enriched the global discourse, but what is most striking is perhaps its theoretical challenge to the liberal constitutional paradigm. Besides demonstrating new paths to legitimacy within the boundaries of constitutionalist

2 Backer actually categorizes five main types of constitutionalism, based on the different normative foundations as well as different sources for the norms, namely nationalist, transnational, natural law, theocratic, and Marxist-Leninist. It seems that Backer does not make a qualitative distinction between the first two types and the last three types; nevertheless, the former might be regarded as vertical and the latter horizontal, with both groups overlapping to some extent.

3 See Backer (2008, 2009a, 2009b, 2009c).

ideology – preserving the democratic character of the state and the avoidance of the cult of personality and individual rules (rule of law in the Western context) through a distinct model – , most importantly Chinese constitutionalism also embodies certain vital superiority over the liberal constitutionalism with fatal consequences.

The liberal confusion of human emancipation and political emancipation

The most prominent flaw of liberal constitutionalism is its confusion of human emancipation with political emancipation. Besides Mark Warren's warning about this danger as discussed in Chapter 3 of this book, Marx's critique should deserve a close review here. To understand it, we first should have a firm grasp of Marx's notions of religion and emancipation, two very important concepts of Marx's philosophy. As we will see below, for both concepts, Marx actually has two visions: first political emancipation is conventionally understood as stemming from religion and second human emancipation stems from Marx's unique understanding of "religiosity."

Thus, Marx distinguishes between political emancipation and human emancipation. As shown in Figure 7.1, political emancipation and human emancipation are located at different stages of human history.

For Marx, "political emancipation is a reduction of man, on the one hand to a member of civil society, and *independent* and *egoistic* individual, and on the other hand, to a *citizen*, to a moral person" (46). This is so, because in the feudal society, there is no civil society and individual in a strict sense, or at least not in the way we understand them today. As Laura Janara nicely phrases it, "[T]he individual life – if 'the individual' can even be imagined in this context – is not autonomous but is, rather, one small node in a larger, seemingly eternal, societal, and historical web of relations" (556). For Marx, this web determines "the relation of the individual to the *state as a whole*; that is, his *political* situation, or in other words, his separation and exclusion from the other elements of society" (44). Because of this alienation, Marx thinks that the feudal individuals are in fact excluded from the body of the state, since "the state as a whole and its consciousness, will, and activity . . . necessarily appeared as the *private* affair of a ruler and his servants, separated from the people" (45). However, because "the elements of civil life such as property, the family,

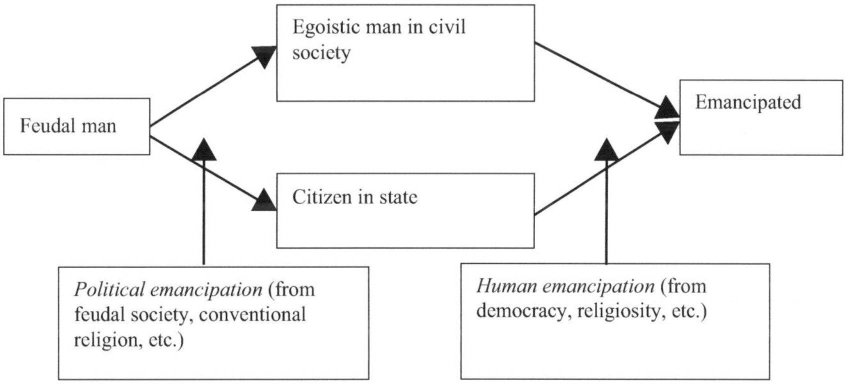

Figure 7.1 Marx's two visions of emancipation and religion in history

and types of occupation had been raised, in the form of lordship, caste, and guilds, to elements of political life," Marx points out that the old civil society retains "a *directly* political character" "at least in the feudal sense" (44). In other words, the political character of feudal society has reached its civil society, but not to its individuals. As we will see, the political revolution changes everything.

According to Marx, the political revolution is also the revolution of civil society (44). It "shattered everything – estates, corporations, guilds, privileges – which expressed the separation of the people from community life" and "made state affairs the affairs of the people, and the political state a matter of general concern" (45). To borrow Janara's nice wording, this revolution "atomizes the individual, signifying release from a highly organized hierarchy into a world of flux" (557). This "swirling disintegration" (Janara, p. 557), according to Marx, on one hand "dissolved civil society into its basic elements" and on the other hand "set free the political spirit which had, so to speak, been dissolved, fragmented, and lost in the various culs-de-sac of feudal society" (45). While the political spirit liberated from civil society were reassembled and made of the general concern of the people, Marx points out that "[T]he bonds which had restrained the egoistic spirit of civil society were [also] removed along with the political yoke" (45). As a result, the feudal man becomes an egoistic individual of civil society and the citizen of the state at the same time. If the political revolution also brought to an end of the state religion in the public sphere, Marx contends, it would not mean that the people would be truly emancipated from religion. In other words, he was not freed from religion, but only received religious liberty (45). According to Marx, the true human emancipation from religion

> will only be complete when the real, individual man has absorbed into himself the abstract citizen; when as an individual man, in his everyday life . . . he has become a *species-being*; and when he has recognized and organized his own powers (*force propres*) as *social* powers so that he no longer separates this social power from himself as *political* power.
>
> (46)

To understand this, we need to understand Marx's vision of religion.

It would seem that Marx has two visions of religion: one is conventionally understood religion and another is a unique vision of his own. When Marx is discussing political emancipation from religion, most of the time, he is using religion in the first vision, the one held by Bruno Bauer. This vision has no difference from today's conventional understanding of religion, such as Christianity, Judaism, etc. When Marx is talking about human emancipation, as well as the reasons why the separation of the state from religion does not liberate people from religion, he is transitioning to the second vision. According to Marx, "[R]eligion is the generalized theory of this world, its encyclopedic compendium, its logic in popular form, its spiritualistic point d'honneur, its enthusiasm, its moral sanction, its solemn complement, its general ground of consolation and justification" (28). It is "the self-consciousness and self-regard of man who has either not yet found or has already lost himself" (Marx 28). To know one's true human nature is thus the sole criteria for one's evasion of religiosity. However, since religion is "the *fantastic realization* of the human essence inasmuch as the human essence possesses no true reality" (Marx, 28), it would seem that, for Marx, few, perhaps only those who have experienced the emptiness of human nature and attained enlightenment as the Buddha, would escape the "opium" of religion. This is also shown in Marx's analysis of the double existence of man: celestial, communal, and terrestrial, personal

(34).[4] As long as people are trapped in "the dualism between individual life and species-life, between the life of civil society and political life," in Marx's view, they would remain religious (39). Understanding this, we then could understand why, for Marx, human emancipation would not be complete until the "sensuous, individual, and immediate existence" of the "egoistic man" in civil society and the "abstract, artificial," "allegorical, moral" existence of the "species-being" in the political state are united, as shown earlier in Figure 7.1.

Risk of fascism re-emerging

Since Marx's solution of a proletariat revolution did not occur in the West, the evolution of the West since then has been a downward spiral towards the abyss of demise. This is well captured by Milbank and Pabst, whose insights are worth close review here. First of all, Milbank and Pabst (2015) point out that the left and right in the Western politics represent two versions of liberalism that are seemingly opposite to each other but actually are in a tacit, secret alliance in engendering illiberalism that they ascribes to non-liberal positions. The two liberalisms may seem to be opposite to each other, since the left version appeals to the state for protection from the forces of market fundamentalism that the right champions, while the right version defends conservative values of family and the nation against multiculturalism and emancipation that the left celebrates. However, just as Milbank and Pabst (2015) rightly observe, far from representing genuine alternatives to each other, the two versions of liberalism are actually mutually reinforcing in the sense of fusing economic-political individualism with bureaucratic-managerial collectivism and social-cultural atomization. This may well be seen in the convergence of policies by the left and right parties throughout the Western world in the past decades. In Milbank and Pabst's words,

> They have now more explicitly fused to proffer the shared creed of the left that recently embraced economic neo-liberalism together with an impersonal statism, and the right that has openly espoused cultural liberalism in scorn of its own natural constituency.
>
> (Milbank & Pabst, 2015)

The illiberalism is then naturally engendered and would lead to meta-crisis of the West. Just as some scholar points out, most people habituated in such a cultural matrix would have merely the illusion of freedom since they would be separated from moral virtue, which is crucial for the nation to sustain its commitment to freedom and equality for all (Dennehy, 2007). Illiberalism is the necessary result largely because the economic and political liberalism advocated by the right has been eroding the social bonds and civic ties on which vibrant democracies and healthy market economies ultimately depend for trust and cooperation, while the cultural and social liberalism held by the left, including some modes of middle-class feminism, has been carelessly underwriting the new cult of market choice in default of its supposedly radical commitments (Milbank & Pabst, 2015). "Since in theory and practice liberalism goes against the grain of humanity and the universe we inhabit," Milbank and Pabst (2015) conclude that "we are facing not merely a cyclical crisis (linked, for example, to economic boom and bust or the decline of representative government), nor even just a systemic crisis of capitalism and democracy, but rather a meta-crisis," which is "the tendency

4 This may shed some light for the receptivity of Marxism into Chinese culture, as one distinguishing idea of the latter is the inseparability of the human and divine, or the terrestrial and the celestial.

at once to abstract from reality and to reduce everything to its bare materiality, leaving an irreducible aporia between human will and artifice, on the one hand, and unalterable laws of nature and history, on the other."

This meta-crisis as manifested in the wider gap between the abstract and the material may actually echo the insights of Marx as elaborated earlier. To put it in metaphorical terms, liberal constitutionalism has straitjacketed people's heads into the cloud, forcing them to see, hear, and contemplate only what Marx calls the "abstract, artificial," "allegorical, moral" world, while leaving their bodies on the rotting ground, which is the "sensuous, individual, and immediate existence" of the "egoistic man" in civil society. This divergence is also well shown in the latest development of capitalism. Just as Milbank and Pabst (2015) point out, contemporary capitalism subjects the real economy of productive activities to relentless commodification and speculation, while at the same time separating symbolic significance from material basis, which is seen increasingly as just an object for arbitrary division, consumption, and destruction. As a result, it renders ecological damage constitutive of our fundamental economic processes. It is for this reason that the authors draw the conclusion the liberalism delves its tombs:

> Thus, liberalism undoes itself and, in so doing, it erodes the polity it claims to save from extremes on both the left and the right. After all, the liberal focus on abstract, general standards (such as subjective rights, commercial contracts or formal, procedural justice) is parasitic upon a culture of universal principles and particular practices of virtue that this obsessive and rigid focus undermines, cutting off the branch on which it sits.
>
> (Milbank & Pabst, 2015)

Clearly, the meta-crisis of the Western constitutionalism is bound to occur, as long as it confuses political emancipation with human emancipation and the gap between the two are getting wider. When that happens, it would not be surprising for fascism to resurface on the earth. In fact, we are already witnessing the widespread emergence of an unhealthy populism in the West, which is a direct result of Western Liberal Constitutionalism, since the lack of human emancipation would by necessity lead to a corrupted mass, that is at risk of being manipulated by demagogues being inevitable under certain conditions. When life is so miserable and not worth living anymore, that is the time the demise of the West will start. The omnipresent symbolic violence, leading to all kinds of perversions of democracy as Pierre Bourdieu has discovered, certainly would contribute to such a dim future (Topper, 2001).

The Chinese way as an alternative

However, the alternative constitutional paradigms of Traditional Confucian Constitutionalism and Sinicized Marxist Constitutionalism do not suffer from these problems. The defining feature of Confucian constitutionalism, for example, lies with its ritualistic dimension and the religious dimension. As we have seen in Chapter 4, in Confucian constitutionalism, ritual plays an important constitutional function in not only constraining power, but also cultivating virtue. The "religious dimension" of Confucian constitutionalism is also different from the theocratic constitutionalism seen in other parts of the world in the sense that the religious aspect of Confucianism is different from that of conventional religions of the West, such as Islamism or Judaism. In fact, the Chinese constitutionalism may well qualify the institutional arrangement Spinoza prescribes for enlightening the mass.

Therefore, with Western Liberal Constitutionalism manifesting more and more of its fatal flaws and unsustainability, the theoretical significance of the Chinese constitutionalism, especially its virtue cultivation aspect, will become clearer. In fact, many scholars have contended that Confucianism provides the sources for an illiberal democracy that could serve as a good alternative to that of liberalism (Ackerly, 2005). Scott Newton (2006) also points out that the mystical doctrine of separation of powers has been fetishized so that other legitimate democratic forms of government such as conciliar democracy have been obscured or prevented from consideration (p. 335). Similarly, while lying at the very heart of the operational legitimacy of the liberal constitutional order, the electoral formulas of Western democracies have been strangely neglected and ignored, leading to very "unscientific" and crude results that are susceptible to manipulation (Newton, 2006, p. 336).

Practical implications

The practical significance of the constitutionalism development in China could be seen in two aspects. First, it may induce some tensions between China and the Western world. Second, it might serve as an attractive alternative for developing countries. Just as anticipated in previous chapter, Sinicized Marxist Constitutionalism would face challenges from both inside and outside forces. If China continues to embody the path of Sinicized Marxist Constitutionalism without falling into instability, the tension might increase. There is no sign of any retreats as shown in reports from both the 18th and the 19th National Congresses. In the reports, Communist Party leadership proclaimed that it would continue to firmly embrace the so-called "Socialism with Chinese Characteristics" and have the latter's theory, path, and institutions further clarified. In its foreign policy, the reports state that it would seek for equal trust, receptive mirroring, and mutual winning cooperation. Nevertheless, ideology still seems to be the biggest barrier for the amelioration of the relationships between China and the West, so it is questionable to what degree these wishes can be realized.

While China's relationships with the West might get more tense as Chinese constitutionalism develops, it may serve as an attractive alternative for many developing countries. Indeed, the interest as well as popularity of China's model among developing countries have been growing in the past decades as China becomes strong yet retains its own regime characteristics. It is perhaps most charming to those authoritarian countries that would also like to retain the native regime yet attain the benefits of capitalism. It would thus have significant soft power among the countries in Latin America, Middle East, Africa, and Asia. Given that the normative frameworks of different constitutionalisms at the global level are largely incompatible and to some extent aggressively competitive, "the great competition between communities of believers for control of legitimating discourse of political organization" would be fierce in those battle grounds, which would be similar to the traditional competition of religions (Backer, 2009a, 112, 175). How this new game at the global level will play out, however, will have to wait for history to be the ultimate judge. However, if we want some plausible and heuristic forecast of the future, it is perhaps helpful to have a careful look at the Ukraine crisis just occurred not long ago, which we will do next.

The Ukraine crisis as a practical example

The Ukraine crisis is arguably the major geopolitical event of recent times. Triggered when then-president Viktor Yanukovych suspended the process meant to bring about an association agreement with the EU, the "Euromaidan" protests ultimately resulted in the president fleeing the country. Protests also spurred unrest in eastern and southern regions of Ukraine and led to the secession of Crimea, followed by its reincorporation into Russia. To date, civil war continues between the post-revolutionary Ukrainian government and pro-autonomy insurgents.

Surprised by the crisis and shocked by Russia's prompt reaction to it, at least in the case of Crimea, Western commentators have almost unanimously blamed Russia for the complex and difficult situation in Ukraine. Nevertheless, as John Mearsheimer points out, the West is actually responsible for the crisis due to the relentless eastward expansion of the EU/NATO as well as the project of "promoting democracy" mounted inside Ukraine by the West. This analysis is more impartial and closer to reality. Ironically, Mearsheimer (2014) as a well-known representative of the "realist" school in international relations argues that the reason why the West is wrong is because it is liberal, while Russia is more "realist":

> Elites in the United States and Europe have been blindsided by events only because they subscribe to a flawed view of international politics. They tend to believe that the logic of realism holds little relevance in the twenty-first century. . . . The crisis there shows that realpolitik remains relevant – and states that ignore it do so at their own peril. (p. 2)

Mearsheimer's critical analysis has been thought-provoking for many in the West, but it betrays the limitations of Western theoretical frameworks. The truth is that the realism displayed by the Russian side has represented a direct response to a succession of threatening Western moves. NATO/EU expansion and the "democracy project" undertaken by the West within Ukraine failed to take Russian strategic interests into consideration, and Western leaders did not show due care in considering the likely consequences. These mistakes have deep historical and philosophical roots. Under US leadership, the West has failed to learn from similar mistakes in the past and has not shown insight into the flawed nature of its own political norms. Worst of all, the West has fallen into the trap that Thucydides correctly identified, a trap whose origins lie in the nature and fate of the multitude. The insights of Thucydides and Spinoza throw a good deal of light on the situation surrounding Ukraine. Accordingly, the main body of this section will be divided into three parts. The first of these parts reviews Mearsheimer's arguments concerning the reasons why the West should be held accountable for the Ukraine crisis. The following part analyzes why the West should be condemned for acting consistently on the basis of a flawed liberalism. The final part concludes with the lessons that can be drawn from this analysis.

Why the Ukraine crisis is the West's fault

While it is understandable that subscribers to Western liberal interventionism should hold Russia responsible for the confrontation in Ukraine, it is quite obvious, on sober reflection, that the guilty party is actually the West. First of all, there is no disputing that the crisis has much to do with the enlargement of NATO and the EU. With the collapse of the former Soviet Union as well as the Warsaw Pact, NATO seized the unprecedented historic opportunity to expand eastward. By 1999, it had incorporated three of the Visegrad countries, the Czech Republic, Poland and Hungary; in 2004 it absorbed Bulgaria, Estonia, Latvia, Lithuania, Romania, Slovakia, and Slovenia. By 2009, all these countries had become members both of NATO and the EU. At a summit in Bucharest in April 2008, NATO considered the addition of Ukraine and Georgia. But due to opposition from Germany and France, which feared such a move would unduly antagonize Russia and spark internal strife within Ukraine and Georgia, these countries were not admitted. NATO did, however, proclaim that the two countries would in time become members of NATO. As Mearsheimer (2014) rightly points out, Putin has made it explicit that the incorporation of Ukraine and Georgia into NATO would pose a "direct threat" to Russia and that Russia would never allow this to happen. Indeed, the Russian invasion of Georgia should have fully demonstrated this determination. Meanwhile, the EU was expanding too; in May 2008, it launched the Eastern Partnership initiative, with the declared goals of fostering prosperity in countries such as Ukraine and of integrating them into the EU economy. Given the way in which the EU and NATO have expanded in lockstep with one another, Russian leaders understandably regarded this move as paving the way for further expansion of NATO.

The West's goal of "promoting democracy" in Ukraine is consistent with the philosophy and values declared by the political elites in the West and also espoused by ordinary people. Western policy-makers, however, are perfectly aware that democracy cannot be imposed from outside. Their strategy has been to support those on the ground in Ukraine who are pursuing the same democratic agenda while keeping pressure on the government through all available channels. The effect of these policies on Ukraine has been thoroughly destabilizing. Victoria Nuland, the US Assistant Secretary of State for European and Eurasian affairs, estimated in December 2013 that the United States alone had invested more than $5 billion in Ukraine since 1991 for "democracy promotion" activities; the National Endowment for Democracy, supported by the US government, has funded more than 60 projects aimed at promoting civil society in Ukraine (Mearsheimer, 2014). These moves certainly contributed to the Orange Revolution, which occurred in Ukraine in 2004. When a regime cannot cope with rapid transformations emerging from the grass-roots level of society, disorder is bound to emerge, and this pattern was well demonstrated in the "Euromaidan revolution." This revolution may be categorized as a *de facto* coup, since the democratically elected president was ousted by obviously illegal means. But the dominant Western media, due to their deeply entrenched prejudice, have never viewed the overturn in this way or used so negative a term to describe it.

Meanwhile, the West, in its drive to expansion, has proved unable to take Russia's strategic interests into serious consideration or to act prudently with an eye to the results of its initiatives. We are entitled to ask: would the Americans permit hostile powers to take its neighbors such as Canada and Mexico into their orbit? Russia, because of its weakness in the early post-Soviet years, may have been unable to resist the early phases of NATO enlargement and EU expansion. Today, however, the situation is different. The Ukraine crisis can be viewed as posing five threats to Russia: it constrains Russian foreign policy choices, it threatens the country's security and sovereignty, it challenges the entire post-Soviet order, it encourages the growth of Ukrainian nationalism, and it threatens domestic stability (Wilson, 2014). It is therefore not surprising that the Euromaidan revolution provoked a strong reaction in Moscow. The West may not have intended to provoke a civil war in Ukraine, but through its myopic policies it has achieved exactly that. Like the mayhem its interventions have created in countries such as Iraq and Syria, the outcomes of its meddling in Ukraine have taught the West nothing about self-restraint.

Why the blundering is inevitable

Lack of the ability to learn from past mistakes

Serious introspection, we may conclude, is simply beyond the capacities of the West. It is common, for example, to see commentaries blaming Russia for the chaos seen in Ukraine since the Euromaidan revolution. As a result, Western writers often advocate that, in order to counter Russian expansionism, the whole West should work together to bolster the democracies of the Eastern Partnership states, develop a safe and secure energy supply for European countries, strengthen the defenses of the front-line NATO states of Central and Eastern Europe, and increase its support for the new Ukraine government (Nix, 2014). For such writers, it is self-evident that

> as the Ukrainian people have fought for their right to live in a democratic system inspired by European values, the EU should continue to support Ukraine in its democratic and European aspirations; this support should not only be in the form of financial packages, but also shown by accelerating the visa liberalization dialogue, which would grant Ukrainians access to what they have fought for – a united Europe.
>
> (Saryusz-Wolski, 2014)

While "visa liberalization" might seem attractive to many Ukrainians, it can also be viewed as simply a way of transforming Ukraine into a reserve army of labor for Western Europe, as has occurred with other countries of the former Soviet bloc, and of converting the Ukrainians into more faithful followers of EU/Western values and norms.

Insofar as US and EU initiatives with regard to Ukraine have been criticized in the West, the dissension has usually focused on a supposed lack of coordination and on policy failures. For example, one author argues that, while democratization has been one of the EU's key objectives for the Eastern Partnership region, EU actions have not always been coordinated, and the bloc's rhetoric has not been backed up by political and financial resources. As a result, the argument proceeds, the EU should enhance the region's democratic prospects by improving coordination and widening the involvement by stake-holders in their countries' democratization (Kobzová, 2014). Another commentator regards the EU Eastern Partnership as a political region-building project that seeks to reconfigure Eastern Europe as a political and economic periphery through a process of assimilating these countries to EU norms and standards. The Ukraine crisis, however, shows that the assimilation project has failed. Instead, it is argued, the EU should explore the potential (and perhaps by now, the missed opportunity) to strengthen political and economic cooperation and infrastructure links between these Eastern Partnership countries so as to reduce their dependence on Russia. As a result of this strategic failure, the region is said to have been fragmented into a multiplicity of territories set to develop into *de facto* dependencies either of Russia or of the EU/West (Bosse, 2014).

For someone like Mearsheimer, such diagnoses of the crisis and prescriptions for resolving it represent undoubted progress over the earlier-cited liberal interventionist views. However, the critiques involved fail to question views and beliefs that are deeply held in the West, including confidence in such political norms as faith in the Western mode of liberal democracy. The analyses by ancient philosophers that will be explored here suggest that this may well be the reason why the blundering by the West is inevitable, and why the countries at fault are likely to commit the same mistakes in future.

Lack of insight regarding political norms

A more fundamental reason why the West commits endless blunders is that it lacks insight into its values and norms, which it regards as self-evident. The insights into political matters of Aristotle, the forerunner of political science as well as one of the founders of Western civilization, are certainly worth our attention here. According to Aristotle (1984), the reason why different types of regimes exist is that society is made up of distinct parts with various purposes; it is the ruling part that defines the regime. Aristotle divided regimes into six types: kingship, aristocracy, polity, tyranny, oligarchy, and democracy (1278b8-12, 1289b27-29). These types of regime are further categorized on the basis of whether the ruling power, exercised by one person, by a few or by the masses, serves the private or public good. Given that human beings aim not just to live together but to live well, Aristotle preferred the rule of a philosopher-king, whom he considered the exemplar of virtue. But since virtue is hard to judge and the wise are always few in number, the most common forms of regime would be oligarchy based on wealth, and democracy based on liberty; if we apply Aristotle's method, the most likely regime in Western countries today would be a mixture of oligarchy and democracy. It is worth recalling that in the ancient world democracy was commonly regarded as the worst possible regime, but over the course of history, this perception has been turned upside down, and democracy has come to be viewed throughout the world as the only legitimate form of rule.

Bearing this in mind, it is clear that during most of recent history the Western regime of liberal democracy has been on the offensive throughout the world, aiming to eliminate all the alternatives. The "offensive" may not necessarily take the traditional form of military action, but in all other fields the "invisible war" is quite obvious. The result in various countries is civil conflicts, or what we would now call "color revolutions." The Ukraine crisis is just another outcome of this offensive, and the fact that the crisis has aroused a vehement response from Russia is not hard to understand. To some extent, it shares the logic that Thucydides revealed as underlying the Peloponnesian War, and it is thus helpful to review his insights on the latter topic.

Falling into the Thucydides Trap, with no way out

Led by the United States, the West has fallen into the trap that Thucydides rightly discerned and has no way out. In recent years the concept of the "Thucydides Trap" has been widely invoked in academic and policy circles, but in a form that misinterprets Thucydides' real meaning. According to the conventional reading of the concept, history shows that a rising power is destined to challenge the established hegemon and that conflict between the two is inevitable. In today's context, and for obvious reasons, the concept is widely used in discussing the Sino-US relationship. However, this interpretation is flawed. A careful reading of Thucydides and an understanding of his thought shows that this dominant interpretation is simplistic and does not reflect Thucydides' original intention. The "Thucydides Trap" that emerges from a proper reading of Thucydides is, in fact, a warning that foresees the inevitable expansion, or over-extension, and decline of a democratic imperialism. Since this insight is highly relevant to our discussion of the sources of the Ukraine crisis, it deserves careful review.

Before we examine the specific content, it is helpful to have an understanding of Thucydides' credentials. Thucydides was an Athenian historian and general, renowned for his *History of the Peloponnesian War*, which recounts the war between Sparta and Athens in the 5th century BC. Thucydides has been dubbed the "father of scientific history" because of his strict standards for evidence-gathering and analysis of cause and effect without reference to intervention by gods. For our purposes here, Thucydides' (1998) *History of the Peloponnesian War*, besides its "unprecedented standards of objectivity and consequent accuracy" (1998, p. xiii), is also "a possession for all time," compiled for those "who wish to look at the plain truth about past events and those that at some future time, in accordance with human nature, will recur in similar or comparable ways" (Thucydides, 1998, p. 14).

It is worth noting how Thucydides argues that similar events will recur in history because of unchanging human nature. For these reasons, we should abstract his diagnosis of human nature and consider whether today's crisis shares the same logic.

The Peloponnesian War of 431–404 BC was fought by Athens and its empire against the Peloponnesian League led by Sparta. The conflict was memorable not only because "both sides came into it flourishing in overall preparedness and on seeing that the rest of the Hellenes were aligning themselves with one or the other," but also because it was

> accompanied by such sufferings as never afflicted Hellas in any comparable period of time. For never had there been so many cities captured or left desolate . . . nor were there so many men exiled or slaughtered, both in the war itself and because of faction. (Thucydides, 1998, p. 3.14)

Thucydides explicitly attributes the war to the expansion of Athenian power: the "increasing Athenian greatness and the resulting fear among the Lacedaemonians made going to war inevitable" (1998, p. 15). On the basis of this passage, many scholars interpret the Thucydides Trap as signifying that the rising power necessarily clashes with the established hegemon. This interpretation, however, is made from the point of view of the hegemon and serves his interests by portraying emerging powers as the cause of the problem, justifying the actions of established powers in taking military action against them. A less tendentious interpretation is that expansion of the democratic imperialism represented by Athens inevitably forced a reaction from Sparta.

It is a common view among classical scholars that, in the course of the Peloponnesian War, Athens gradually evolved into an expansionist empire (Bruell, 1974; Foster, 2010), and there are three complementary explanations as to why it did so. The first is a political-economic reading such as that of the British classical scholar Cornford (1907, p. 59), who sees in the Athenian state a picture of class antagonism between rural elites, wealthy and conservative aristocrats, radical-minded citizens of the Piraeus harbor area, and poor lower classes. While the elite strata opposed war because they feared destruction, the Piraeus radicals, engaged in industry and commerce, serving as naval oarsmen and with their interests and fate closely bound to sea trade and the navy, favored it. The tragedy was that the latter gradually become the leading force determining Athenian domestic and foreign policy, which led the city-state to embark on the road of imperialist expansion.

A second explanation advanced for the Athenian expansion has to do with the city's national character. Many historians have contended that the cause of Athenian imperialism lay in the "daring" and impetuous nature of the city's population (Forde, 1986; Bluhm, 1962; Connor, 1984, p. 39; Cornford, 1907, p. 167; Ehrenberg, 1947, p. 47; Finley, 1967, p. 143; Shorey, 1893, pp. 72–73; Thibaudet, 1922, pp. 113–114). Indeed, Thucydides repeatedly emphasizes this trait of Athenians in his book. The Athenian general Pericles, for example, is recorded as praising the "daring" character of Athens, considering it responsible for the greatness of the city's empire. Pericles even went so far as to boast that the Athenians had "compelled" every sea and land to allow access to their daring, enabling them to leave "immortal" monuments to themselves "everywhere" (quoted in Forde, 1986, p. 434). It is worth noting that to denote the concept of "daring," Thucydides uses the word *tolma*; this term has a wider semantic scope than "courage," suggesting something close to recklessness. The "daring" of the Athenian character is seen by Thucydides as having three manifestations. First of all, the Athenians as a race are said to be characterized by a native daring that allows them, without effort, to be the equal of others who take great pains to cultivate virtue

(Thucydides, 1998, 2.39.4). Second, the Athenians are said to be "daring" in the sense that they abandoned their city and embarked on their ships, becoming a sea-borne people in the literal sense (Thucydides, 1998, 1.18.2). This experience may have had a profound impact on the formation of the Athenian character, since the people of the city were forced to give up their homeland as well as all their fixed moorings, including the shackles of tradition and piety toward ancestors and gods. This leads to the third manifestation of the Athenians' "daring" character, their "erotic passion." Present in Thucydides' account only as a concealed thread, this concept nevertheless has important implications. As Forde (1986) points out, even though the word *eros* and its derivatives appear only seven times in Thucydides' book, each of these is at a crucial juncture, playing a significant role in the ancient writer's treatment of Athenian imperialism and of the political psychology of Athens (p. 439). The reason is that the Athenians, having largely forsaken the traditional devices used to support community and patriotism, needed to have recourse to extraordinary devices to bind an individualistic, intemperate people together for an imperialist endeavor. These devices included appealing to *eros*, which was "individualistic, even egoistic, yet leads to the most intense devotion and willingness to sacrifice" (Forde, 1986, p. 439). As a result, Athenian imperialism for Thucydides was "compounded out of a volatile combination of erotic passion and daring, qualities woven into the fabric of the Athenian regime." The devotion to democracy was not "dedication to the common good as such, but rather to a kind of private freedom from restrictions of all sorts, a freedom to follow where one's passion might lead" (Forde, 1986, p. 441).[5]

A third explanation advanced for Athenian expansion relates to the city's democratic regime. It is perhaps hard for many in the West to understand how a democracy founded on principles such as liberty, equality, and the rule of law could engage in imperialism. This apparent paradox is explained with some precision by one author who argues that democrats tend to be zealous about their values and institutions, on whose behalf they show a strong compulsion to preach. Understanding this puts us in a better position to appreciate how the Athenians justified their empire. They felt that the empire assured peace and bound together the city's dependencies, protecting them from invasion and rule by dictatorial peoples such as the Persians and helping them to maintain or establish democratic regimes (Romilly, 1963, p. 95). Further, the Athenians also believed that their empire was welcomed by its subjects because the latter were guaranteed more justice by the Athenian rule of law than by naked force (Thucydides, 1998, pp. 1.75.1, 1.77.2). Along with these arguments, proclaimed by the Athenians themselves, Galpin (1983) suggests two further rationales that the Athenians could have used to try to reconcile the contradictions between their internal democracy and external imperial rule. The first is that the Athenians needed the wealth the empire provided if they were to maintain time-consuming democratic practices at home, and the second is that the empire satisfied the domestic need for honor and power; as we saw earlier, this is well captured by Thucydides.

While these explanations tend to explain the Athenian expansion from one perspective only, all of them shed some light on the issue, and together they have the potential to form a full picture. Behind a complex phenomenon such as the emergence of a democratic empire, there are certainly reasons that relate to political economy, national character, and

5 This insight may remind us of Shakespeare's wisdom in capturing the same human nature in his long poem *The Rape of Lucrece*: "while Lust is in his pride, no exclamation can curb his heat or rein his rash desire, till like a jade self-will himself doth tire. (p. 125)"

the political regime. It is in this sense that the three explanations complement each other. For many people, the similarities between the US-led democratic empire and the imperialism led by Athens are no doubt obvious. One could argue that the reasons leading Athens to engage in imperialist expansion also apply to the present-day US. For example, the need of the US empire to exploit overseas markets and resources provides a strong political and economic drive to expansion. Indeed, there are numerous works that criticize the US from this perspective for its launching of the Iraq War. As a national entity that has little attachment to tradition, the US also displays characteristics of daring and impetuosity. This is well demonstrated by the various wars in which the West has engaged under US leadership. There are also striking similarities in the way both the Athenian empire and the US-led Western liberal empire have preached democracy. Even the dilemmas faced by the two empires, and the justifications advanced for their existence, are strikingly analogous.[6] For these reasons, it is not hard to see the logic behind the view that in the case of the Ukraine crisis, the US-led West has fallen into the Thucydides Trap, and has no way out.

These comparisons may be queried. For example, some may object that the Athenian political system cannot be regarded as having been democratic, since it rested on slavery. That is a legitimate question, but one that is resolved if we subscribe to Aristotle's conception of regime types. There are certainly profound differences between the ancient and contemporary regimes, but so long as the defining features are the same, the differences are not decisive. Aristotle's analysis is mainly philosophical in the sense that it transcends local contexts as well as specific eras. For some, the defining features of regimes are whether political power is distributed according to virtue, wealth or freedom, and I think these criteria still apply to contemporary regimes. Modern Western democracies consider that the traditional concept of inner virtue has no place in public affairs and that modern politics should be based on a general franchise of equally free individuals. Certainly, wealth still plays an important role in Western democracy, so the contemporary Western regime could well be taken as a mixture of oligarchy and democracy, something foreseen by Aristotle.

Origins on the "dark side" of the multitude

As well as utilizing the insights of Thucydides to understand the logic behind the Ukraine crisis, we can also turn to the political thought of Spinoza to lend support to this reading. Scott Newton (2006) has written an insightful article analyzing the similarities in the logic behind constitutionalism and imperialism from a Spinoza perspective. For Newton, such a perspective on contemporary world affairs is relevant not only because Spinoza's central preoccupation is with the legal-institutional character of the New World, but also because it is "not just post-Christian and post-liberal, but post-Marxist as well" in its power of inspiring contemporary imaginations.

Viewed from the Spinozan perspective, Western Liberal Constitutionalism and imperialism are deeply interconnected and often go together, because they follow the same logic of power-alienation and institution-entrenchment.[7] The power-alienation and institution-entrenchment dimension of imperialism is not hard to grasp; meanwhile, the case of the

6 The differences between the two states are obvious, but whether these differences suffice to undermine the similar logic of the two cases is another question that would take an extensive article to elaborate.

7 It is worth noting that in the original Latin of Spinoza's works, the term that is variously translated as "state" or "sovereignty" is *imperium*, which may remind us of broad set of analogies between the nature and working mechanisms of a national *imperium* and of a colonial *imperium*.

constitutional state demands closer examination. First of all, there is inevitably a "bunch of guys" who "man" (the terminological gender is not accidental for obvious reasons) and instrumentalize the institutions, standing over the people governed (Newton, 2006). That is why Newton contends that Lincoln's famous, endlessly invoked slogan "government of the people, for the people, *by the people*" (italics added), even while sounding good, makes only limited sense. According to Newton, constitutions in this regard "are dangerous because they entail the alienation-via-institutionalization of *potentia*,[8] freeze an existing configuration of relations of social power in institutions immunized against change and deform or constrain the development of political subjectivity" (Newton, 2006, p. 332). Spinoza is aware of the "affective and rational necessity of juridical institutions, as indispensable building materials of political imagination and reason," but he is more concerned about "their false transcendence, their capacity to bewitch the multitude and lull the learned, to appear on high or over against us, in the awe-inspiring but imaginary majesty of *potestas*, with its residual aura of divinity" (Newton, 2006, p. 331). For Spinoza, this "core of mystification is extraordinarily resilient, and the ideological effects it exercises are extraordinarily powerful," operating "through the doctrine and practice of constitutionalism, which runs the risk of the fetishization and reification of constitutions" (Newton, 2006, p. 334). The current worldwide zeal for Western Liberal Constitutionalism would then be a good example of such a mystification and fetishization.

Besides this explanation, drawing on Spinoza, of what Habermas termed "constitutional patriotism,"[9] another crucial linkage between imperialism and constitutionalism has to do with their common origin in the concept of the "multitude." Within Spinoza's political thought, this is a central and notably complex idea. For purposes of simplification, the multitude may "be conceived as a generative matrix for collective and individual political subjectivity, a uniquely plastic and totipotent (in the embryological sense) social 'tissue'" (Newton, 2006, p. 349). In plainer language, it may be taken as equivalent to the "mass," which is the defining class base of contemporary liberal democracies, echoing Aristotle's political theory as reviewed earlier. It is thus conceivable that the mass part of a society might be better able than the elite part of that society to provoke, echo, invoke, or unite the similar mass part of another society, since this is determined by their nature. The mass has neither the virtue nor the knowledge required to engage in sober reflection and self-constraint. To borrow the vivid terminology of Spinozan physics, the situation is conditioned by "a matter of adjacency that is both physical and political"; it arises "when numerous bodies find themselves adjacent to one another in space that thereby becomes common" (Newton, 2006, p. 350).

This metaphorical reading of the concept of "multitude" is quite instructive if we are to understand the Ukraine crisis in the context of the US-led Western empire. Just as Newton (2006) points out,

> Nothing, then, theoretically limits the magnitude of the multitude. . . . It is a capacity that is inherent in the sheer force, the *potentia* itself, of the multitude. Bodies can unite,

8 *Potentia* and *potestas* are two crucial and complicated concepts of Spinoza's political thought, but for the sake of simplicity, the former may be taken as "constituting power" and the latter as "constituted power."

9 Constitutional patriotism is the idea that people should form a political attachment to the norms and values of a pluralistic liberal democratic constitution, rather than to a national culture or cosmopolitan society. Habermas played a key role in developing and contextualizing the idea of constitutional patriotism and in spreading the idea to English-speaking countries. See Müller and Scheppele (2008).

> and the bodies that those united bodies form can unite in their turn. The only limits to a multitude would be physical. . . . The only ultimate physical limits are those of the globe itself. . . . Thus, viewed in relation to the multitude's *potentiae*, the demarcation of territory is always just artificial or conventional (p. 350).

As a result, we have witnessed the emergence of an empire as a new form of imperialism in today's globalized world, which is "capillary, horizontal, acephalous, rhizomatic, and emphatically not metropolitan"; it is "not sited anywhere: it is everywhere" (Newton, 2006, 355). That is why Newton (2006) maintains:

> Imperialism, then and now, is constitutionalism, then and now, writ large. . . . If Imperialism in the late and post-colonial phase had become a motor for the propagation of individual, local "constitutionalisms" rather than one grand metropolitan version, the arrival of Empire witnesses an unprecedented renewal of pressures on "local constitutionalisms" for convergence on a very limited set of institutional models. . . . Constitutionalism lives and thrives as never before, for better and worse. The force of juridification, the fetishization and reification of particular institutional arrangements, endures (pp. 326, 354–355).

Lessons to be learned

This analysis allows us to see why the Ukraine crisis is the West's fault and why the blundering has been inevitable. These conclusions follow compellingly if we diagnose each event through locating and comprehending it in relation to the deeper historical trend of which it is part, rather than contenting ourselves with superficial investigations. If we remain at the surface level, then, as Russian novelist Leo Tolstoy suggests, we will find that "an incalculable number of causes present themselves . . . and each separate cause or whole series of causes appears to us equally valid in itself and equally false by its insignificance compared to the magnitude of the events" (quoted in Burns, 2003, p. 14). If we want to understand events accurately and insightfully, we need to delve into the sources, capture the main trends, and hence avoid being misled by the nuances.

The mass prejudices of the Western mainstream, of course, are not easily overcome. Near four decades ago, another Russian novelist, the Nobel laureate Alexander Solzhenitsyn (1980, p. 59) commented on the deeply held prejudices of the West:

> [the mass media] gives birth to strong mass prejudices, to a blindness which is perilous in our dynamic era. An example is the self-deluding interpretation of the state of affairs in the contemporary world that functions as a sort of a petrified armor around people's minds, to such a degree that human voices from seventeen countries of Eastern Europe and Eastern Asia cannot pierce it. It will be broken only by the inexorable crowbar of events.

For some, the 9–11 terrorist attack, the chaos of the Iraq War, and so forth, have all failed to break the "petrified armor around people's minds." That is why Solzhenitsyn (1980, p. 172) contends that "The West is very afraid of hearing the truth – any truth. The West is much given to reassuring self-deception." These judgments, though made some decades ago, are still capable of provoking our further reflection and introspection.

Meanwhile, the similarity between Athenian imperialism and the workings of today's US-led Western empire have to be considered striking and deserving of further research. Just as the example of ancient Athens signifies for us a regime that sought to extend individual freedom to the widest scope possible, "the liberal-individualist tradition [of today] sets few roadblocks and signposts to the legitimation of wants as needs because its very credo validates the rights of humans to break through restrictions" (Burns, 2003, 144–145).

Finally, we should be mindful of this perspective and prepare for the worst possible scenario. Perhaps it is wise for me to conclude this article with the vivid words of Nietzsche (1998, p. 18):

> Let's submit to the facts: the people were victorious – or "the slaves," or "the mob," or "the herd," or whatever you like to call them . . .[10] there never has been a people had a more world-historic mission. "The lords" are cast off; the morality of the common man has been victorious. . . . The "redemption" of the human race (namely from "the lords") is well under way; everything is Jewifying or Christifying or mobifying as we watch (what do the words matter!). The progress of this poisoning through the entire body of humanity appears unstoppable, from now on its tempo and step may be slower, more refined, less audible, more thoughtful – one has time after all.

The hope, as Nietzsche (2002) suggests, is that

> There are heights of the soul from which even tragedy ceases to look tragic; and rolling together all the woe of the world – who could dare to decide whether its sight would necessarily seduce us and compel us to feel pity and thus double this woe? (Part Two, Section 30)

Our task, perhaps, is to seek to attain this height of the soul!

10 For Nietzsche, the words "people," "slaves," "mob," "the herd," "Christians" and "Jewish" all imply the same referent, which is similar to Spinoza's usage of the term "multitude." I should point out here that I neither share nor support Nietzsche's anti-Jewish attitudes and sentiments.

Appendix

Zhuangzi's view of non-action as the panacea of peace

Introduction

Even though the world has entered the new millennium near two decades ago, it does not seem to be more peaceful than before. No matter whether we consider the Iraq and Afghanistan wars in the early stage, or the uprisings and changes of the Middle East and North Africa in the past years, or the emergence of right-wing extremism throughout the world, there are reasons for a pessimistic view towards the prospect of peace in the 21st century. Nevertheless, people seem not to have found the real root of the various conflicts and wars. Perhaps, as some great thinkers such as Toynbee, Shaw, and Tagore have pointed out, humanity must seek answers from ancient Chinese thought if it wants to avoid committing suicide. This short appendix marks such an attempt in this direction by first introducing Zhuangzi's view on right and wrong and then seeking inspiration from it for understanding and maintaining world peace today.

Zhuangzi's view on right and wrong[1]

Regarding right and wrong, Zhuangzi may seem to be a relativist, since his writings are full of passages that have challenged and subverted various conventional norms; nevertheless, if we study his words carefully, we may find that he is actually an absolutist, which is well shown in his statement that "non-action could serve as the ultimate judge of right and wrong" ("Ultimate Joy" chapter of *Zhuangzi*). What is Zhuangzi's actual view on right and wrong? What does he mean by "non-action"? These are the questions this section will seek to explore.

In order to understand Zhuangzi's view on right and wrong, it is crucial to first clarify his distinction between the human and the heavenly. For Zhuangzi, right and wrong is only a matter of the human realm, rather than the heavenly realm. The two realms are very distinct, with the former following an active yet base rule while the latter following a non-action yet venerable rule. In Zhuangzi's view, all the norms we have taken for granted, such as right and wrong, benevolence and justice, are concepts of the human realm rather than the heavenly realm. The heavenly realm has transcended these values and could only be borne by the sage-kings. The concepts closely related to the heavenly realm include "Chaos," the "Way," "non-action," "Empty and Tranquil," and so on.

1 Zhuangzi is an influential Chinese philosopher who lived around the 4th century BC during the Warring States Period.

Zhuangzi's view on right and wrong is well elaborated in his "Qiwu Chapter." In a nutshell, Zhuangzi thinks that all things have their realities and merits, and there is nothing that does not have some merits. For him, all things have their opposites, and one could not have a clear view if one only focused on its opposite and forgot itself. True knowledge thus requires self-knowledge. From a non-static view, the two sides are also mutually transforming towards the opposite side, just as the birth of a new thing also marks the beginning of its journey towards death. Zhuangzi calls that which does not have an opposite the Pivot of the Way and thinks that only it could respond to all the situations. For all other things, either side has its right and wrong, which could be endless, so the best way of judgment is to have a dialectic view of it.

Zhuangzi's elaboration here is actually quite profound in meaning. First of all, he resonates Laozi's dialectic thought as well shown in the *Daodejing*, especially in its chapter 2. Second, Zhuangzi also reveals the secret principle of the opposite sides' mutual transformations, just as that of the yin and yang. Finally, due to the incompatibility of each side's right and wrong, Zhuangzi suggests that one could only transcend this by adopting a heavenly perspective, which is equivalent to the Western notion of the "God's Eye" perspective. This perspective will thus take a non-action approach and just let all things evolve according to their nature.

Another characteristic of Zhuangzi's view on right and wrong is that they could not be discovered through argumentation. Just as Zhuangzi vividly asks, if two persons engage in a debate, and one wins in the arguments, does that mean the winner is right and the loser wrong? Does it mean that one must be right and the other wrong, or are both right and both wrong? How could we find someone to be a fair judge, since he might take only one of the four positions, namely agreeing with one side, agreeing with the other side, agreeing with both sides, or disagreeing with both sides, which are equally unable to let him or her be an objective judge. Therefore, there will be no fruit for debates, and the opposition in arguments will not be able to stand just like the opposition in things themselves could not stand.[2] If a value is truly right, and a thing is genuinely authentic, their rightness and authenticity then require no argumentation. As a result, the best thing we can do is to follow their nature and let them all evolve accordingly. That is why Zhuangzi thinks the best strategy towards argumentation is to remain silent, and the best way to determine right and wrong is to take no action. These are then Zhuangzi's thoughts on right and wrong, and next, we will have a look at world peace from this perspective.

Zhuangzi on world peace today

There is perhaps little question that today's world is not very peaceful, but people disagree on the causes of the various conflicts and wars. It is true that any historical event is caused by myriad causes, as Tolstoy points out at the end of *War and Peace*, but we perhaps could agree that the assertion of each side's right and wrong is a major factor. As Zhuangzi says,

> [T]he sage does not have conflicts because he does not stick to/assert the universal truth, even though it is most justified, while the common people are often in conflicts because they hold non-universal knowledge yet assert them to be universal.
>
> ("Lieyukou chapter" of *Zhuangzi*)

2 For Zhuangzi, things do not oppose to each other, since at a very abstract level, they are all the same; this is the main idea of his "Qiwu" (齐物) thesis.

If we review the major wars that have occurred in the past 10 years, we can see that the assertion of right and wrong has played a significant role. But where do those right and wrong views come from? To a large extent, they come from their respective cultures and civilizations. This actually echoes Huntington's forecast that the main conflicts of the 21st century will largely be conflicts between civilizations. Nevertheless, Huntington failed to realize that the actual cause of the conflicts along cultural lines is actually the spreading of Western civilization. Next, we will elaborate such a reading based on Zhuangzi's thoughts.

If we look around the major civilizations of the world, we could say that Western civilization is the most assertive and perhaps even the most zealous about its notion of right and wrong to some extent. Here Western civilization is a loose and overarching concept covering the civilization that is pillared on Judaism, Christianity, and Islam. The assertive and zealous nature of Western civilization is partly due to the impact of its religions' monotheism. For the European-American civilization developed from the base of Christianity, which we conventionally call the "Western civilization," its philosophical tradition of epistemology also further reinforces the assertiveness and extremism. On this, Nietzsche has provided a sophisticated analysis in his *Genealogy of Morality*. For example, in it, he shows how the ancient Greek philosophers have secretly transformed the previously dialectic yet uniting relationship of "good and bad" into the mutually exclusive relationship of "good and evil." In his diagnosis of the English Civil War, Hobbes also traces the root back to the philosophical tradition inherited from ancient Greece. One of the major reasons, according to Hobbes, is the over-reliance of the philosophical tradition on logic and speech, and one of the pitfalls of this epistemology is the assertiveness of their painstakingly discovered results. For Hobbes and others who hold a similar view, the poetic tradition of epistemology of the East is certainly more open and flexible. Nevertheless, very few in the world today seem to have realized this vital difference.

A further problem is that each perspective could develop a self-sufficient knowledge system, which is hard to break from outside. For example, on the matter of right and wrong, the West has a great deal of very sophisticated elaboration as well as proofs of the universal nature of their norms. As a result, the mainstream in the West does not agree with Zhuangzi that there is no universal standard regarding values, and in their eyes, the main problem has to do with dictators or authoritarian governments that try to prevent their people from embracing the Western universal norms. Regarding "non-action," the West also thinks that its "small government/big society" mode is closer to this principle and points to the various freedoms the Western people enjoy as well as the popularity of the West as the destination of foreign immigrants as evidence. Nevertheless, the "non-action" of the West actually has some fundamental problems. First of all, in their sub-conscience, sometime in their actions, they usually despise those who do not share their universal norms, and even have the instinct to annihilate them if they not only do not accept, but also oppose their values as well as rulings. Even in the "original position" of John Rawls' thought experiment, those who do not subscribe to a minimal standard of liberal democratic norms are considered "unreasonable" despite the fact that they could still be rational, and consequently they need to be dictated or exiled. Second, if they do use Zhuangzi's non-action principle to justify liberal democratic norms, they then fundamentally miss Zhuangzi's original intentions. In fact, Zhuangzi's non-action principle has a vital prerequisite, which is that no negative forces should influence the health of the people's body and mind. That is why Zhuangzi warns the rulers not to disturb the people's mind-heart but to censor carefully those materials that could have an impact on them. If we recall the action of Socrates, the founder of Western civilization, who often went out to the street to challenge and subvert conventional opinions among the youth, as well as the former Soviet Union Nobel laureate Solzhenitsyn's condemnation of the Western media's dumping of trivial gossips and vulgarity into people's innocent minds, (Solzhenitsyn, 1980, p. 52) we would not be surprised by the distance between those two versions of the "non-action" principle. In an era when market forces particularly stimulate the lower instincts and desires of people, the non-action of the government actually means evading responsibility, with serious long-lasting harm.

If we trace back into a deeper level, we could find that the problem of the West lies with its confinement to the human realm in a dualistic "heaven-human" framework. They could not transcend the thought mode and norms of the human realm and, hence, cannot be silent and non-active as the heavenly way demands. Again, the difference between the human realm and the heavenly realm is like that between the petty men's realm and the sages' realm. This distinction's manifestation today would be the assertiveness of the superiority of "human rights" over sovereignty, as well as the instinct of "new interventionism." In fact, the founders of America actually had set the goal of the US as the "lighthouse" of the world following a non-action principle. This is why the then US president told the Greeks during their war of independence against the Ottoman empire that the US's heart will be with them, but it does not go out to seek and destroy the monsters (Kissinger, 2002, p. 238). Nevertheless, US foreign policy has since then deviated more and more from its "non-action" principle: first came the carving out and intervention of the Western Hemisphere through the "Monroe Doctrine" and the "Roosevelt Corollary"; then emerged the proposal of the Wilson administration for full involvement in world affairs, which was not realized until the end of World War II; and finally America's full determination to search for monsters and have them destroyed worldwide. The evolving trajectory of US foreign policy cannot be more obvious. If we subscribe to Zhuangzi's view that only "non-action" could serve as the ultimate judge of right and wrong, the deep root of the world's peace problem is then clear. Seen from this perspective, the Chinese government's consistent "non-interventionism" as well as its emphasis of winning the world through moral example then would serve as a good contrast and reference. This is certainly worth more consideration by the world.

Conclusion

To sum up, we have first reviewed Zhuangzi's view on right and wrong and its basis in the human-heaven distinction, as well as its irrelevance to argumentation and then discussed the assertive tendency of Western civilization and its self-sufficient system, as well as its confinement to the human realm, as the major cause of the challenges world peace currently faces. From this perspective, we could have three inspirations. First of all, we should make great efforts to advocate Zhuangzi's "non-action principle" as the norm of the world community. This principle echoes certain principles of the UN Charter, but it is unclear how much of it could still be followed by the Western countries. Certainly this challenge is partly due to the impracticability of the principle in today's globalized world. Second, we should promote communications between cultures and civilizations. "As the pi (否) and tai (泰) hexagrams of the I Ching reveal, communication would bring harmony while closeness could only result in conflicts. Nevertheless, even though we could hope for the best, we need to be realistic, and this leads to the third inspiration we could draw, namely to have a realistic forecast of world situations. Given that the Western leadership is not justified from the Zhuangzi perspective, we could then expect that disobedience as well as objection would become more common as the processes of globalization further spread Western norms throughout the world. For this, we should have a clear mind as well as good preparations.

References

Ackerly, B. A. (2005). Is liberalism the only way toward democracy? Confucianism and democracy. *Political Theory*, *33*(4), 547–576.

Adams, M., & van der Schyff, G. (2010). Political theory put to the test: Comparative law and the origins of judicial constitutional review. *Global Jurist*, *10*(2), 1–37.

Angle, S. C. (2005). Decent democratic centralism. *Political Theory*, *33*(4), 518–546.

Aristotle. (1984). *The politics* (C. Lord, Trans.). Chicago: University of Chicago Press.

Backer, L. C. (2008). God(s) over constitutions: International and religious transnational constitutionalism in the 21st century. *Mississippi College Law Review*, *27*.

Backer, L. C. (2009a). From constitution to constitutionalism: A global framework for legitimate public power systems. *Penn State Law Review*, *113*, 671–732.

Backer, L. C. (2009b). The party as polity, the communist party, and the Chinese constitutional state: A theory of state-party constitutionalism. *Journal of Chinese and Comparative Law*, *16*(1), 101–165.

Backer, L. C. (2009c, Winter). Theocratic constitutionalism: An introduction to a new global legal ordering. *Indiana Journal of Global Legal Studies*, *16*(1), 85–172.

Backer, L. C. (2010). A constitutional court for China within the Chinese Communist Party: Scientific development and a reconsideration of the institutional role of the Communist Party of China. *Suffolk University Law Review*, *43*(3), 593–624.

Balme, S., & Dowdle, M. W. (Eds.). (2009). *Building constitutionalism in China*. New York: Palgrave Macmillan.

Bao, W. (1998). Confucianism and Protestantism: The native complex and cultural resistance of constitutional construction in the past century (儒教与新教：百年宪政建设的本土情节与文化抵抗). *Peking University Law Review* (北大法律评论), *1*(2), 505–575.

Bell, D. A. (2008). *China's new Confucianism: Politics and everyday life in a changing society*. Princeton, NJ: Princeton University Press.

Benewick, R. (1998). Towards a developmental theory of constitutionalism: The Chinese case. *Government and Opposition*, *33*(4), 442–461.

Bluhm, W. T. (1962). Causal theory in Thucydides' Peloponnesian War. *Political Studies*, *10* (1): 15–35.

Bosse, G. (2014). The eastern partnership and the disintegration of Eastern Europe: The end of the region-building project? *European View*, *13*(1): 97–108.

Brady, J. P. (1982). *Justice and politics in People's China: Legal order or continuing revolution*. London: Academic Press.

Bruell, C. (1974). Thucydides' view of Athenian Imperialism. *The American Political Science Review*, *68*(1): 11–17.

Burns, J. M. (2003). *Transforming leadership: A new pursuit of happiness*. New York: Grove Press.

Cabestan, J. (2005). The political and practical obstacles to the reform of the judiciary and the establishment of a rule of law in China. *Journal of Chinese Political Science*, *10*(1), 43–64.

Cai, D., & Wang, C. (Eds.). (2010). *China's journey toward the rule of law: Legal reform, 1978–2008.* Leiden, Netherlands & Boston, MA: Brill.

Chaibong, H. (2001). Confucian rituals and the technology of the self: A Foucaultian interpretation. *Philosophy East and West, 51*(3), 315–324.

Chaihark, H. (2003). Constitutionalism, Confucian civic virtue, and ritual propriety. In D. A. Bell, & H. Chaibong (Eds.), *Confucianism for the modern world* (pp. 31–53). Cambridge, UK: Cambridge University Press.

Chaihark, H. (2009). Ritual and constitutionalism: Disputing the ruler's legitimacy in a Confucian polity. *American Journal of Comparative Law, 57*(1), 135–204.

Chan, J. (2007). Democracy and meritocracy: Toward a Confucian perspective. *Journal of Chinese Philosophy, 34*(2), 179–193. doi:10.1111/j.1540-6253.2007.00408.x

Charter 08. (2008). *Unpublished manuscript.* Retrieved August 14, 2011, from www.2008xianzhang.info/

Cheminant, W. L., & Parrish, J. M. (Eds.). (2011). *Manipulating democracy: Democratic theory, political psychology, and mass media.* New York: Routledge.

Chen, A. H. Y. (2007). Is Confucianism compatible with liberal constitutional democracy? *Journal of Chinese Philosophy, 34*(2), 195–216. doi:10.1111/j.1540-6253.2007.00409.x

Chen, F. (2003). *The research outline of Chinese constitutional history (*中国宪政史研究纲要*).* Guiyang: Guizhou People's Press.

Chen, G. (2009). On intuitionism in ancient China's legislation (浅议中国古代立法中的直觉思维). *Hebei Law Studies, 27*(8), 190–194.

Chen, H. (2004). Some reflections on the problem of constitutionalism (关于宪政问题若干思考). *Political Studies, 3*, 1–11.

Chen, M. (2008). On Confucianism and constitutionalism (儒家思想与宪政主义试说). *Journal of Hunan University (Social Sciences) (*湖南大学学 *(*社会科学版*))*, *6*, 17–20.

Chen, X., & Jin, Y. (2009). People-centered: Centered on what kinds of people and what of a person (以人为本: 以"什么样的人"和"人的什么" 为本?). *Marxist Philosophy, 8*, 15–21.

Cheng, C. (2000). The origins of Chinese philosophy. In B. Carr, & I. Mahalingam (Eds.), *Companion encyclopedia of Asian philosophy* (pp. 493–534). New York: Routledge.

Cheng, Y. (2008). Liberalism in contemporary China: Ten years after its "resurface". *Journal of Contemporary China, 17*(55), 383–400.

Chinese Government. White paper of the News Office of the State Council. (2008). The Building Up of China's Rule of Law (中国的法治建设).

Chu, J. (2006). *One-party constitutionalism: The new path of Chinese constitutionalism (*一党立宪：中国宪政新路*).* Retrieved November 10, 2010, from http://chinaelections.net/newsinfo.asp?newsid=99982

Chu, Y., Diamond, L., & Nathan, A. J. (Eds.). (2008). *How East Asians view democracy.* New York: Columbia University Press.

Clarke, D. C. (2008). *China's legal system: New developments, new challenges.* Cambridge, UK: Cambridge University Press.

Connor, W. R. (1984). *Thucydides.* Princeton: Princeton University Press.

Constitution. (2009). In *Encyclopedia Britannica.* Retrieved June 23, 2009, from Encyclopedia Britannica Online at search.eb.com/eb/article-22061

Cornford, F. M. (1907). *Thucydides Mythistoricus.* London: Edward Arnold.

Dai, B. (2010). Persist in taking the peaceful development path (坚持走和平发展道路). *Contemporary World, 12*, 4–8.

Dallmayr, F. (Ed.). (2010). *Comparative political theory: An introduction.* Hampshire, UK: Palgrave Macmillan.

Davis, M. C. (1998). Constitutionalism and political culture: The debate over human rights and Asian values. *Harvard Human Rights Journal, 11*, 109–147.

De Luca, T., & Buell, J. (2005). *Liars! Cheaters! Evildoers!: Demonization and the end of civil debate in American politics.* New York: New York University Press.

Deneen, P. J. (2005). *Democratic faith.* Princeton, NJ: Princeton University Press.

Deng, Lilan (邓丽兰). (2010). *Western thoughts and the evolution of republican constitutional movements (《西方思潮与民国宪政运动的演进》).* Tianjing: Nankai University Press.
Dennehy, R. L. (2007). The illusion of freedom separated from moral virtue. *Journal of Interdisciplinary Studies, 19*(1/2), 19.
Douzinas, C. (2000). *The end of human rights: Critical legal thought at the turn of the century.* Portland, OR: Hart Publishing.
Du, D. (2003). From the principle within a thing to the essence felt from its aroma: The turn of ancient Chinese intuitionism' objects from philosophy to arts (从"物中之道"到"味外之旨" – 中國古代的直覺思維對象從哲學向藝術的演化). *Chinese Culture Research, 4,* 106–114.
Dunn, J. (2005). *Setting the people free: The story of democracy.* London: Atlantic Books.
Dynon, N. (2008, July). "Four civilizations" and the evolution of post-Mao Chinese socialist ideology. *The China Journal, 60,* 83–109.
Ehrenberg, V. (1968). *From Solon to Socrates.* London: Methuen & Co.
Fan, R. (Ed.). (2008). *The Confucian society and renaissance of Dao: Dialogues with Jiang Qing (儒家社会与道统复兴 – 与蒋庆对话).* Shanghai (上海): Eastern Normal University of China Publishing House (华东师大出版社).
Fang, Ke-li (方克立). (2006). Three letters about the current problem of neo-Confucianism on the mainland (关于当前大陆新儒学问题的三封信). *Academic Exploration (学术探索), 2.*
Fang, K. (2010). Marxist soul, Chinese *ti* and Western *yong*: A realistic path of China's cultural development ("馬魂、中體、西用":中國文化發展的現實道路). *Beijing University Journal (Philosophy and Social Science), 4.*
Fang, S. (2011). *Chinese model in essence is a "new republicanism" ("中国模式"本质上是一种"新共和制").* Retrieved May 30, 2011, from www.chinaelections.org/NewsInfo.asp?NewsID=203223
Finley, J. H. Jr. (1967). *Three essays on Thucydides.* Cambridge, MA: Harvard University Press.
Forde, S. (1986). Thucydides on the causes of Athenian Imperialism. *The American Political Science Review, 80*(2): 433–448.
Foster, E. (2010). *Thucydides, Pericles, and Periclean Imperialism.* Cambridge: Cambridge University Press.
Frank, J. (2006). Aristotle on constitutionalism and the rule of law. *Theoretical Inquiries in Law, 8*(37), 37–50.
Fung, E. S. K. (2008–2009, Winter). Were Chinese liberals liberal? Reflections on the understanding of liberalism in modern China. *Pacific Affairs, 81*(4), 557–576.
Gadamer, H. (2004). *Truth and method* (2nd ed., J. Weinsheimer, & D. G. Marshall, Trans.) London & New York: Continuum.
Galpin, T. J. (1983). The democratic roots of Athenian Imperialism in the fifth century BC." *The Classical Journal, 79*(2): 100–109.
Gao, J., & Tong, D. (Eds.). (2010). *Chinese style democracy (中国式民主).* Tianjing: Tianjing People's Press.
Geertz, C. (1977). *The interpretation of cultures.* New York: Basic Books.
Gilley, B., & Holbig, H. (2009). The debate on party legitimacy in China: A mixed quantitative/qualitative analysis. *Journal of Contemporary China, 18*(59), 339–358.
Ginsburg, T. (2002). Confucian constitutionalism? The emergence of constitutional review in Korea and Taiwan. *Law and Social Inquiry, 27*(4), 763–799.
Goldberg, J. (2011). *Hillary Clinton: Chinese system is doomed, leaders on a "fool's errand".* Retrieved May 27, 2011, from www.theatlantic.com/international/archive/2011/05/hillary-clinton-chinese-system-is-doomed-leaders-on-a-fools-errand/238591/
Gordon, S. (1999). *Controlling the state: Constitutionalism from ancient Athens to today.* Cambridge, MA: Harvard University Press.
Gunde, R. (2003). *Distinguished Chinese political activists discuss constitutionalism & political reform: Noted "neo-liberals" ponder the choices facing China.* Retrieved November 10, 2010, from www.international.ucla.edu/asia/article.asp?parentid=3243

Han, D. (2005). *A study of the constitutionalism of new democracy (《新民主主义宪政研究》)*. Beijing: People's Press.

Han, D. (2007). *Initial exploration of the categories of Marxist political philosophy* （《马克思主义政治哲学诸范畴初探》）. Changchun: Jilin Publishing Corporation.

Han, D. (2008). *The 1954 Constitution and Chinese constitutionalism (《1954 年宪法与中国宪政》)*. Wuhan: Wuhan University Press.

He, B. (2010). Constitutionalism and transcending the competition of the left and the right (宪政和超越左右之争). *Jinyang Journal*, *4*, 21–24.

He, X. (2009). Administrative law as a mechanism for political control in contemporary China. In S. Balme, & M. W. Dowdle (Eds.), *Building constitutionalism in China* (pp. 143–161). New York: Palgrave Macmillan.

Hermeneutic circle. (2004). In Nicholas Bunnin, & Jiyuan Yu (Eds.), *Blackwell reference online [The Blackwell dictionary of Western philosophy]*, Blackwell Publishing. Retrieved May 11, 2011, from www.blackwellreference.com/subscriber/tocnode?id=g9781405106795_chunk_g97814051067959_ss1-42

Hipkin, B. (1984). Book review of justice and politics in People's China: Legal order or continuing revolution by James P. Brandy. *Journal of Law and Society*, *11*(1), 124–127.

Holloway, K. W. (2009). *Guodian: The newly discovered seeds of Chinese religious and political philosophy*. New York: Oxford University Press.

Hou, H. (2010). *Marx's ideological critique and contemporary China (马克思的意识形态批判与当代中国)*. Beijing: China Social Science Press.

Hou, Y. (2009). *The political reform in early 20th century's China: The history of the late Qing Constitutional Movement (《二十世纪初中国政治改革风潮：清末立宪运动史》)*. Beijing: Renmin University of China Press.

Hucker, C. O. (1959). Confucianism and the Chinese censorial system. In D. S. Nivison, & A. F. Wright (Eds.), *Confucianism in action* (pp. 182–208). Stanford, CA: Stanford University Press.

Ivanhoe, P. J. (2007). Heaven as a source for ethical warrant in early Confucianism. *Dao: A Journal of Comparative Philosophy*, *6*(3), 211–220.

Ivanhoe, P. J. (2000). *Confucian moral self cultivation* (2nd ed.). Indianapolis, IN: Hackett Publishing Company.

Jiang, Q. (2009). Reflections on "Confucian theocratic constitutionalism" (关于"儒教宪政"的思考). Paper presented at *Reform, opening up and China's future: The principles, value, motivation, and contemporary exploration of Confucianism* (改革开放与中国前途 –儒家的义理，价值，动力及当代探索) Qufu, Shandong (山东曲阜).

Jiang, S. (2009). The unwritten constitution of Chinese constitution: A new perspective to understand Chinese constitution (中国宪法中的不成文宪法 – 理解中国宪法的新视角). *Opening Times (开放时代)*, *12*, 10–39.

Jiang, W. (2011). *Has Wen Jiabao decided to leave the stage? (温家宝去意已决？)*. Retrieved May 23, 2011, from www.chinainperspective.org/ArtShow.aspx?AID=11250

Jiang, Y. (1997). *The Great Ming Code: A cosmological instrument for transforming "all under heaven."* (Unpublished dissertation, University of Minnesota, Minneapolis).

Jiang, Y. (2007). The current situation and future of liberalism (自由主义的处境与未来). *Intellectuals*. Volume 7. Retrieved June 5, 2018, from http://www.aisixiang.com/data/22736.html.

Jin, G., & Liu, Q. (2010). *A study of conceptual history: The formation of the important political concepts of modern China* (《观念史研究：中国现代重要政治术语的形成》). Beijing: Law Press.

Jin, G., Liu, Q., & Lam, L. (2005). From "republicanism" to "democracy": China's selective adoption and reconstruction of modern Western political concepts (1840–1924). *History of Political Thought*, *26*(3), 468–501.

Jing, Y. (2007). Representative theory and Chinese politics: A study from comparative perspective (代表理論與中國政治 – 一個比較視野下的考察). *Social Science Research*, *3*, 16–21.

Jung, H. Y. (Ed.). (2002). *Comparative political culture in the age of globalization: An introductory anthology*. Lanham, MD: Lexington Books.
Killion, M. U. (2003). China and neo-liberal constitutionalism. *Global Jurist Frontiers*, *3*(2), 1–48.
Kim, J. (2007). Tuning: Constitutional emplotment under the Confucian rule of ritual. *The 65th Annual Conference of the Midwest Political Science Association*, Chicago.
Kim, S. (2009). Self-transformation and civil society: Lockean vs. Confucian. *Dao: A Journal of Comparative Philosophy*, *8*(4), 383–402.
Kissinger, H. *Does America Need A Foreign Policy? Toward A Diplomacy for the 21st Century*. New York: Simon & Schuster, 2002, p. 238.
Kobzová, J. (2014). Can the EU support democracy in the Eastern partnership? *European View*, *13*(1): 109–114.
Kofmel, E. (Ed.). (2008). *Anti-democratic thought*. Exeter, UK: Imprint Academic.
Kupperman, J. J. (2004). Tradition and community in the formation of character and self. In D. Wong, & K. Shun (Eds.), *Confucian ethics: A comparative study of self, autonomy and community* (pp. 103–123). New York: Cambridge University Press.
Legal Studies Institute of the Chinese Academy of Social Sciences. (2008). *Thirty years of China's rule of law (《中国法治30年, 1978–2008》)*. Beijing: Social Science Academic Press.
Legge, J. (1880). *The religions of China: Confucianism and Taoism described and compared with Christianity*. London: Hodder and Stoughton.
Li, B. (2006). *Constitutionalism and China*. Beijing, China: Law Press.
Li, G. (2005). Legal aesthetics as humanistic studies (法美学是人学). In W. Zhang (Ed.), *Forum on the frontier of legal studies* (4th vol., pp. 1–38). Beijing: Science Press.
Li, H. (2001, Spring). The political Stalinization of China: The establishment of one-party constitutionalism, 1948–1954. *Journal of Cold War Studies*, *3*(2), 28–47.
Li, L., & Zhu, K. (2005). The transcendental dimension of constitutionalism and the constitutional meaning of "people-centredness" (宪政的超越之维 – – 兼论"以人为本"的宪政意义). *The Journal of Henan Politics and Law Cadre Management School*, *1*.
Lin, F. (2000). *Constitutional law in China*. Hong Kong: Sweet & Maxwell Asia.
Lin, L., & Zhu, C. (2009). The conceptual history of Chinese "constitutionalism" (中國式"憲政"的概念發展史). *Tribune of Political Science and Law (政法論壇)*, *27*(3), 38–49.
Ling, J. (2007). Plan the domestic and the international grand games in one entirety (统筹国内国际两个大局). *Study of Party-Building*, *11*, 69–75.
Liu, C. (2009). *The isomorphism of the heart and the king: A prototypal study of the history of ancient Chinese political thought (《心君同构 – 中国古代政治思想史的一种原型范畴分析》)*. Tian Jing: Nan Kai University Press.
Liu, J., & Yang, Z. (2004). "People-centredness" and constitutional civilization (以人为本与宪政文明). *Jiangxi Social Science*, *5*.
Lu, Y. (2010, November 3). *Hong Kong professors: Liu Xiaobo represents war not peace (香港教授：刘晓波代表战争而非和平)*. Retrieved November 25, 2010, from www.voanews.com/chinese/news/20101103-Liu-Xiaobo-stand-war-not-peace-106614033.html
Lubman, S. (2000). *Bird in a cage: Legal reform in China after Mao*. Stanford, CA: Stanford University Press.
Luo, H., & Song, G. (2009). *Soft law is also law: Public governance calls for rule of soft law (软法亦法:公共治理呼唤软法之治)*. Beijing: Law Press.
Ma, X. (2006). Reflection on China's one hundred years' constitutionalism (百年中国宪政反思). *Shanghai Normal University Journal (Philosophy and Social Science Edition)*, *35*(4), 30–41.
Maddox, G. (1989). Constitution. In T. Ball, J. Farr, & R. L. Hanson (Eds.), Political Innovation and Conceptual Change. Cambridge: Cambridge University Press, pp. 50–89.
Maletz, D. J. (2002, August). Tocqueville's tyranny of the majority reconsidered. *The Journal of Politics*, *64*(3), 741–763.
Marx, K. (1994). *Marx's selected writings* (Simon Ed.). Indianapolis, US: Hackett Publishing Company.

Mearsheimer, J. (2014). Why the Ukraine Crisis is the West's fault: The liberal delusions that provoked Putin. *Foreign Affairs*, September–October, 1–12.

Milbank, J., & Pabst, A. (2015, April 13). *The downward spiral*. Retrieved November 19, 2016, from the European Magazine at www.theeuropean-magazine.com/john-milbank/10019-the-meta-crisis-of-liberalism

Mo, J. (2003). The challenge of accountability: Implications of the censorate. In D. A. Bell, & H. Chaibong (Eds.), *Confucianism for the modern world* (pp. 54–68). Cambridge, UK: Cambridge University Press.

Newton, S. (2006). Constitutionalism and imperialism *sub specie Spinozae. Law Critique*, *17*, 325–355.

Ni, D. (2009). *A study of sinicization of Marxism* (马克思主义中国化研究）. Beijing: Central Documents Publishing House.

Ni, L. (1996). The censorship system and power checking mechanism of ancient China (中国古代监察制度与权力制衡机制). *Xinjiang University Journal (Philosophy and Social Science Edition) (《新疆大学学报》（哲学社会科学版））*, *24*(2), 64–65.

Nietzsche, F. (1968). *The will to power* (W. Kaufmann, & R. J. Hollingdale, Trans.). New York: Vintage Books.

Nietzsche, F. (1998). *On the genealogy of morality: A polemic* (M. Clark, & A. J. Swensen, Trans.). Indianapolis, IN: Hackett Publishing Company.

Nietzsche, F. (2002). *Beyond good and evil: Prelude to a philosophy of the future*. Trans. H. Zimmern. Retrieved November 3, 2016. from http://users.compaqnet.be/cn127103/Nietzsche_beyond_good_and_evil/bge_ch2_the_free_spirit.htm.

Nix, S. (2014). Responding to the Russian invasion of Crimea: Policy recommendations for US and European leaders. *European View*, *13*(1), 143–152.

Pan, W. (Ed.). (2009). *Chinese model: Understand the 60 years of PRC*. Beijing: Central Translation and Compilation Press.

Peerenboom, R. (2002). *China's long march toward rule of law*. Cambridge, UK: Cambridge University Press.

Peerenboom, R. (Ed.). (2009). *Judicial independence in China: Lessons for global rule of law promotion* (1st ed.). Cambridge, UK: Cambridge University Press.

Peerenboom, R. (2010). *Social foundations of China's living constitution*. Unpublished manuscript. Retrieved June 5, 2018, from SSRN: https://ssrn.com/abstract=1542463 or http://dx.doi.org/10.2139/ssrn.1542463

The Politics and Law Committee of Communist Party of China Central. (2009). *Socialist legal ideas reader* (社会主义法治理念读本）. Beijing: China Chang'an Press.

Qi, S. (2010). *On the Chinese model* (《中国模式论》）. Beijing: Zhongguo Fangzheng Press.

Qian, Y. (2007). The moral order and social imaginary of Liberalism (自由主义的道德秩序观与社会想象). *Intellectuals*. Volume 7. Retrieved June 5, 2018, from https://www.douban.com/group/topic/29308944/.

Qing, Q., & Ye, H. (2008). *A study of socialist constitutionalism (《社会主义宪政研究》)*. Jinan: Shandong People's Press.

Qiu, Y. (2006). *The history of ancient Chinese censorate system (《中国古代监察制度史》)*. Shanghai: Shanghai People's Press.

Ren, X. (2010). The developmental prospects of socialist constitutionalism with Chinese characteristics-from Mao, Deng to Jiang. *The Theory and Practice of Socialist Constitutionalism with Chinese Characteristics*, Changsha, Hunan, China.

Romilly, J. de. (1963). *Thucydides and Athenian Imperialism*. Translated by P. Thody. New York: Barnes & Noble.

Rousseau, J. (1987). *The basic political writings* (D. A. Cress, Trans.). Indianapolis, IN: Hackett Publishing Company.

Saryusz-Wolski, J. (2014). "Euromaidan: Time to draw conclusions." *European View*, *13*(1), 11–20.

Schaberg, D. (2010). The *Zhouli* as constitutional text. In B. A. Elman, & M. Kern (Eds.), *Statecraft and classical learning: The rituals of Zhou in East Asian history* (pp. 33–63). Leiden, Netherlands: Brill.

Shakespeare, W. (1988). The Complete Works. Oxford, UK: Oxford University Press.

Shambaugh, D. (2008). *China's Communist Party: Atrophy and adaptation.* Oakland, CA: University of California Press.

Shorey, P. ([1893] 2003). On the implicit ethics and psychology of Thucydides. *Transactions of the American Philological Association*, *24*, 66–88.

Shultziner, D. (2003). Human dignity: Functions and meanings. *Global Jurist Topics*, *3*(3).

Solzhenitsyn, A. I. (1980). *East and west.* New York: Perennial Library.

Song, J. (2009). The *Zhouli* 《周禮》 and constitutionalism: A Southern Song political theory. *Journal of Chinese Philosophy*, *36*(3), 424–438.

Sun, J., & Feng Yong (冯勇). (2010). *The power checking mechanism in ancient Chinese bureaucratic politics (*《中国传统官僚政治中的权力制约机制》*).* Beijing: Beijing University Press.

Tang, S. (2003). Confucianism and the ideology of righteousness (儒家学说与正义观念). *Studies of International Politics* （国际政治研究）, *4*, 25–35.

Taylor, R. L. (1998). The religious character of Confucian tradition. *Philosophy East & West*, *48*(1), 80.

Thibaudet, A. (1922). *La Campagne avec Thucydide* [The campaign with Thucydides]. Paris: Editions de la Nouvelle Revue Fransaise.

Thucydides. (1998). *The Peloponnesian War.* Translated by S. Lattimore. Indianapolis: Hackett Publishing Company.

Tian, C. (2005). *Chinese dialectics: From Yijing to Marxism.* Lanham, MD: Lexington Books.

Tong, D. (2010). Introduction. In J. Gao, & D. Tong (Eds.), *Chinese democracy.* Tianjin: Tianjin People's Press.

Tong, Z. (2009). Chapter six: China's constitutional research and teaching: A state of the art. In S. Balme, & M. W. Dowdle (Eds.), *Building constitutionalism in China.* New York: Palgrave Macmillan.

Tong, Z. (2015). *A review of the recent debate on China's Constitutionalism Path* (《近年来中国宪政道路之争评说》). Retrieved June 6, 2018, from http://www.calaw.cn/article/default.asp?id=11055.

Topper, K. (2001). Not so trifling nuances: Pierre Bourdieu, symbolic violence, and the perversions of democracy. *Constellations*,(1), 30–56.

Tribe, L. (2008). *The invisible constitution.* Oxford, UK: Oxford University Press.

Waluchow, W. (2007). *Constitutionalism.* Retrieved July 2, 2009, from http://plato.stanford.edu/entries/constitutionalism/

Wang, J. (2003). The relationship between political civilization and constitutionalism (政治文明与宪政的关系). *Chinese Legal Studies*, *6*, 33–40.

Wang, X. (2004). A few issues on the study of ancient Chinese censorate history (中国古代监察制度史研究的几个问题). *Explorations (*《求索》*)*, *12*, 233–237.

Wang, Y., & Chen, H. (2004). The opinions and reasons for not using the notion of constitutionalism (关于不可采用"宪政"提法的意见和理由). *The Trend of Theoretical Studies* （《理论研究动态》）.

Warren, M. (1989). Liberal constitutionalism as ideology: Marx and Habermas. *Political Theory*, *17*(4).

Wartenberg, T. E. (1982). "Species-being" and "human nature" in Marx. *Human Studies*, *5*(2), 77–95.

Wilson, A. (2014). "The Ukraine Crisis brings the threat of democracy to Russia's doorstep." *European View*, *13*(1), 67–72.

Wong, K. C. (2006). Human rights and limitation of state power: The discovery of constitutionalism in the People's Republic of China. *Asia-Pacific Journal on Human Rights & the Law*, *7*(1), 1–37.

Wu, H. (2006). The literary meaning of "the heavenly way as paradigm" and its evolution ("神道设教"的文字意义及其演绎). *Sun Yat Sen University Forum, 26*(8), 3–5.

Wu, Q. (2006). Translator's preface. In Q. Wu (Ed.), *The decline of the West* (Q. Wu, Trans., pp. 1–46). Shanghai: Sannian Books.

Xi, W. (Ed.). (2007). *A study of socialist political civilization with Chinese characteristics (*中国特色社会主义政治文明研究*)*. Beijing: The Communist Party of China Party History Press.

Xiao-Planes, X. (2009). Of constitutions and constitutionalism: Trying to build a new political order in China, 1908–1949. In S. Balme, & M. W. Dowdle (Eds.), *Building constitutionalism in China* (pp. 37–57). New York: Palgrave Macmillan.

Xie, P. (2006). *The basic contents of the "socialist legal ideas" (*社会主义法治理念的基本内容). Retrieved January 3, 2011, from http://theory.people.com.cn/GB/49150/49153/4149328.html

Xie, Y. (2004). Could constitutionalism be used as a fundamental political concept of China (能不能把"宪政"作为我国的基本政治概念). *Political Studies, 3*.

Xing, G. (2009). Hu Jintao's political thinking and legitimacy building: A post-Marxist perspective. *Asian Affairs: An American Review, 36*(4), 213–226.Xu, J. (2007). Political Liberalism or Comprehensive Liberalism?(政治自由主义，还是整全性自由主义？). Intellectuals. Volume 7. Retrieved June 5, 2018 from http://www.aisixiang.com/data/22746.html.

Xu, X., & Xie, L. (2005). The institutional condition for realizing the constitutional ideal of "people-centred" socialism: A reading of Marx's whole-person development theory from the constitutional perspective ("以人为本"的社会主义宪政理念实现的制度条件 – 从宪政的视角看马克思人的全面发展学说). *Philosophy Study, 7*.

Yan, J. (2011). *The governance of Chinese government in changes*. Governance and Political Leadership in East Asia, Seoul, Korea.

Yang, Y. (2007). The cultural order and the political order: A political-cultural interpretation of the Confucian China (《文化秩序与政治秩序 – 儒教中国的政治文化解读》). Beijing: Chinese University of Politics and Law Press.

Yovel, Y. (2002). Spinoza: The psychology of the multitude and the use of language. In G. Y. Segal Yirmiyahu (Ed.), *Spinoza* (1st ed., pp. 435–463). Surrey, UK: Ashgate Pub Ltd.

Yu, R. (1998). The conflicts and integration of natural law, state laws, and commonsensical sentiments of the people: The inner core of Confucian law and traditional resources of modern legality (天理、國法、人情的沖突與整合——儒家之法的內在精神及現代法治的傳統資源). *Chinese Cultural Forum, 4*.

Yu, R. (2006). Seeking of the middle way: The spirit of Confucian law and its universal value (尋求"中道" – 儒家之法的精神及其普世價值). *Modern Legal Studies, 6*.

Yu, X. (2009). Western constitutional ideas and constitutional discourse in China, 1978–2005. In S. Balme, & M. W. Dowdle (Eds.), *Building constitutionalism in China* (pp. 111–124). New York: Palgrave Macmillan.

Yuan, J. (2010). "People-centredness" and constitutionalism (以人为本与宪政). *Theoretical Investigation, 6*.

Zang, F. (2009). *An introduction to Marx's political philosophy*. Beijing: Central Translation and Compilation Press.

Zhang, Q. (2001). Tradition and modern: On the constitutional nature of *Li* (传统与现代: 论"礼"的宪法学定性). *Journal of Jinling Law (*金陵法律评论*), 1*, 119–127.

Zhang, Q. (2008). Reflection on China's one hundred years' constitutional journey and its prospects (中国百年宪政历程的反思与展望). *Legal Studies, 4*.

Zhang, S. (2008). The efforts and limitations of re-institutionalizing Confucianism (儒学再制度化的努力与限制). *Journal of Yunnan University (Social Sciences Edition) (*云南大学学报*(*社会科学版*)), 2*.

Zhang, X., & Jiang, Z. (2002). The Three-represents thought: The foundation of China's constitutional thoughts ("三个代表"思想: 中国宪政创新之基础). *Wuhan University Journal, 55*(6), 641–647.

Zhang, Z. (2010). Traditional Chinese jurisprudence summarized: Its significance to construct contemporary Chinese jurisprudence (**概括的**传统中国的法理观 – **以中国法律**传统对建构中国法理学的意义为视点). *Jurist, 2*, 56–67.

Zhao, S. (1996). *Power by design: Constitution-making in nationalist China*. Honolulu, HI: University of Hawaii Press.

Zhao, Y. (2009). Semiological culture study: Current status and future trend. *Journal of Southwestern Ethnic University (Social Science Edition)*, *12*(220), 169–172.

Zheng, Y. (2004). *Will China become democratic? Elite, class, and regime transition*. Singapore, London & New York: Eastern Universities Press.

Zheng, Y. (2010a). *The Chinese Communist Party as organizational emperor: Culture, reproduction, and transformation*. London, UK: Routledge.

Zheng, Y. (2010b). *The Chinese model: Experience and dilemma* (《**中国模式的**经验与困局》). Hangzhou: Zhejiang People's Press.

Zhou, Y. (2005). Power structure modes and constitutionalism (权力结构模式与宪政). *China Legal Science*, *6*, 3–15.

Zhuangzi. Zhuangzhi Zhushi (《庄子注释》). Wang Shixun ed. Jilan: Qilu Press.

Zhu, S. (2000). Sending Law to the Countryside: Research on China's Basic-level Judicial System. New York: Springer Publishing Company.

Index

Kolibri 360 GmbH
Ferdinand-Jühlke-Straße 7
99095 Erfurt, Deutschland
produktsicherheit@kolibri360.de